# CAREER PATHWAYS
# IN ACTION

# CAREER PATHWAYS IN ACTION

## CASE STUDIES FROM THE FIELD

Edited by

**Robert B. Schwartz**
**Amy Loyd**

Harvard Education Press
Cambridge, Massachusetts

**WORK** AND **LEARNING SERIES**

Series edited by Robert B. Schwartz and Nancy Hoffman

**OTHER BOOKS IN THIS SERIES**

*Vocational Education and Training for a Global Economy*
Edited by Marc S. Tucker

Paperback ISBN 978-1-68253-379-6
Library Edition ISBN 978-1-68253-380-2
Library of Congress Cataloging-in-Publication data is on file.

Published by Harvard Education Press,
an imprint of the Harvard Education Publishing Group

Harvard Education Press
8 Story Street
Cambridge, MA 02138

Cover Design: Wilcox Design
Cover Photo: kali9/E+/Getty Images
The typefaces used in this book are Adobe Garamond Pro and Milo OT.

# CONTENTS

# FOREWORD

The volume you are about to read is the second in a series of books we are curating for the Harvard Education Press (HEP) under the title Work and Learning. The first book, *Vocational Education and Training for a Global Economy*, is a set of cases profiling the vocational education systems of four countries: China, Singapore, Switzerland, and the United States. This book, also a collection of case studies, focuses on the United States. It is designed as a follow-up to our 2017 HEP volume, *Learning for Careers, The Pathways to Prosperity Network*. In that book, a history, overview, and analysis of the strategies at play in the Pathways Network, we could touch only lightly on what that work looks like on the ground in several of the most promising states, regions, and locales in our network. Consequently, we commissioned a set of case studies to give readers a more in-depth understanding of what it takes to develop and implement career pathways systems designed to equip young people with the combination of academic knowledge, technical skills, and professional/social skills to get started in the labor market and prepare them for an uncertain future. These cases represent the diversity of a national network. They come from five different regions of the country; two focus on states, two on regions, and one on a single locality.

Why case studies? We are often asked, "Where is the Pathways work happening well at scale?" and "What data do you have to show that this work makes a difference?" While our field partners are admirably grappling with the challenges of cross-sectoral and longitudinal quantitative data, we will not have any data that follow youth into the labor market until a decade or more into our work, and we may never have definitive causal data because this complex work has too many variables, too many players, and too many data-related challenges to allow for the definition of a clear baseline to enable meaningful before-and-after comparisons. Consequently, we believe that our Pathways work to date is better shared through the stories and qualitative analysis found in these case studies.

A second question that readers may be asking is, who actually does the work that is described here? As the introduction notes, the Pathways Network that formed in 2012 meets twice a year to take part in powerful peer learning. At a Network Institute, it's always inspiring to look out at a hotel ballroom filled with around two hundred people from across the country, a good number of whom have been members of the Pathways Network from the start. They are from rural, suburban, and urban communities; they work at jobs as different as leading a nonprofit to advising a governor, to placing interns in work sites, to designing pathways reaching back to high schools from the perch of a community college. Yet they come together in their understanding of the need for pathways and their commitment to doing the hard work to create and sustain the cross-sector alliances that are required to put pathways in place. These are unsung champions of the young people who benefit and whose communities will be healthier places in which to grow up and thrive because of the thoughtfulness and persistence of these hardworking adults.

As for the young people who benefit from early career experiences, their voices are always worth hearing. Here are the words of a young man reflecting on the internship set up by his Delaware high school in partnership with Delaware Technical Community College: "I was at a chemical company. I didn't know when I started what I'd think, but by the end, I thought, 'This is really interesting.' I did something new every day; I got to go out in the field and do maintenance and work hands on . . . I really liked that. The team was welcoming, but they told me to stay in school. They wished they'd done that so they could improve their lives. I'm going to go to college in electrical engineering."

—Robert B. Schwartz and Nancy Hoffman

# INTRODUCTION

*Amy Loyd*

Seven years ago, we were in the early stages of designing and launching the Pathways to Prosperity Network at JFF, largely in response to the surge of interest generated by the Harvard Graduate School of Education's report, *Pathways to Prosperity: Meeting the Challenge of Preparing Young Americans for the 21st Century*. We recognized the immense disconnects between our education systems and workforce needs, the realities of young people struggling in the labor market, and the difficulties business and industry face in hiring skilled talent. In an experimental effort to ameliorate these challenges, we initially brought together leaders from five states to consider how they might individually and collectively learn to create more strategic systems of college and career pathways through forming the Pathways to Prosperity Network. While we expected that our work would be helpful to the field in the short term, we did not know whether the network we launched in 2012 would continue to grow and thrive; nor did we anticipate that our pathways work would provoke a national movement in this critical space.

The Pathways to Prosperity Network has indeed proved to be a valuable addition to the field—not as yet another reform agenda for states to contend with, but rather as an authentic and strategic, locally driven realignment of state and regional education, workforce development, and economic development systems. We initially planned that the network would consist only of state members but quickly received requests from metropolitan regions to join, soon followed by urban communities. Over the years, we have partnered with eighteen formal members of our network and done related career pathways work in another thirteen states. We've learned that the power of the network is the network itself—and the powerful peer learning that results from systems-level cross-sector leaders coming together to share their effective policies and practices, to brainstorm and co-create innovations, and to problem solve solutions to their thorniest challenges. In our increasingly politically polarized nation, our pathways work is soundly bipartisan and provides a neutral, trusted, and common ground for learning across differences. Our network comprises large states and small states; red, blue, and purple states; and rural regions and urban centers; and it serves communities of all sizes and demographics. Yet, despite—or *because* of—the diversity in our network, we find that the end goal of creating more effective educational pathways that are aligned to industry resonates in all contexts. The lessons learned from our network, highlighted in this book, can be applicable to any state or region considering college and career pathways as a lever for systems building and transforming education and workforce outcomes.

This collection of case studies follows the first book about our work, *Learning for Careers*, in which my colleagues Nancy Hoffman and Robert Schwartz describe the work across our network and the emerging learnings from it. Since then, our network members have demonstrated ambitious vision and goals, and are transforming how teaching and learning take place to better prepare *all* young people for the future of work.

We start this book with two cases of exemplary Pathways to Prosperity Network states, Delaware and Tennessee. Delaware experienced a gubernatorial leadership transition during the period covered by the case; Tennessee, more recently. Tennessee also experienced leadership transitions in its Department of Education: Danielle Mezera, the protagonist in the case study, left the department in 2017, and with the election of a new governor, Bill Lee, in 2018, Education Commissioner Candice McQueen also resigned. However, the strength and depth of the pathways systems in both states suggest that this work will continue to be a priority for new leaders as it was for their predecessors.

Delaware's competitive advantage is its small size and its collaborative relationships that result from everyone knowing each other well. Delaware Pathways has had consistent leadership from the Rodel Foundation and both governors, a single community college system with a clear vision and mission for partnership and targeting priority industry sectors, and a strong public-private governance structure that is co led across key partnering agencies and organizations. When Delaware joined the network, it had one pathway in manufacturing that served fewer than thirty high school students; it is now on target to enroll twenty thousand students, half of the state's high school population, in high-quality pathways by 2020.

Tennessee was the first state to step forward and ask to join our network. At the time, it was a state with a long-standing commitment to career and technical education (CTE), but it needed to align and modernize its offerings and structures to meet current and future industry demands. The Tennessee Department of Education set high expectations for its Tennessee Pathways, insisting that programs of study be high quality, rigorous, and vertically aligned with postsecondary offerings and industry opportunities. It analyzed all CTE courses and programs of study to identify those that needed to be phased out or revitalized to better reflect the needs of the state's economy. It also engaged our JFF Pathways team to lead asset mapping in all nine of the state's economic development regions to identify region-specific strengths and needs so that the state could better support and advance pathways on the ground. Tennessee is also a leader in cross-institutional alignment, including through other pathways-related state initiatives such as the Governor's Workforce Subcabinet, Workforce 360, Drive to 55 (its postsecondary credential attainment goal), Work-Based Learning, Tennessee Promise, and Tennessee Reconnect.

The next case study highlights a cross-state pathways initiative in the Great Lakes region. The four sites engaged in this initiative—the northwest suburbs of Chicago and Rockford, Illinois; Central Ohio; and Madison, Wisconsin—had all been engaged in our Pathways to Prosperity Network for at least two years when they were invited to submit a proposal to the Joyce Foundation to join the Great Lakes College and Career Pathways Partnership (GLCCPP). JFF is a technical assistance provider to GLCCPP and assisted the foundation in scanning, identifying, and recommending the regions in which equitable, high-quality pathways were already developing and could benefit from an additional investment to deepen and accelerate their work. Each region has distinct characteristics, and their infrastructure, demographics, industry sectors, and approaches vary accordingly. The four regions regularly meet in a community of practice to share learnings, collectively working toward ensuring that historically marginalized students or underrepresented groups in the Great Lakes region thrive in college, career, and beyond.

The final two case studies focus on two regions engaged in pathways: the rural Central Valley of California with The Wonderful Company, and Marlborough in the suburban/urban Greater Boston area.

Wonderful Agriculture Career Prep is an example of a highly ambitious, employer-led, comprehensive, and tight approach to developing pathways systems. With a focus on agriculture—and the cutting-edge technology, science, and business savvy it requires—The Wonderful Company is singlehandedly defining and designing the high expectations it holds for college and career pathways. The students, schools, and colleges partnering with Wonderful sign on to non-negotiable terms for engagement. In turn, Wonderful provides strong funding, committed staffing, intensive supports, and smart thought partnership to its pathways partners. Its results to date are impressive, and its keen attention to detail and data keeps it sharply focused on continuous improvement.

Marlborough's work with JFF precedes the Pathways to Prosperity Network: in 2009, with American Recovery and Reinvestment Act and federal Race to the Top funding, Marlborough became a STEM-focused early-college high school, receiving technical assistance from JFF to do so. When we launched the network, Massachusetts was one of the first states to join, and Marlborough was the leading region in the state, eager to take a stronger career focus in its early college. In 2014, the JFF Pathways team was awarded a federal Youth CareerConnect grant that funded Marlborough's work, including purchasing state-of-the-art tools and resources for its industry sector–aligned pathways, such as advanced manufacturing; and receiving ongoing and intensive JFF technical assistance in its pathways design, implementation, and improvement. The region benefits from consistent leadership, the coherence of one middle and one high school engaged in the STEM early-college and career pathways work, committed higher education partners, strong employer partners located near their schools, an engaged workforce development board that serves as a youth work-based learning intermediary, and extensive teacher professional development.

Where are we now with the Pathways to Prosperity Network, and where is it headed? A motto we commonly use when describing our Pathways to Prosperity work is *"Not just faster horses."* This is adapted from an adage mythically attributed to Henry Ford: "If I had asked people what they wanted, they would have said faster horses." We are not encouraging states and regions to do the same work they have always done, only more of it and faster. Instead, we are challenging our network partners to reinvent *how* education takes place altogether, which requires students, families, and educators alike to make substantive, and sometimes cognitively dissonant, mind-set shifts—akin to the leap from using tried and true horses to unknown and uncertain cars for transportation. Instead of perceiving career-focused pathways as a last resort, we want high-quality pathways in in-demand fields to become first-choice options—and we want *all* high school students to be held to the high expectations of earning college credit through dual enrollment and participating in ongoing career advising, coupled with authentic work-based learning experiences.

We have learned some hard lessons through our work. The systemic transformation we seek in states and regions does not happen overnight, and it is constrained by the ossified structures of existing education and workforce systems. Changing policy, practice, and partnership structures is hard work that often spans more than one political election cycle. Furthermore, it requires committed cross-sector leadership, so that the work is truly co-designed and co-owned by the stakeholders essential for such pathways, that is, K–12, higher education, workforce development, and business and industry. However, this shared leadership is not commonly practiced, especially across entities with different time frames, constituencies, and bottom lines—and instead we frequently see one organization defining and leading the work, and then inviting other key stakeholders to engage in a predetermined vision for pathways, which does not typically yield deep and sustained systems that effectively serve young people. We also often hear "But we're already doing this!" as a common refrain in the field, but as stakeholders better understand the nature of building pathways *systems, not programs*, they begin to recognize that this work is more complex than it may first appear.

While we are proud of the seven years of this work, we cannot yet declare victory and march off the pathways field. We have deepened our expertise and built a compelling evidence base for our work, and we continue to learn from the field as it grows. We are exploring and engaging in emerging considerations, modifications, and innovations in college and career pathways; some of our newer areas for consideration include:

- *How can we integrate the liberal arts and humanities into career pathways?* Many of our JFF Pathways team members bring strong liberal arts backgrounds to our work, spanning philosophy, performing arts, history, comparative Renaissance literature, sociology, community justice, and gender and women's studies. We know firsthand that the critical thinking, creativity, communication, and other skills we developed in our studies are valuable in the workplace and readily transferable to any industry sector. We want to ensure that college and career pathways provide a balanced and holistic education, and are not overly focused on utilitarian technical skill development.
- *What role does happiness play in career selection?* Our country is founded on the notion of life, liberty, and the pursuit of happiness as unalienable rights. At JFF, we are committed to pathways that lead to a living wage with economic advancement opportunities, yet research indicates that money and happiness are not directly correlated above a certain income level. Several of our JFF Pathways team members are also parents (and two are grandparents!), and ultimately our yardstick for measuring high-quality education is whether or not we would enroll our own young family members in the pathways we espouse and help to create, and their happiness is close to our hearts.
- *How does the future of work impact pathways systems?* Jobs, the new economy, and the nature of work itself are changing. Automation is changing the labor market in fundamental ways, and reshaping the types of jobs that will be available in the future. Jobs that do not rely

on sophisticated social skills and are routine in nature are those most likely to be automated, and these are often the jobs held by young people and low-skilled adults as they enter the workforce and gain the skills needed to advance along a career ladder. These trends suggest that a successful career arc in the near and long terms will require mastery of a body of transferable skills (i.e., professional skills) that can be deployed in a variety of job settings. We want all young people to develop this foundation of transferable skills, coupled with the ability to pursue lifelong learning and nimbly adapt to change.

- *How might we need to rethink our education systems to better prepare young people for the future?* Currently, forty-seven states and the District of Columbia include college in high school in their state Every Student Succeeds Act plans, and thirty-seven states incorporated it into their state accountability plans. We are considering the increasingly blurred line between secondary and postsecondary education, and how we might reinvent a new form of higher education that integrates the two. Our current systems do not serve all young people well, and the jobs of the future—and of today—require some form of postsecondary credential beyond high school, but the gap between credential attainment and market demand for credentials is still too wide, especially for first-generation college goers, students of color, and low-income students.

- *What is the role of intermediary organizations in credibly convening and connecting cross-sector stakeholders to build and sustain pathways systems that equitably serve young people?* Intermediaries are the hidden yet essential glue that bring together and mobilize the key players in pathways ecosystems and support the development of cross-sector partnerships. But many pathways leaders do not fully understand why such linking organizations are necessary, and even those who do value their role do not know how best to build and support them. Yet the cultural and structural divide between employers and educational institutions requires not only a translation function, but also a new structure to carry out responsibilities that few educational institutions or employers have the capacity to put in practice on their own.

- *How do we pivot to best serve a rapidly changing pathways field?*
  When we first started our network, most states and regions were in
  the design and planning stages for changing pathways systems and
  entered our network at approximately the same starting point and
  trajectory in their work. As the pathways movement and the capacities of the field grow, we are becoming more sophisticated in our
  work with partners, and better at identifying the unique entry points
  into the work and tailoring our services to meet their specific needs.
  We are also observing that regions and cities are increasingly delving
  deeper into pathways-related work—and the work itself is different
  in kind when it starts with local leadership that is situating the work
  on the ground in practice, rather than leading with state agencies and
  state-level policy.

Our hope is that these case studies will serve as useful inspiration to
the field, demonstrating what is possible to accomplish in a short seven
years or less. All of the strategies in these cases are replicable, but they
are not necessarily adoptable wholesale for immediate implementation; instead, quality strategies for college and career pathways systems should be
grounded in best practice but adapted to local education and workforce
needs. We value the complexity and nuance that goes into any of the strategies described in these chapters, are encouraged by the achievements of
our network to date, and are eager to tackle the new challenges in college
and career pathways in partnership with our network. We invite you to
join us in this exciting work.

## CHAPTER 1

# GETTING TO SCALE THROUGH STRATEGIC PARTNERSHIPS
## Delaware Pathways

*Robert Rothman*

Andrew Flynn had long dreamed of working as an engineer. As a high school junior, his dream began to come true.

Andrew enrolled in an advanced manufacturing career pathway program at his school, William Penn High School in New Castle, Delaware. Under the program, he took classes in technology and engineering at Delaware Technical Community College (Delaware Tech), which used state-of-the-art equipment and had teachers with experience in the industry. He then had an opportunity to work during the summer before his senior year at the Kuehne Company, a chemical manufacturer. A plant manager at Kuehne, Alan Rogers, was impressed with Andrew's work: "He will be an asset to a company one day."

The program gave Andrew a better sense of his future. He is continuing his education to become an electrical engineer and knows he will be prepared for his career when he graduates: "I know what the competition is like and what I need to do to succeed."

Andrew's classmate Joe Zecca is on a different trajectory. He too went through the advanced manufacturing pathway and worked in a company before his senior year. By the time he graduated, though, he wanted to go into the workforce. Fortunately, he had several options with three companies that wanted to hire him. He chose AstraZeneca, the pharmaceutical company, because he liked the range of equipment it had and the opportunities that were available. There was one catch: AstraZeneca did not have a job opening, but the company hired him as a consultant until one opened. "They really wanted me," Joe said.

Andrew and Joe are two of nearly nine thousand Delaware students—and counting—who have benefited from a statewide initiative designed to provide college and career preparation for Delaware youth. Under the program, students who enroll develop needed skills, get real work experience, and earn certificates that qualify them for employment when they graduate. At the same time, participating businesses get a steady supply of skilled workers who are job ready.

"The more we satisfy skill needs, the better off the state will be, and the better off individuals will be," said former governor Jack Markell, who launched the initiative in 2014. "We want people to stay here. And the more people stay here, the more employers want to stay here. It's a virtuous circle."

Markell noted that the initiative represents a strong and diverse partnership that includes the K–12 system, businesses, higher education, and community agencies and organizations. Although Delaware is a small state, and many of the partners know one another and have worked together in the past, the partners have also worked hard to create an infrastructure that will remain in place and meet its goals for students and for employers.

The goals are ambitious. Markell pledged to increase the proportion of Delaware residents with college degrees or postsecondary credentials to 65 percent (up from 40 percent) by 2025, and to enroll half of all Delaware high school students in career pathways by 2020.

The initiative faces challenges in meeting those targets. For one thing, it has been unable to secure dedicated funding from the state, which has faced budget deficits over the past few years. But Markell believes that its early success bodes well for the future. "The fact that we were able to grow from twenty-seven [students in the initial cohort] to nearly nine thousand in three years is a pretty good indication we have been able to move forward," he said.

## A CHANGING LABOR MARKET

As with most states, Delaware's economy has undergone significant changes over the past few decades. These transformations have had profound effects on the job market, creating a need for individuals with higher levels of skills than ever before.

Traditionally, Delaware's economy rested on what local residents call "the three Cs": credit cards, chemicals, and chickens. These industries remain the backbone of the state's economy, but they are changing.

Financial services have been a key element in Delaware's economy since 1981, when the state legislature passed the Financial Center Development Act. The legislation provided tax incentives for financial services companies to locate in the state and removed usury caps, allowing the companies to charge market-based interest rates. In the years since, many of the world's largest financial firms, such as Barclays, Capital One, Citibank, and Wells Fargo, have established major operations in the state.

The chemical industry in Delaware is largely synonymous with Du-Pont, one of the largest chemical companies in the world and a Delaware presence for more than two hundred years. But the industry also includes a number of smaller firms and has expanded to include pharmaceuticals, plastics, and other synthetic products.

Chickens are a symbol for the state's large agricultural industry, which dominates the southern part of the state. Delaware ranks first nationally in the dollar value of agricultural products per farm, according to the US Department of Agriculture, and by far the largest revenue producers in the agriculture sector in Delaware are broilers and roasters.[1]

Technology and globalization have transformed these and other industries. For example, much of the work in financial services is technology-related, such as the development of online platforms, rather than call-center responsibilities. Similarly, agricultural businesses are increasingly moving to specialized foods and processing, which require advanced manufacturing skills.

The Great Recession also transformed the state's economy and job market. In 2009, the last two automobile manufacturing plants in the northeastern United States, a Chrysler plant in Newark and a General Motors plant near Wilmington, shut down, wiping out thousands of jobs. And in 2015, DuPont announced that it was merging with Dow Chemical and splitting the combined company into three units; two of the units would be headquartered in Delaware and one in Michigan, Dow's home. The merger resulted in the loss of seventeen hundred jobs in Delaware.[2]

The result of these and other changes in the state's economy is a skills gap. Traditional low-skilled but high-paying jobs, such as auto manufacturing and call-center work, are being eliminated, while the growing areas of the economy demand higher levels of skills. Yet while employers are looking for people to fill the higher-skilled jobs—particularly the so-called "middle-skill" jobs that require some postsecondary training but not a four-year degree—they are finding a shortage of candidates. Middle-skill jobs in Delaware offer an average salary of $44,960 a year, compared with low-skill jobs, which offer an average salary of $26,350 a year.

"There is no more frustrating conversation a governor could have than with an employer who wants to hire people, but can't find people with the right skills," Markell said. "There has never been a better time to be a person with the right skills, and no worse time to be somebody without the right skills."

State employment data illustrate the magnitude of the problem. Overall, officials estimate that Delaware will hire or replace 30 percent of its workforce by 2024. Of that total, 22 percent, or 104,267 workers, will replace those who retire. The rest, 8 percent, or 39,326 workers, will come from new jobs. The total increase, 143,593, is larger than the state's K–12 student population.[3]

Moreover, most of the employment will be in middle- and high-skill jobs. Middle- and high-skill employment accounts for 62 percent of all Delaware jobs and represents 69 percent of all projected openings from job growth through 2024. By contrast, low-skill jobs will grow more slowly. That means the state must do more to ensure that young people are qualified for the jobs that are growing.

In the past, Delaware companies could mask these skills gaps by hiring workers from nearby states, like Pennsylvania, Maryland, and New Jersey. But, increasingly, firms prefer to hire workers from within the state—and

**FIGURE 1.1** Delaware Employment Projections, 2014–2024

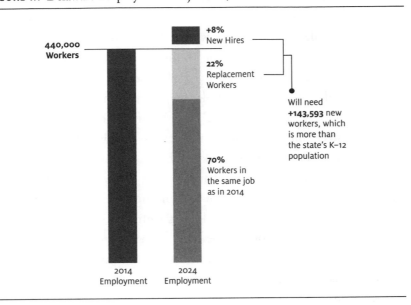

state officials want this as well. That way, more local residents will get jobs and remain in the state, and firms can spend less on recruiting from nearby states. (See figure 1.1.)

## ENTER DELAWARE PATHWAYS

Delaware Pathways is intended to address talent supply in the state by giving young people opportunities to develop the competencies needed for middle-skill jobs and by providing employers with ways to recruit and train a steady supply of needed workers. The goal is to create true pathways from school to career.

After hearing a presentation about Pathways to Prosperity by Robert Schwartz in 2014, Markell became interested in having Delaware join the network. He believed that the network's focus on building pathways systems for students through partnerships of educators, business leaders, and government officials fit well with his goal of increasing the postsecondary attainment rate in the state. (See appendix A for more about the Pathways to Prosperity Network.)

Markell called together leaders from K–12, higher education, business, and community organizations to discuss creating a Delaware Pathways system. They quickly agreed, and with seed money of $25,000 each from the Rodel Foundation of Delaware, a local philanthropy that supports education reform, and the Delaware Business Roundtable, a nonpartisan, volunteer consortium of business leaders, Delaware became part of the Pathways to Prosperity Network and began building its system.

The members of the group that met with the governor and planned the initiative were not strangers to one another. A decade before, Rodel had convened a coalition of state leaders from the same sectors to outline a vision for education for the state. That group continued to meet regularly, although some of the individuals had changed over the years. Thus, the partnership could begin immediately, without taking time for introductions.

One of the first steps for the partners was creating a strategic plan. With such a plan, they could be clear about what they needed to do and who would be responsible for each step. The plan could also serve as a communications tool to engage the public in the initiative. A draft was released in February 2016, at the second annual Delaware Pathways meeting. The final plan laid out five broad areas of work:

1. *Build a comprehensive system of career preparation that aligns with the state and regional economies.* Expand Delaware's model of career preparation and continuing education to include all secondary and postsecondary partners (grades 7–14). These efforts must support a diverse group of students as they enroll in career pathways that reflect the needs of the state and regional economies. The efforts must also lead to an industry-recognized credential, certificate, or license that holds value at the professional or postsecondary level. Lead agency/organization: Delaware Department of Education

2. *Scale and sustain meaningful work-based learning experiences for students in grades 7–14.* Establish a statewide workforce intermediary.

This intermediary will link educators and employers to better scale work-based learning experiences for secondary and postsecondary students. These efforts must leverage industry sectors and employer associations. In doing so, they will build the professional capacity of employers to recruit and onboard student talent as well as design work-based learning activities that enrich and advance school-based instruction. Lead agency/organization: Delaware Technical Community College

3. *Integrate education and workforce development efforts and data systems.* Align the education and workforce system to create postsecondary options for all students, including the expansion of apprenticeship and support services for individuals with disabilities or other barriers to employment. These efforts will underpin a workforce data-quality campaign that provides partners with the necessary information to ensure Delaware's human capital can compete in a global economy. Lead agency/organization: Delaware Department of Labor

4. *Coordinate financial support for Delaware Pathways.* Engage the public, private, and philanthropic communities to garner the initial and ongoing capital necessary to implement and scale the Delaware Pathways initiative. These financial and in-kind resources will be applied to address the most pervasive issues in our education and workforce system and also guarantee that partners have a shared stake in the educational outcomes of students. Lead agency/organization: United Way of Delaware and Rodel Foundation of Delaware

5. *Engage employers, educators, and service providers to support Delaware Pathways.* Develop a communication and partnership strategy to expand visibility, facilitate public support, and brand Delaware Pathways. These efforts must build support for youth employment so that the next generation of Delaware's workforce has the skills and work experience required to achieve the Delaware Promise. Lead agency/organization: Delaware Workforce Development Board

The leaders of the organizations met monthly to chart progress and refine strategy. They also took the strategic plan to dozens of community organizations and events to gather feedback and support. Two issues emerged: the need to engage a broader range of community organizations, and the need to support students with disabilities and those at risk. In response, the group developed plans to work with organizations such as the Boys & Girls Clubs and libraries to provide after-school services for youth, and with organizations that represent exceptional children and the state Department of Labor's Division of Vocational Rehabilitation.

The group also took steps to formalize its governance structure. In August 2016, Markell signed an executive order, which defines Delaware Pathways as "a collaborative workforce development partnership which will create a fluid relationship between our public education system, post-secondary education, non-profit, and employer communities to ensure that the pathway to college and a well-paying job is accessible for every Delawarean."[4] The executive order also established a steering committee to oversee and be accountable so that: (1) the program's sustainability and adaptation aligns to the needs of the workforce and individuals who participate; and (2) budgetary priorities are identified and outlined in a transparent and collaborative manner. The steering committee consists of fourteen members, including the cabinet secretaries of education, labor, economic development, and health and social services; the president of Delaware Tech; the chair of the Delaware Workforce Development Board; the president of the State Board of Education; two school system superintendents; two business representatives; and three members of community organizations. Mark Brainard, president of Delaware Tech, was appointed to chair the steering committee, which held its first meeting in October 2016.

This cross-agency structure is unusually strong. In addition to the steering committee, the working group of deputies continues to meet twice monthly, once in person and once on the phone, and work together through the day-to-day issues with Delaware Pathways. All of the members understand one another's work and how their work contributes to the initiative.

One outcome of this collaborative effort is the integration of Delaware Pathways with a number of state programs. The Workforce Development Board has made pathways a key element in its strategy, and the vision process led by the Rodel Foundation of Delaware includes pathways as a key element.

## SYSTEM OF CAREER PATHWAYS

At the heart of the pathways initiative are the pathways themselves, which are intended to link high school, postsecondary education, and employers into a seamless system that enables young people to develop the skills they need, gain valuable experience, and move into productive careers.

To accomplish this, the Delaware officials decided to create structures in which students, some in middle school, would be able to learn about and explore career options. Then as high school sophomores or juniors, the students would take courses related to careers and, concurrently, enroll in an institution of higher education for a two- or three-year career-related program of study. In the summer before their senior year and during their senior year, students would participate in a paid internship for approximately 240 hours at a work site in their chosen field. When a student graduates from high school, he or she would have a high school diploma, six to fifteen college credits, an industry-recognized credential, and work experience. The student would then have the option of pursuing further postsecondary training or moving right into the workplace. Markell commented: "The secret to its success is the collaboration between K–12, institutions of higher education, and employers. Without employers playing a leading role in defining the skills that are required, it would not be successful."

To select the type of pathways, state Department of Education officials worked with officials from higher education and industry to examine labor market data and identify fast-growing fields that required some postsecondary training and paid relatively high wages. These included the health sciences sector, which is expected to grow by 15.4 percent by 2024, and the information technology sector, which is expected to grow by 13.2 percent by that time. The three partners then developed a course of study to train for the skills necessary for entry-level employment.

But developing the courses proved more challenging than the partners originally thought, said Mark Brainard, president of Delaware Tech. When they were putting together the advanced manufacturing pathway, educators from Delaware Tech and representatives of the manufacturing industry met to spell out the competencies needed for entry-level employment and a curriculum that would produce those outcomes. But putting the pieces together took time, he said. "I assumed that, for a sector telling people they couldn't find employees, they could identify the competencies," he explained. "But it took four months. It involves the business community communicating with us in a way we never communicated before."

In some cases, the business partners also helped make sure that the materials and equipment used in the courses represented the state of the art in the field—at least indirectly. In 2016–2017, for example, Delmarva Power, the leading energy company in the state, financed the creation of a career pathway in renewable energy and energy efficiency. For the renewable energy courses, the funding helped pay for kits that would help students to understand the concepts of the field. The kit manufacturer worked with Delmarva Power to make sure it provided up-to-date information, according to Gary Stockbridge, Delmarva's president, who is also the chair of the Delaware Business Roundtable education committee and the Delaware Workforce Development Board. "That entity works with the business community to make sure the kits are relevant," he said.

The state Department of Education supports pathways development and invited school districts to apply to participate, using a competitive grant process with funds from the federal Carl D. Perkins Vocational and Technical Education Act. Those selected received seed money; the department also provided professional development for teachers. Once selected, the schools spent a year planning before implementing the pathway programs. The schools then recruited students they identified as those who might benefit from the initiative and encouraged them to enroll.

In some pathways, students take all of the career-related coursework at an institution of higher education, where they earn college credits. In others, students take some courses at their high school and others at a college or university. The students earn college credits and can apply them to degree programs once they graduate from high school. For example, in the nurse assisting pathway, high schools offer courses in fundamentals in health sciences, essentials of anatomy and physiology, and certified nurse assisting. These credits can be applied to an associate's degree program or to programs leading to certification in allied health fields.

Asking schools to volunteer to take on the pathways means that only schools that are prepared to offer them do so. But one result of this practice is that not every school offers every pathway, noted Kim Joyce, the associate vice president for academic affairs at Delaware Tech. "If you're at Cape Henlopen High School and you want to be a nurse practitioner, you're out of luck," she said.

The initial pathway was in *advanced manufacturing*, the program that Andrew Flynn and Joe Zecca entered on their way toward their future. Some groundwork was already underway; the Delaware Manufacturing Association, in partnership with Delaware Tech, created a certificate in the field, and Delaware Tech established a dual-enrollment program with one high school. For this pathway, the partners created two programs of study: manufacturing logistics technician and production technician. The manufacturing logistics technician program included four courses, taken over two years at Delaware Tech: principles of manufacturing; manufacturing quality, safety, and practices; manufacturing processes and production; and advanced handling and logistics. Initially, forty students signed up for the pathway; after some left their schools, twenty-seven ended up completing it in 2016.

Teachers for the courses had extensive industry experience. At one Delaware Tech campus, for example, one of the teachers in an electronics lab had worked at General Motors for twenty-three years.

During the 2014–2015 academic year, the state added pathways in *allied health* and computer science. Allied health included coursework in such topics as human anatomy and physiology and prepared students for careers such as respiratory therapist, nurse, physical therapist, dental hygienist, and medical lab technician. Students could earn up to nine college credits, giving them a head start on an associate's degree. In its first year, six high schools offered this pathway.

The *computer science* pathway included coursework in algorithm development and programming. To develop it, state officials looked at programs that were piloted in Chicago and Los Angeles and by a private organization, code.org. The program offered nine college credits.

During the 2015–2016 academic year, the state offered pathways in *engineering, finance*, and *CISCO networking*, and in 2016–2017, the state developed pathways in *environmental science*, teaching, certified nursing assistant, and energy. Education department officials are particularly enthusiastic about the *teaching* pathway because this will facilitate school districts to serve as employers, as well as providers for the program, and thus model the kinds of activities they want other employers in the state to undertake. The program of study was developed in consultation with former state Teachers of the Year and teacher-preparation institutions, and will allow students to graduate with twelve to eighteen college credits, a paraprofessional certificate, and work experience. Students will also take the Praxis examination, a requirement for entering teacher education. "I see this flying off the shelf," said Luke Rhine, the director of career and technical education/STEM initiatives for the state Department of Education.

The development of the *energy* pathway shows how nimble the initiative has been. Delmarva Power offered the state a $750,000 grant to create the pathway in June 2016, after Delmarva's parent company, Exelon, merged with Pepco, another energy company. Company officials then worked with educators from the state Department of Education and Delaware Tech to develop the curriculum and have it in place by September. Christiana High School in Newark offered to pilot the pathway. The department also waived a requirement that schools announce courses well in advance of the summer before the school year.

The pathway called for three three-credit courses: Introduction to Energy Management; Excel Level I; and Society and Sustainability, along with seventy hours of workforce training in areas such as lighting and energy audits. Originally, only Society and Sustainability was scheduled to be offered at Delaware Tech, but since the high school teacher who planned to teach the Excel course was unable to do so, the course was moved to

Delaware Tech. That meant, too, that Christiana High School had to arrange its schedule so students in the pathway could spend a block of time on the community college campus. The high school also had to arrange transportation for the students. (The grant paid for a bus to take students to and from the campus.)

Recruiting students proved challenging, according to Cory Budischack, the chair of the energy technology department at Delaware Tech. "The most challenging aspect was finding qualified students," he said. "Students in this county are the most disadvantaged in the state. They lack math and ELA skills. We're working on building them up."

In addition, since the program was announced late in the school year, many students who might have been interested in energy careers could not to take it in the first year because they had already signed up for other coursework. Indeed, some of the students in the first year of the program said they enrolled because it offered them a chance to get college credit, not because they planned to pursue energy careers; nevertheless, they found the coursework valuable.

In its first year, the pathway did not offer work experience. But Budischack said he is considering having the pathway students join college students in the energy technology program on their internships, in which they conduct energy audits for small businesses.

In 2016–2017, 13 percent of Delaware high school students (5,072 students) earned credit in a pathway, up from 5 percent (1,850 students) in the prior school year. The goal is to ensure that 50 percent of all high school students (20,000 students) are completing pathways by 2020–2021.[5]

## Support for the Pathways

In addition to working with partners to identify pathways and develop programs of study, the state Department of Education has provided policy support in a number of ways. For example, the department issued waivers to school districts so they could hire people from industry who lack teaching certification to teach the career-related courses. The department also revised the School Success Framework, its school-accountability system, to reflect school participation in pathways. Under the revision, schools report the number of students who earn early college credit, attain industry credentials, or participate in work experiences as part of the pathway programs.

Additionally, the department developed a program to help underprepared students take college coursework. Under the program, known as Readiness with a Purpose, students who score below certain benchmark scores in English language arts on the PSAT or SAT will receive targeted assistance. Those who are far below the benchmark scores will take the course Foundations of College English. Those who are close to the benchmark will take modular coursework based on their needs. Under an agreement with all of the state's colleges and universities, students who successfully complete the course or the modules will be exempt from remedial classes in English language arts and can enroll in credit-bearing courses.

The program was implemented in 2017–2018 for students in the allied health pathway, which is in place in six high schools. To Rhine, the program demonstrates the high standards that the pathways initiative maintains for students. "This is an example of how we are clear with children about the prerequisite expectations for jobs," he said. "If you are interested in health care, you need to know English exceptionally well."

Rhine added that the program will benefit students and their parents by reducing the need for remedial coursework in college. Students who take remedial courses are less likely to complete their degrees, he noted. "Everybody wins," said Rhine. "The kid wins because the likelihood of completing is substantially higher. And there's value added for parents and kids because they are not paying for remedial coursework."

Partners are also creating supports for students in the pathways. The United Way is taking the lead to ensure that the most disadvantaged students in the state can benefit from the initiative, according to its president and chief executive officer, Michelle Taylor. "We want to make sure there is an equity component," she said. "We want to be sure that kids who come from high-needs communities have opportunities and can be on the way. We want to see what wraparound services are needed to better support young people."

## Local Pathways

While state officials have been working to develop pathways by engaging employers and developing courses of study, they have also been encouraging local schools that have the capacity to do so to develop their own pathways. Ultimately, the local pathways will be the main part of the system, according to Rhine. "I want to get out of the development business and into the support business," he said.

One of the most extensive local pathways programs is in the Appoquinimink School District, a fast-growing district in the central part of the state. There, the district has organized each of its two high schools into nine "schools": agriculture and natural resources; business and economics; culinary arts and hospitality; education and human studies; health sciences; language, literature, and human development; military and civic leadership; performing and design arts; and science, technology, engineering, and math. Each school includes one or more pathways; there are twenty-four pathways in all.

Incoming freshmen choose a pathway and take courses related to it, often beginning in ninth grade. To guide student choices, the district has hired a college and career counselor to manage an annual college and career fair and bring in adults from the business community to give guest lectures and provide opportunities for job shadowing. The counselor also gives presentations in middle schools to familiarize students and parents with high school options.

Additionally, the district provides students and parents with a course catalog that describes the pathways, including the occupations these pathway prepare students for and the sequence of courses needed to complete the pathway. The occupations in the computer science pathway include applications analyst, business analyst, computer engineer, data modeler, information technology manager, software applications architect, and software engineer.

The district also has formed partnerships with the University of Delaware, Wilmington University, and Delaware Tech so students can take college courses while in high school and earn both high school and college credit. According to school leaders, the goal is for each pathway to have at least one dual-enrollment option or one Advanced Placement course, and every pathway will give students the opportunity to garner work experience.

Matthew Burrows, the district's superintendent, said the pathways program has been enormously popular in the district because it makes high school relevant to students: "It answers the age-old question—when will I use this?"

## Future Directions

Like the district officials in Appoquinimink, state officials are working to strengthen school counseling in the middle grades, and perhaps earlier, to provide students with a greater awareness of potential careers and prepare them to enter pathways in high school. The goal is to engage students, parents, teachers, and counselors to expand students' awareness of career options and to help them match future careers with their interests.

In addition, state officials are monitoring the demographic data of students enrolled in the pathways to maintain gender and racial and ethnic balance. They say that they do not want computer science pathways to be overwhelmingly male, for example. While there are no set targets for balance, they are working to reinforce that student enrollment reflects the community the school district serves. State officials are also collecting information and sharing it with schools to encourage them to provide equal opportunities to all students.

"We have to be conscious we are not reinforcing socioeconomic strata," said Paul Herdman, president and chief executive officer of the Rodel Foundation of Delaware. "We want to create a broad set of options for folks." Herdman also noted that the state leaders are looking carefully at the quality of the pathways programs as the program grows. "Any time you grow fast, there is the issue of capacity and quality," he said. "We have to be vigilant."

## WORK-BASED LEARNING EXPERIENCES

A key element of the Pathways to Prosperity Network is work-based learning. By providing students with opportunities to apply their knowledge and skills in actual work sites, students gain the skills and experience they need to begin their careers. And companies gain workers who are capable of starting effectively on day one.

In countries such as Switzerland, these opportunities are routine. Some 70 percent of young people participate in a dual system in which they spend time as apprentices in a wide range of industries while they take courses in school. The Swiss system is a major factor in that country's strong economy; the per capita gross domestic product in Switzerland in 2013 was $80,528, the fourth highest in the world.[6]

In the United States, which lacks the guild tradition that has led Switzerland and other countries to develop highly sophisticated apprenticeship programs, many employers have been reluctant to provide work-based experiences for young people. In part, this reluctance reflects the fact that many employers are ill-prepared to provide the mentorship and supervision needed for teenagers, who may lack experience in any work setting, particularly settings with sophisticated equipment and demanding timelines. Many employers are also wary of providing training for young workers who may end up getting full-time jobs with their competitors. In those cases, the employers believe, they incur the expenses without reaping the benefits.

In Delaware, many employers have been eager to provide work-based learning experiences for youth, according to Markell. The employers see the experiences as a way of helping fill the skills gap by training a cadre of potential employees who are simultaneously gaining valuable skills and knowledge in the classroom, Markell said. "So far, they've seen the light. Employers recognize they get a lot of value out of this. We're not asking them to do this out of charity—we're asking them to do it out of their self-interest. When they do, they see the value of doing this."

Stockbridge of Delmarva Power acknowledged that some employers might be reluctant to hire high school–aged interns, but said there is a growing recognition that the practice will help develop a talent pipeline, which is badly needed in the state. "At Delmarva, we have found that it is easier to do internships at the college level than at the high school level," he said. "At the high school level, it's more about helping the individual student than it is about the student helping the business. At the college level, you get benefits back—they are more senior, more able to work on their own. But you are developing a talent pipeline, so you spend more time [with high school students] helping them understand the soft skills. Businesses have to understand that."

Employers who have hired students as interns said they have been impressed with the knowledge and enthusiasm the young people bring to the job. "They have passion, drive, they want to know more," said Meg Gardner, the owner of the Blue Moon restaurant in Rehoboth Beach, who has hired five students under the pathways program. "They want to get all the experiences. They want to do more than they were hired to do."

Joshua Grapski, the owner of a group of restaurants in Rehoboth Beach, agreed that the workers are eager to learn and added that their coursework provides a nice complement to the hands-on experience they get while working as interns. "I'm impressed with how well the curriculum fits with what the industry needs," he said. He added that the students learn cooking techniques as well as business and management. "That's something I wish I had in high school," Grapski said. "It's applicable if they want to own a restaurant some day or be a general manager. They know marketing, financing."

Still, he and others acknowledged that there are some limits to what high school–aged interns can do in the workplace. Youth under age nineteen cannot serve alcohol in restaurants, for example. And there are liability concerns involving potentially dangerous equipment.

In some cases, the partners have worked with other agencies to address these issues. For example, in setting up the advanced manufacturing pathway, the partners learned that some businesses cannot hire a youth under eighteen. So they worked with Goodwill Industries, which agreed to act as the employer of record. In that way, the youth would be paid by Goodwill but would work at the site.

Stockbridge noted that there are other ways besides hiring interns that businesses can provide work-based experiences for young people in the pathways. For example, business leaders can serve as mentors for youth by working one-on-one with them and explaining what they do and helping them navigate career options. Technology opens up the possibility of "cyber-mentoring," in which youth and adults in a business conduct live chats and email conversations, not limited by geography.

Delmarva Power and other businesses have also created job-shadowing experiences, in which businesses invite students in for a day to see how the business works and talk to employees. Recent job-shadowing events at Delmarva Power focused on information technology and managing through a storm, Stockbridge noted. "As we think about work-based experiences more broadly, internships may not be for everybody," he said. "There are lots of opportunities for work-based experiences."

## Intermediary Organizations

Delaware Tech is the lead agency in charge of arranging the work-based experiences. Because of the college's long experience in working with employers, administrators there have close relationships with businesses and a vast amount of knowledge about the capacities of the businesses to work with young people.

In the spring of 2017, Delaware Tech hired a director for work-based learning and made plans to hire a team to work with her to take on the intermediary role. The college has studied two successful examples of organizations that link schools and businesses. The Boston Private Industry Council (PIC), perhaps one of the best-known and most successful intermediaries in the country, has coordinated job training efforts in the city since 1979 by creating summer job and internship opportunities for students in the Boston Public Schools. The Boston PIC was a leader behind the Boston Compact, a series of agreements among the schools, higher education institutions, and businesses to provide support and improvements to education and career preparation.

The other model for Delaware Tech's work is the Philadelphia Youth Network, which since 1999 has worked with more than two hundred organizations in the city to provide opportunities for youth development and employment for more than 160,000 young people.

However, unlike those organizations, Delaware Tech is planning to rely on technology to match students and employers. "We don't have the funding to support forty to fifty people to connect students to jobs" as the Boston PIC and the Philadelphia Youth Network do, said Paul T. Morris Jr., the assistant vice president for workforce development and community education at Delaware Tech. "We'll use technology to do that. That's where the matchmaking will happen. There will be connections beyond that, but the [electronic] platform will do the heavy lifting connecting students to employers."

The electronic platform Delaware Tech will use is already in place. Success Pathways and Roads to Careers (SPARC) is an online resource designed to enable students to learn about career options and connect with employers as well as provide a channel for employers to let students know about work-based learning opportunities.[7]

By signing onto SPARC, students can match their interests to available careers and connect with a career coach from industry who can provide virtual mentoring. The site, which was developed by the Delaware Business Roundtable education committee, the Delaware Department of Education, and the United Way of Delaware, also contains downloadable resources to help schools conduct career fairs. Resources include invitation letters to employers and a how-to guide for career panels.

Currently, some seventy-six employers have signed on to SPARC, with ninety-two company-based career coaches. State officials plan to link the site to Delaware JobLink, a state-run website on which job seekers can post résumés.

Under the plan, Delaware Tech will link to SPARC to connect schools and businesses by matching the services the schools need with those the employers can provide. The services can range from supplying guest speakers to offering job shadowing to providing internships and apprenticeships. Delaware Tech will take care of the logistics and legal arrangements. "All schools have to do is plug and play," said Morris.

The operation will also benefit businesses, which often find that they do not know whom to contact to provide services to schools, Morris said. This is particularly important in a state like Delaware where most businesses are small. In addition to maintaining the linking service, Delaware Tech will help form industry councils representing broad sectors of the economy to advise schools on business trends and help guide curriculum and programming decisions. The goal is to create six to eight councils, which will meet once or twice a year with representatives from high schools, Morris said. To provide additional support, Delaware Tech will also employ coordinators in each of the three counties in the state to put out fires and work directly with schools and businesses.

While Delaware Tech is taking the lead in connecting schools and businesses, other organizations in Delaware have also played intermediary roles in the pathways initiative and will continue to do so. The Delaware Manufacturing Association was instrumental in bringing leaders of the industry together to help develop the curriculum for the state's first pathway, in advanced manufacturing, and then enlisted employers to provide work-based experiences for students. The Delaware Restaurant Association played a similar role for the culinary and hospitality pathway.

Junior Achievement, a financial literacy nonprofit, has also helped arrange job shadowing for Delmarva Power, said Stockbridge. And the United Way of Delaware convened a breakfast for employers in Wilmington to showcase best practices. "Partners are starting to evolve, making it easier for the business community," he said.

## WORKFORCE AND DATA SYSTEMS

While the pathways initiative is providing important experiences and skill development for youth, leaders of the initiative recognized that it will be most effective if it is integrated into the state's system for workforce development. In this way, the pathways can provide an entry into further education and training and help the state meet its employment needs.

To that end, the state's departments of labor and education worked to classify occupations into high-skill, middle-skill, and low-skill areas. The agencies could then use the Department of Labor's economic projections to determine which of the high- and middle-skill occupations were growing and at what rate. That enabled them to develop a more sophisticated investment strategy across the education and workforce system and to appropriate funds to develop new pathways.

The resulting classification is posted on a private website, the Economic Development and Employer Planning System (EDEPS). Through EDEPS, the agencies—and employers—can see quickly which occupations are high skilled, high wage, and high demand. This work is now being incorporated in the Department of Labor's labor market information website and the Delaware Pathways website. (See table 1.1.)

### Connection to Adult Education and Training

Pathways leaders have also taken steps to connect the initiative to the state's adult education and training system. For example, they have expanded a data-sharing agreement between the state's departments of labor and education to integrate student-level data into Delaware's Workforce Innovation and Opportunity Act (WIOA) system, which will help connect students who have earned employment certificates to postsecondary and adult education opportunities.

In addition, the Delaware Department of Labor is developing a way to grant advanced standing in apprenticeships to students who have completed pathways. And in late 2016, the state received a grant from the US Department of Labor that will allow the expansion of an apprenticeship program from a thousand to thirteen hundred participants. Apprentices are hired as full-time employees and receive pay while they are learning career skills. "That's another postsecondary opportunity for youth," said Rhine.

### Support for Students with Disabilities

When the leaders of Delaware Pathways solicited public comments on their strategic plan, one of the most consistent comments they received was about the need to strengthen support for students with disabilities. In response, the leaders asked the state Department of Labor's Division of Vocational Rehabilitation to join the planning team to help develop a more concerted strategy for that population.

As part of that effort, the state sought a US Department of Labor Disability Employment grant to create on-ramps for students with disabilities to help them participate more easily in the pathways. It also plans to work with other agencies to identify services for students with disabilities and

TABLE 1.1 Delaware: Labor market summary data by career clusters

| Career Cluster | Middle-Skill Jobs | High-Skill Jobs | High-Wage Jobs | High-Demand | Employment 2015 | Employment Change 2014–2024 | Employment Growth 2014–2024 | Avg. Wage 2015 |
|---|---|---|---|---|---|---|---|---|
| Agriculture, Food & Natural Resources | • | | | | 3,370 | 26 | 0.5% | $59,758 |
| Architecture & Construction | • | • | • | ✓ | 24,740 | 3,561 | 12.7% | $48,763 |
| Arts, Audio/Video Technology & Communications | • | • | • | | 2,810 | 160 | 4.8% | $54,166 |
| Business Management & Administration | | • | | ✓ | 70,960 | 2,635 | 3.6% | $52,482 |
| Education & Training | | • | • | ✓ | 25,810 | 2,730 | 10.2% | $57,020 |
| Finance | • | • | • | ✓ | 23,640 | 2,427 | 9.2% | $79,800 |
| Government & Public Administration | • | • | • | ✓ | 3,950 | 399 | 8.6% | $56,828 |
| Health Science | • | • | • | ✓ | 42,580 | 6,922 | 15.4% | $63,447 |
| Hospitality & Tourism | • | | | ✓ | 57,690 | 5,112 | 8.9% | $24,274 |
| Human Services | | • | | ✓ | 16,370 | 2,272 | 13.1% | $35,359 |
| Information Technology | | • | • | ✓ | 12,540 | 1,743 | 13.2% | $86,932 |
| Law, Public Safety, Corrections & Security | • | | • | ✓ | 15,820 | 950 | 5.1% | $65,168 |
| Manufacturing | • | | • | | 25,690 | 713 | 2.9% | $43,172 |
| Marketing | • | • | | ✓ | 49,760 | 3,393 | 6.5% | $42,314 |
| Science, Technology, Engineering & Mathematics | | • | • | ✓ | 4,090 | 483 | 6.2% | $102,347 |
| Transportation, Distribution & Logistics | • | | | ✓ | 28,560 | 2,527 | 8.2% | $37,995 |

Source: Economic Development and Employer Planning System (Wilmington: Delaware Department of Labor, n.d.), http://www.edeps.org/.

map them against the schools that are participating in the pathways programs. Additionally, it will conduct training for teachers, counselors, and special education coordinators to support students with disabilities.

## COORDINATION OF FINANCIAL SUPPORT

When the pathways leaders developed their strategic plan in 2016, they created a budget that allocated projected spending and resources according to the five elements in the plan. That way, the partners would understand exactly what they needed for each element and seek funding to fill targeted gaps.

This braided funding strategy has let the state make the best use of available funds. Because of the strong cross-agency collaboration, when one agency or organization receives funding from the federal government or a private philanthropy, it immediately starts a conversation about how it will support the pathways work.

Much of the money on hand is from government sources. Under Rhine, the state's career and technical education office used funds from the federal Carl D. Perkins Vocational and Technical Education Act to support the development of pathways. The funds went to curriculum development and teacher professional development, along with staff time for coordination.

In 2016, the initiative received a number of additional private grants, for a total of $3,275,000. These included:

- $250,000 from Strada Education Network (formerly USA Funds) to develop the Readiness with a Purpose program to support college readiness in English language arts.
- $720,000 from Delmarva Power to develop the energy pathway.
- $100,000 from Capital One to launch the workforce intermediary by enabling Delaware Tech to hire an intermediary director.
- $50,000 from Bank of America to scale Delaware Pathways.
- $50,000 from the Delaware Business Roundtable Education Committee to support continued membership in the Pathways to Prosperity Network and support the workforce intermediary.

- $55,000 from United Way of Delaware to support the SPARC platform.
- $2.05 million from JPMorgan Chase & Co. and the Council of Chief State School Officers. Delaware became one of ten states to win a three-year grant under the New Skills for Youth initiative, which supports the development of statewide career and technical education systems—precisely the kind of system that pathways is aiming to become.

In addition, Delaware Tech won a $3.5 million grant from the US Department of Labor to support certification programs in advanced manufacturing and information technology, and the Delaware Department of Labor received $800,000 from the federal Department of Labor to expand apprenticeship programs.

While these and other fund-raising efforts were successful and permitted the work to continue, the leaders were less successful in securing state funding for the initiative. The governor included funds for pathways in his 2016 budget, but the legislature cut the funding—along with all other new funding—because of a $75 million deficit. The state had a deficit in 2017 as well, and although spending rose somewhat in 2018, new state funding for pathways is unlikely.

Herdman of the Rodel Foundation of Delaware said state funding is essential. "For long-term sustainability, we need to figure out the public-sector side," he said. "We've talked to districts, and we're working with the economic development office and higher education. As we build the case for this, we are working on a matrixed strategy to get there. We have to be creative."

As they pursue options for state funding, the leaders are also coordinating their strategy for finding private dollars. The goal is for 60 percent of the funding to come from public sources and 40 percent from private sources by 2019. Building on their success in fund-raising, the United Way of Delaware and the Rodel Foundation of Delaware are leading efforts to identify potential sources of funding and coordinate the development of grant applications.[8]

Because they have been careful about linking funds to their strategic goals, the partners can direct their fund-raising efforts to their needs. If the funds do not come through, they will slow their expansion plans. But they do not need to cut back on the initiative, commented Rhine. "This is a best-case scenario budget," he said. "We will engage in work that maintains or improves current status. If we are not able to confirm [additional funding], that work will flow back to the next year, when we believe we will garner money to accomplish that activity."

## COMMUNITY ENGAGEMENT

Delaware Pathways leaders knew from the beginning that they would need to engage the broader community in the effort if it were to succeed. Schools would have to sign up to participate, students would have to enter the pathways, and businesses would have to provide work-based learning for youth. The leaders needed to make sure as many people as possible knew about the program and supported it.

As a first step, the leaders cast a wide net to solicit public comment on the strategic plan, which was published in draft form in February 2016. In dozens of face-to-face meetings and public forums, the leaders explained the program and invited reactions. They also posted it online and made it possible for people to submit comments via the internet.

In all, they received more than eight hundred comments, and as noted previously, the comments led to changes in the program. Specifically, the leaders created a course for students who needed additional help to meet college-level English language arts requirements, and they enlisted other agencies to provide additional support for students with disabilities participating in the pathways.

However, the partners did not engage in a broad-based engagement strategy until early 2017 when they secured funding for such efforts through the New Skills for Youth grant from JPMorgan Chase & Co. According to Robert Ford of the Workforce Development Board, the trajectory of community engagement for the pathways initiative resembles a hockey stick: flat and then rising sharply.

As part of their efforts, the leaders hired a local communications firm, Strongpoint Marketing, to conduct a communications audit to determine effective outreach strategies. Based on the audit, Strongpoint drafted a communications plan. Key elements of the plan included:

- Upgrading the Delaware Pathways website (delawarepathways.org) to provide clear information about the initiative for students, parents, and employers
- Producing tool kits for employers and parents with information about pathway programs and participating schools
- Developing materials for schools to promote pathways programs
- Launching a social media outreach campaign

The leaders also agreed to produce an annual outcomes report to hold themselves accountable for the success of Delaware Pathways.[9] The leaders went through several iterations before agreeing to a report that provides data on the most important outcomes, said Rhine. "It was a hard conversation—is the information valid and reliable? How do we find the thing that influences all others—what moves the needle most?" In the end, the report card is blank in a couple of areas where data do not yet exist, Rhine said.

According to Markell, winning support for the initiative has not been a great challenge. Parents are beginning to recognize that a four-year university degree is not the only path to success for young people, and this offers a better way, he said. "The business model of paying $40,000 a year for a mediocre four-year college that may not get you qualified for a career is broken. Credentials are more important."

## PATHWAYS TO SUCCESS

Pathways leaders are confident that they can reach their goal of expanding the initiative so that half of all high school students are enrolled in a pathway by 2020. All the pieces are in place.

Already, the initiative has produced a number of accomplishments. The biggest beneficiaries, of course, are the students who have gone through the pathways, like Andrew Flynn and Joe Zecca. They now have skills, work experience, and a credential that will enable them to pursue further education or a career. And there are thousands more with those advantages.

But the initiative has also produced some ancillary benefits, some of which might not have been expected at the outset.

### Redesigning High Schools

For decades, education reformers have urged an overhaul of high schools to make them more relevant and engaging for students. Although the graduation rate has been rising, many students continue to drop out of high school, and surveys continually show that high school students remain bored and disengaged in school. The academic performance of high school students has been flat for years, according to national tests like the National Assessment of Educational Progress and international tests like the Programme for International Student Assessment.[10]

The pathways initiative has accelerated high school redesign in Delaware. As previously noted, the Appoquinimink School District reorganized its high schools into "schools," each of which includes one or more career pathways. Each of the pathways offers opportunities for students to take Advanced Placement courses or dual-enrollment options, and each provides work-based learning experiences with business and industry partners.

Burrows, the district's superintendent, said the redesign was aimed at supporting all students, including those who did not intend to go on to four-year colleges. "For a long time, we have been saying 'college and career readiness,'" he said. "We've done a wonderful job on the college piece. We want to do a better job on the career piece." Burrows added that the district had had career pathways for seven years, but the state effort propelled them forward. "It has accelerated high school redesign," he said.

In addition, the work has spread to the middle schools. Some pathways, like engineering and computer science, begin in middle school. And middle school teachers are working with high school teachers to align coursework to improve the preparation of students. Best of all, Burrows said, the work is spreading to other districts. "The highest form of flattery:

other districts have taken our course catalog and tried to duplicate it," he said. "That's great. It's great for kids—the more kids have access to that, it's a good thing."

### Linking Schools, Colleges, and Employers

The vision of the pathways initiative was to create a seamless system in which students moved from high school through postsecondary education to employment. Achieving that vision requires the three sectors to work together in ways they seldom have throughout the history of American education. The pathways initiative has indeed made that happen.

In Delaware, the leaders of the sectors knew one another and had worked together to craft a statewide vision for education. But the initiative has also led to partnerships on the ground that had not been in place before.

For example, business leaders and educators from Delaware Tech and the K–12 sector worked closely together to develop the pathways curricula. This was not an easy task; business leaders had complained for years that students lacked the skills they needed for entry-level employment, but they had not articulated the precise skills that were necessary, nor had they worked on a program of study to teach students those competencies in a systematic way. Now such programs of study are in place.

Similarly, there are now more partnerships than ever between schools and businesses. Schools partner with businesses to hold career fairs, and businesses send representatives to schools to discuss careers, as well as invite students and teachers to job-shadowing experiences in the workplace. With the launch of the intermediary at Delaware Tech, these activities will accelerate rapidly.

K–12 and higher education leaders have also worked together to try to create a better connection in academic content. In developing the Readiness with a Purpose program, which provides support to low-performing students in English, the two sectors collaborated to confirm that the coursework students took in high school was equivalent to the expectations for college entry. The partners are developing a similar program in math.

### Changing Expectations for Youth

Much of the education reform rhetoric in the past decade has focused on getting more students to go to college. In part, this reflects a greater recognition that the workplace in the coming decade will require students to attain some form of postsecondary education; the wage gap between college graduates and those with a high school diploma or less is large and growing.

However, success does not necessarily require a four-year degree, and because of the pathways initiative, Delawareans increasingly recognize this. In large part, this is because pathways redefined career and technical education in the state after Rhine took over the department in 2014.

"The pathways work opened the door to rethinking how we think about careers and college," said Herdman of Rodel. "It could be a one- or two-year certificate program. Kids [who take that route] are doing just fine or better in terms of income and quality of life. For the 70 percent of people who didn't finish college, their life choice was validated."

## CHALLENGES AHEAD

While the initiative has been successful, the partners face some challenges moving forward. These challenges do not threaten to unravel the initiative, but the leaders need to address them to ensure that it continues to accomplish its goals.

### Changes in Leadership

Markell, who set the initiative in motion, stepped down as governor in January 2017 because of term limits. His appointed secretary of education also stepped down. In many cases, the loss of two key leaders can threaten an initiative because new leaders want to put their own stamp on policies and not necessarily carry out the policies of their predecessors.

In this case, that does not look likely. The new governor, John Carney, spoke at the annual Delaware Pathways conference in March 2017. His comments focused on the essential role the Delaware Pathways initiative plays in the state's economic development strategy. Since taking office, Carney has restructured the state's economic development agency, creating a more nimble public-private partnership focused on the twenty-first-century economy. In a visit following the conference to Appoquinimink School District's pathways program, Carney pledged his support for expanding and strengthening Delaware Pathways.

The new secretary of education, Susan Bunting, is also an enthusiastic supporter of the initiative. She was previously superintendent of the Indian River School District, where two high schools, Indian River High School and Sussex Central High School, operate the engineering pathway. The leadership transition appears smooth.

## Uncertain Funding

The gap between planned programming and secured funds is large: more than $3 million (see figure 1.2). Fortunately, the leaders have been effective in securing private funds, and they have a strategy for pursuing grant opportunities where they exist. They also have designed the initiative so that existing funds support current programming; expansions will be delayed if funding does not materialize.

A bigger challenge is in securing state funds for pathways. While the partners have been very successful in using federal funds to support the initiative and have secured millions of dollars in private grants, they all recognize that a reliance on those sources of funding alone cannot sustain

**FIGURE 1.2** Total Delaware Pathways budget, 2017–2019

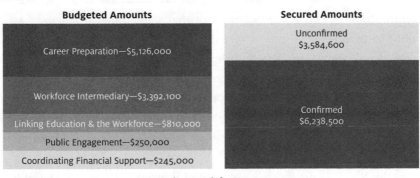

| Budgeted Amounts | Secured Amounts |
|---|---|
| Career Preparation—$5,126,000 | Unconfirmed $3,584,600 |
| Workforce Intermediary—$3,392,100 | |
| Linking Education & the Workforce—$810,000 | Confirmed $6,238,500 |
| Public Engagement—$250,000 | |
| Coordinating Financial Support—$245,000 | |

**Budget Total: $9,823,100**

the program. Only with a steady stream of state funds can they put down roots and build an infrastructure. The state's budget deficit has blocked that stream, at least for the time being.

### Inadequate Student Preparation

Delaware Pathways provides opportunities for students, but students have to be prepared to take advantage of those opportunities. In order to take pathways courses and earn college credit while in high school, students must be ready for college-level work. But a large number of Delaware students lack that preparation.

According to a state report, 40 percent of Delaware high school graduates were required to take remedial coursework in college in 2016, and the gaps in remediation rates between white students and students of color, and affluent and low-income youth are high: only 34 percent of white students were required to take remedial courses in college, compared to 50 percent of Hispanics, 59 percent of African Americans, and 53 percent of low-income students. Forty-three percent of Delaware's class of 2014 did not attend college at all.[11]

But the warning signs for this lack of preparation appear earlier than college. On the SAT, which as of 2016 is required for all eleventh graders in the state, only 27 percent of Delaware students met the benchmark in either math or English language arts. (Students who meet the SAT benchmark are much less likely to be required to take remedial courses than those who do not.) And, again, the gaps are large. While 37 percent of white students met the benchmark in math and English language arts, only 14 percent of Hispanics met the benchmarks in either subject area, and just 12 and 10 percent of African American students met the benchmark in English language arts and math, respectively.[12]

Pathways leaders recognize this challenge, and they have secured funding to develop a course to accelerate the English language skills for students who fail to achieve the benchmark score on the SAT. They are developing a similar course in math.

But Rhine of the state Department of Education recognizes that this is a "Band-Aid strategy." Ultimately, he said, colleges and secondary schools need to work together to align coursework so that all students learn what they need in high school to be prepared for postsecondary education. "I don't want to be doing this in five years," he said.

## THE NEW SWITZERLAND?

These challenges are formidable, but the Delaware Pathways leaders are aware of them and have plans to address them. In the meantime, they have much to show the rest of the nation.

The number of students enrolled in pathways—nearly nine thousand in 2017—has grown astronomically and is projected to continue to grow, to reach the target of 50 percent of the state's high school students by 2020.[13]

The number of businesses providing work-based learning has increased rapidly—seventy-six companies are entered into the online resource SPARC—and the intermediary structure at Delaware Tech will accelerate the process.

Although the partners have been unable so far to secure state funding, they have been successful at raising private and federal funds and using them strategically to advance the initiative.

The partners have constructed an infrastructure that includes high-level support to manage the initiative and steer its growth.

At the statewide Delaware Pathways conference in March 2017, Pathways to Prosperity cofounder Robert Schwartz noted that he has frequently taken Americans interested in a seamless career pathways system to Switzerland, which he has called the "gold standard" in career and technical education. In fact, Herdman from Rodel and Rhine from the state Department of Education accompanied Schwartz on a trip to Switzerland at the outset of the Delaware Pathways initiative. In the not-too-distant future, Schwartz predicted, he might not have to take visitors all the way to Europe. He might be able to bring them to Delaware.

Delaware Pathways is a long way from Switzerland's system, which has five hundred years of history behind it. But the state is off to a promising start.

## CHAPTER 2

# BALANCING BOLD STATE POLICY AND REGIONAL FLEXIBILITY

## Pathways Tennessee

*Richard Kazis*

In 2008, Lillian Hartgrove began working at the Highlands Economic Partnership in Cookeville, Tennessee, charged with leading economic development in the Upper Cumberland region, halfway between Nashville and Knoxville.

Hartgrove knew the area well: she had moved to the region in 2003 and understood its strengths and weaknesses through her work as senior vice president of a regional bank. Experience taught her that the primary barrier to regional growth was not the cost of land or buildings, but rather the challenge of finding skilled workers for new and expanding businesses, particularly in manufacturing and assembly.

The local chamber of commerce launched the Highlands Economic Partnership in 2006 and received attention for two high-visibility studies that raised important red flags about the region's future. The first study documented low high school graduation rates among at-risk students. The second, a labor market assessment, underscored the gap between the skills and education levels of the region's workforce and the expectations and needs of its growing economy. In 2011, Hartgrove created a Highlands Workforce Development and Educational Development Committee, with an influential vice president and dean at Tennessee Technological

University as chair. Together, they tapped their connections among educators, employers, and civic leaders to form the committee, which began trying out different ways to get parents, educators, and public officials working together to build a stronger pipeline from K–12 schools and local colleges into the regional economy. Support was immediate: "If you're in, we're in, Lillian," people told her.

A year earlier, in November 2010, Republican Bill Haslam, the very popular mayor of Knoxville, was elected governor of Tennessee, replacing term-limited Democrat Phil Bredesen. Bredesen threw himself and his administration into improving the state's educational performance—and reputation—after a 2007 US Chamber of Commerce report gave Tennessee K–12 education a failing grade for "truth in advertising" of state standards, accountability, and performance. Bredesen organized the state agencies to compete for a federal Race to the Top grant. Tennessee was awarded one of the first two grants, bringing the state a half-billion dollars in exchange for a commitment to raise K–12 standards, strengthen accountability metrics, and address the problem of low-performing schools. In his final year, Bredesen turned to higher education, helping to secure passage of the Complete College Tennessee Act of 2010 that set goals for improved college completion and made changes in college funding, developmental education, and higher education transfer policies. In his last State of the State address, Bredesen told legislators that, if he were able to serve a third term, he would have made higher education improvement a top priority.

Haslam took the baton from Bredesen. Asking employers what it would take for them to relocate to or expand operations in Tennessee, Haslam heard that the state needed a more qualified, well-trained workforce. In 2013, he launched Drive to 55, an initiative to increase the number of Tennesseans with postsecondary degrees or certificates to 55 percent by 2025, aligning the state's educational system with the needs of Tennessee's high-growth industries. Under Haslam's leadership, Tennessee has become a highly regarded model for other states, implementing creative strategies to significantly increase postsecondary access and success for recent high school graduates and working adults. Haslam's legacy includes Tennessee Promise and Tennessee Reconnect. Tennessee Promise is a last-dollar scholarship, launched in 2014, that guarantees Tennessee high school graduates two years of technical or community college without tuition or fees—the nation's first statewide "free community college" program. The Tennessee Reconnect initiative, which in 2014 began offering adults an opportunity to attend Tennessee's Colleges of Applied Technology tuition-free, expanded in 2017 to include community colleges as well as technical training.

Late in 2011, Danielle Mezera left her job as the educational adviser to Nashville mayor Karl Dean to help drive education reform at the state level. On New Year's Day 2012, Mezera began her new position as assistant commissioner for college, career, and technical education in the Tennessee Department of Education. Although she didn't have much experience with the inner workings of career and technical education (CTE) policy or funding, she was certain that CTE in Tennessee had plenty of potential to improve. Her Nashville experience had impressed upon her the need to better connect high school students to both postsecondary learning and employer demand—and to make it easier to map efficient routes to decent careers. Mezera brought in a Nashville colleague, Casey Wrenn, to be her chief of staff. They began to plan in earnest how to use state policy and resources to drive reform across the state.

These three strands of activity—local organizing to strengthen the workforce pipeline, gubernatorial leadership to better link education programs and incentives with economic priorities, and state education policy reform to modernize CTE—took root somewhat independently in Tennessee. Over the past five to seven years, though, they have come together into a multipronged, synergistic campaign to improve the educational and economic prospects of Tennessee residents, both those coming out of K–12 schools and working adults looking to complete credentials and advance their careers.

Pathways Tennessee is a statewide effort to provide Tennessee students, starting in high school, with access to rigorous academic and career pathways aligned to local and state economic and labor market needs. Launched in 2012 by Mezera and her team at the Tennessee Department of Education, Pathways Tennessee's framework and strategy were greatly influenced by the then-new Pathways to Prosperity Network, which Tennessee was among the first states to join (see appendix A for more information about the Pathways Network). Hartgrove's Highlands Economic Partnership was one of the first two regional entities encouraged and supported by the state to implement Pathways Tennessee. As the effort has expanded across Tennessee's nine economic development regions, Pathways Tennessee has become increasingly integrated into Haslam's Drive to 55 initiative.

The evolution of Pathways Tennessee offers lessons for innovators in other cities, regions, and states who want to build better aligned and more transparent pathways to college and careers for high school students. As one of the states that has gone furthest in implementing this high-school-through-postsecondary career pathways model, Tennessee has learned through experience and trial and error about strategies for tackling important—and inevitable—design choices, resource challenges, and implementation dilemmas. These include lessons on:

- Balancing bold leadership and distributed authority
- The importance of both people and policy in making change
- How top-down and bottom-up strategies can be linked
- What it takes to break down policy and practice silos to create effective, sustainable regional partnerships

Pathways Tennessee leaders have also learned a great deal about how long regional or state-level change takes, how uneven this change often is, and the calibration of expectations for implementing a model relatively untested in the United States and built on the fly.

This chapter draws out lessons both for Tennesseans invested in the different components of their statewide reform effort—of which Pathways Tennessee is a part—and for those in other states and regions working toward similar goals.

## DATA ON PATHWAYS TENNESSEE AT STATE AND REGIONAL LEVELS

Pathways Tennessee has been built at three levels: (1) state activity guided by the Tennessee Department of Education and a cross-agency state planning team; (2) regional infrastructure and partnerships; and (3) activities and pathways programs that change the student experience. Data on progress are incomplete and difficult to compile. A grant from JPMorgan Chase & Co.'s New Skills for Youth initiative is helping the state and regions collect more useful and integrated data on pathways. For now, here are some markers that provide a provisional picture of state, regional, and student-level activities related to Pathways Tennessee.

### STATE-LEVEL SNAPSHOT

- Sixteen employer-led industry councils established.
- New CTE programs established, including human resource management and cybersecurity in 2017.
- New occupational certification approved in animal science; additional certifications planned in horticulture science, dietetics and nutrition, and social health services.
- Seventy-seven percent of high schools offering dual-enrollment courses.
- Number of students who are CTE concentrators (take three or more courses in a career cluster): close to forty thousand per year—nearly half the students in the 2016 graduating class.

### REGIONAL INFRASTRUCTURE PROGRESS

- All nine regions mapped for education and economic assets and needs.
- Intermediaries selected in eight of nine regions and in one additional county (Rutherford).
- Three industry councils established in Upper Cumberland; five in Rutherford County.

### PATHWAYS-RELATED ACTIVITIES ENROLLING STUDENTS

- Career exploration activities: in Upper Cumberland, 3,400 seventh and eighth graders participated (unfortunately, data are unavailable on other regions or statewide).

- Dual-enrollment and other early postsecondary opportunities (ESPOs): more than 40 percent of 2015 Tennessee graduates had enrolled in at least one of eight EPSOs (including AP and dual enrollment); 19 percent of these had enrolled in a dual-enrollment course.
- Tennessee students enrolled in work-based learning capstone course: 7,219 from 2012 freshman cohort (75 percent of these were CTE concentrators).
- Tennessee students participating in the pilot work-based learning portal in 2016: 3,480 students, looking for matches with 1,600 participating employers.
- Tennessee students earning an industry certification in 2015–2016, as reported by CTE teachers: 2,160 (7 percent of CTE concentrators).
- Tennessee students who concentrated in a high-priority career cluster in 2016 (advanced manufacturing, health care, information technology) and completed a work-based learning capstone:
  - Advanced manufacturing: 153
  - Health sciences: 353
  - Information technology: 285

## ECONOMIC AND EDUCATIONAL PERFORMANCE

Tennessee's population of 6.6 million places it seventeenth among US states, even though it is only thirty-sixth in size. With a population density twice the national average, Tennessee is characterized by great regional and metropolitan diversity.

Four cities anchor large metro regions: Knoxville, Chattanooga, Nashville, and Memphis. Much of the state though is rural, with some of it quite mountainous and isolated. Originally populated by Cherokee and several other Native American tribes, English and Scotch Irish pioneers settled across the state. Tennessee is currently 75 percent white, but Memphis, the state's largest city, is majority African American. The Hispanic population, though small, is the state's fastest-growing demographic group.

After the Second World War, Tennessee made huge strides in shifting from an agrarian and natural resource–based economy to one based on high-value-added manufacturing. Pursuing a New South strategy of low taxes, wages, and cost of living, accompanied by active recruitment of large firms, by 1975 Tennessee boasted a manufacturing industry that employed a higher proportion of the state workforce than the national average. In the 1980s, Tennessee attracted huge new Nissan and Saturn car assembly plants. Related parts and equipment manufacturers followed. Transportation equipment and industrial and commercial machinery became the state's second- and third-largest industries, respectively.

In the 1990s, Tennessee enjoyed stronger economic growth than the rest of the United States, building from its position as the third-largest manufacturing state. However, the momentum of the postwar period began to stall. Firms relying on low-skilled labor started to move overseas, while more profitable firms invested in productivity-enhancing automation, raising the demand for higher-skilled workers in the modernizing manufacturing sector. Between 2000 and 2010, these broad trends combined with the Great Recession to reduce manufacturing employment by 36 percent.

Today, Tennessee's economy presents a mixed picture. The state is home to twenty-three of the *Fortune* 1000 firms, including FedEx, Dollar General, Eastman Chemical, and AutoZone.[1] The state's population and economy have both been growing faster than the national average. Labor force participation is up; unemployment dropped to a record low of 3.4 percent in July 2017. In one study of the fastest-growing cities in 2016, five Tennessee cities landed in the top twenty-five. In the past two years, Tennessee was recognized as first in the nation for advanced-industry job growth, first in direct foreign investment, and second in the growth of household median income.[2] Employment in education, health services, and leisure and hospitality has jumped since 2000, though wages in these sectors are significantly below those in manufacturing.

Despite the state's growth, personal and family income levels are still relatively low: the 2015 median household income of $47,275 was $8,500 lower than the national average and put Tennessee in the bottom quintile of states.[3] In 2014, Tennessee was forty-fifth in the nation in terms of the percentage of residents living below the federal poverty level (18 percent).

Wealth and poverty are unevenly distributed. While some regions are booming, many Appalachian counties are depopulating and exhibit little economic vitality. Other communities, like Shelby County, which includes Memphis, are characterized by stark extremes of poverty and affluence.

While some sources argue that Tennessee is one of the healthiest state economies, others argue it is one of the weakest. The conservative American Legislative Exchange Council rated Tennessee the fifth strongest in the nation in 2017, up from seventh the prior year, based on its assessment of fifteen policy variables emphasizing low tax burdens, competitive wages, and a pro-business regulatory climate.[4] The State New Economy Index of the Information Technology and Innovation Foundation—based on twenty-five indicators of the extent to which state economies are "knowledge-based, globalized, entrepreneurial, IT-driven, and innovation oriented"—ranked Tennessee thirty-second in the nation in 2017.[5] The difference between these two positions hinges on what the source argues makes a state competitive in today's global environment.

In anticipation of a more skill-driven economic environment, Tennessee has worked to improve educational outcomes significantly and leapfrog other states that tend to accompany it near the bottom of state performance rankings. Progress has been impressive.

Tennessee's high school cohort graduation rate was 89 percent in 2017, placing it eleventh highest in the nation and second among the Southern Regional Education Board's (SREB) sixteen member states.[6] The graduation rate has risen 3.6 percentage points since the 2010–2011 school year.[7] Since 2011, Tennessee's fourth- and eighth-grade National Assessment of Educational Progress (NAEP) scores in math and reading have risen faster than those of any other state.[8] Eighth-grade reading scores have climbed above the national average; math scores are only three points below the national average.

There is still a long way to go. Scores on the ACT exam—which all Tennessee juniors take—are lower than the national average, and Tennesseans score lower on all ACT subject exams than test takers from other SREB states.[9] And while enrollments in public higher education rose during the recession and again in the first year of implementation of the

Tennessee Promise, graduation rates have been flat in community colleges and have edged up only slightly in four-year institutions during the past decade.[10]

According to the US Census, Tennessee has not yet turned the corner in addressing a very significant skills gap: in 2015, only 25 percent of Tennessee residents age twenty-five or older held a bachelor's degree, well short of the 58 percent of jobs projected to require a bachelor's degree in the next few years.[11] As figure 2.1 indicates, associate's and bachelor's degree attainment rates vary greatly by race and ethnicity, perpetuating the economic and racial disparities that already exist within the state. The supply of educated and skilled workers is not sufficient to meet the needs of the evolving state economy, which could constrain growth in industries and occupations projected to grow across Tennessee in the years ahead.

**FIGURE 2.1** Degree attainment rates among Tennessee residents (aged 25–64) of at least an associate's degree, by population

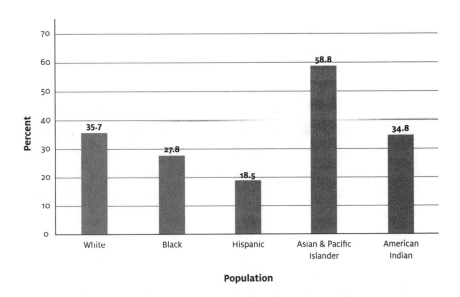

*Source*: Lumina Foundation, 2017, http://strongernation.luminafoundation.org/report/2018/#state/TN.

## MODERNIZING CTE: PATHWAYS TENNESSEE AS A STATEWIDE STRATEGY

When Danielle Mezera took over the CTE division of the Tennessee Department of Education, she set out to end the marginalization of CTE and "to enable it to be what it should always have been: vertically aligned with and reflective of the expectations of both postsecondary institutions and of employers and the labor market."

Mezera felt that repositioning CTE would enable students pursuing a career-related concentration to meet the same rigorous standards as other Tennessee high school graduates and give them a leg up on their peers in terms of college and career preparation and trajectory. But for this to happen, new relationships would need to be developed at the local level among K–12 systems, local technical schools and community colleges, and key employers and their industry-based organizations.

Mezera and her division would also have to design and implement the appropriate state roles to encourage and support this repositioning. She requested that the CTE division be allowed to add an Office of Postsecondary Readiness and Early Postsecondary. State Education Commissioner Kevin Huffman approved the change, giving Mezera oversight of the only office in the Tennessee Department of Education explicitly linked to postsecondary partners.

A few months later, Mezera and Huffman hosted a meeting at Volkswagen's plant in Chattanooga to discuss the role of industry in education. At the meeting, Robert Schwartz, Pathways to Prosperity Network cofounder, introduced a new national effort to encourage states to improve pathways into high-demand industries. "I left that meeting thinking, 'This makes sense for Tennessee.' This is what I wanted to create," explained Mezera. She had been sharpening her ideas for a statewide CTE reform campaign: rigorous coursework; industry certifications with value in the labor market; early and effective career exposure; and guidance to help students understand their options and choose among clear pathways into postsecondary programs and, ultimately, careers.

"There was nothing in the DNA of our division that was not in the DNA of the pathways model—and vice versa," said Mezera. Huffman and

Mezera pleaded Tennessee's case to join the fledgling Pathways to Prosperity Network. In their justification for Tennessee's inclusion, they laid out a vision of a statewide system of rigorous CTE integrated with core academic standards and learning, aligned with postsecondary credentials and with robust supports for work-based learning experiences. Tennessee's application was accepted; Mezera had the framework she was looking for.

Her first step was hiring a full-time staff member to build out Pathways Tennessee. Without a dedicated person working to make it happen, Mezera believed, the effort would not develop sufficient momentum and notice within state government. Nor would practitioners feel that the state was serious about doing things differently.

Nick Hansen was working for a start-up distillery in Nashville when he heard about the new position. He thought his business-oriented background and start-up experience would be a good fit. He liked the role's emphasis on advising, reaching out to employers, and figuring out how to leverage state policy to support local change. Mezera hired Hansen in 2012. According to Hansen, "We had an idea more than we had a strategy. But we knew we wanted to move beyond a stand-alone project, beyond the stigma of CTE and even of K–12 education, to something that made sense to other agencies, to employers, and to community leaders focusing on economic growth."

Mezera and her team launched an ambitious three-phase campaign to modernize CTE in Tennessee and integrate it with general and academic education. In phase one, they reorganized the state's CTE "program areas" to align with sixteen nationally recognized CTE career clusters and related labor market data so that the new program areas responded to the state's economic needs rather than the legacy and interests of CTE faculty and administrators. Phase two involved a painstaking, detailed revision of standards for each program of study, ensuring that each prepared graduates for both college and careers. Phase three, involving the development of course exams for CTE programs, is currently in development. In addition, the team dramatically redesigned the state's work-based learning policies so that student experiences in the workplace would add value and reinforce in-demand technical and professional skills.

When Mezera's tenure began, Tennessee's CTE programs were organized into seven overly broad program areas, such as trade and industry, agriculture, and health sciences. Program areas didn't line up well with regional postsecondary programs of study or employment opportunities. Over the years, high school programs multiplied rapidly, numbering over two hundred. Courses were duplicated in inefficient ways: welding might be offered in architecture, but also in trade and industry. According to Heather Justice, former executive director of the Office of Career and Technical Education, "We did a full scrubbing of all the courses to identify duplications and gaps." Mezera and her team retired programs (such as two- and four-cycle engines) that had no postsecondary program to link to and no demand from the field. Realizing that Tennessee had no program of study in government and public administration, they undertook a statewide analysis of need and opportunity, and then designed and created a new program. They collapsed programs that differed by one or two courses and ultimately reduced the 212 approved programs of study to fewer than 70. Most importantly, they grouped programs under the sixteen nationally recognized career clusters, a tested framework that aligns more easily with postsecondary technical programs.

Mezera and the team then proceeded to establish content standards for over three hundred individual CTE courses taught across Tennessee. To accomplish this, they used a backward mapping process, beginning with the skills and knowledge students were expected to learn in a four-course sequence, and then deriving standards for each course as it aligned with the rest of the sequence. Literacy, numeracy, critical thinking, and other core academic skills were embedded in the CTE courses. The process took three years. It is now repeated annually to ensure that standards stay rigorous and relevant.

In this painstaking process, Mezera and her team saw an opportunity to change the relationship between core academics and CTE. Traditionally, for example, CTE science courses did not qualify as general education science courses in Tennessee high schools: schools might offer both a CTE version of anatomy and physiology and a general education version. Justice and Wrenn began meeting regularly with their peers focused on general education at the Tennessee Department of Education, committed to raising CTE course rigor and eliminating disparities across courses. Today, statewide, seventeen CTE courses also qualify as general education courses, meeting graduation requirements for science, social studies, and fine arts.

Not surprisingly, a number of longtime employees within the CTE division were uncomfortable with the new direction. Some were wary of any change. Others did not believe that CTE students could succeed in an environment of higher standards and argued for "protecting their students" through lower expectations. Mezera made a number of personnel decisions designed to bring new energy and flexibility to the division: "It wasn't pleasant, but the changes had to be made. We ripped the Band-Aid off as quickly as we could."

Mezera had full support from Huffman; when the current commissioner of education, Candice McQueen, took over in 2015, Mezera made sure she was comfortable with their direction and approach. One reflection of that support was the decision to change the Division of Career and Technical Education to the Division of College, Career and Technical Education.

At the school and district levels, some faculty were afraid they would lose courses they enjoyed teaching or lose their jobs altogether. Family and consumer science instructors were particularly concerned that the changes would "take fundamental life skills away" from those who were not college bound. Mezera and her staff stood firm. According to Wrenn, "We told them that all graduates will need these skills, even stay-at-home moms. Our public responsibility was not just to get students to walk across the stage but to prepare them for the postsecondary learning they would need to have more choices and be successful."

Another piece of the reform agenda was to redesign the delivery of work-based learning for Tennessee high school students: creating learning experiences at workplaces or using work situations to advance students' development and mastery of in-demand workplace skills. The statewide policy in place when Mezera joined the Tennessee Department of Education was too much about the logistics of "checking students out of school for the afternoon," according to Chelsea Parker, whom Mezera hired to be the executive director of work-based learning.

By statute, the Tennessee Department of Education oversaw the provision of work-based learning and the training of work-based learning coordinators. Mezera and Parker appreciated the challenges of scheduling work-based learning opportunities and training coordinators, but they saw a deeper problem. No one was asking what students who engage in work-based learning should actually be expected to learn as part of their CTE programs—and how anyone would know whether they were learning or not. "We decided to flip the script," said Parker.

They defined the transferable skills they thought should be learned through work experiences and the kinds of connections to adults that students should develop. They promoted policy changes that would encourage early industry engagement with districts in planning work-based learning activities, from industry tours to job shadows to capstone experiences such as internships, clinicals, and practicum experiences for credit.

The State Board of Education adopted a work-based learning framework in 2015 to govern all work-based learning experiences; the Tennessee Department of Education revised its policy guide to align with the new framework, setting clear expectations for district efforts, student experiences, and learning outcomes. The framework specified state support for regional Pathways Tennessee efforts and industry engagement. It emphasized the alignment of student work-based learning experiences with programs of study so that technical and employability skills could be learned in context. Districts are free to meet the new standards as they see fit. The Tennessee Department of Education has beefed up its data collection system for tracking work-based learning availability and access across the state so that it can make good on its goal of "developing 21st-century skills through work-based learning experiences." Enrollment in capstone courses has increased steadily since the revitalization of the state policy, climbing from under six thousand in 2013–2014 to over eight thousand two years later.

Mezera wanted to position Pathways Tennessee as a cross-sector initiative: "We never wanted Pathways to be an appendage to one agency. That is how these things go away. It had to be more central." Early on, she advocated for a state planning team outside the Tennessee Department of Education to engage other relevant state agencies. By winter 2012, that group was in place and meeting regularly. It included high-level decision makers from the Tennessee departments of Economic and Community Development (TNECD), Labor and Workforce Development, and Education, as well as the Tennessee Higher Education Commission, the Tennessee Independent Colleges and Universities Association, the Tennessee Board of Regents, the State Board of Education, the governor's office, the Tennessee Business Roundtable, and an influential statewide education advocacy group called SCORE (State Collaborative on Reforming Education).

The planning group focused first on information sharing and on common definitions and language that all partners would use. The group did not go immediately to questions of resources. According to Mezera, "From the beginning, we wanted to secure agreement from stakeholders that they would work together, not just get together and ask things of each other. We wanted to weave Pathways Tennessee into the day-to-day workings of the education department and its sister agencies." The strategy was to make it hard for future policy makers to unwind Pathways Tennessee because its definitions, standards, and priorities would be cooked into many agencies' plans.

Local planning and execution was organized according to TNECD's nine economic development regions. The Tennessee Department of Labor inserted the pathways definition into its state plan for use of federal workforce dollars. Department leaders instructed local workforce boards to participate in regional pathways conversations and, where possible, to align funding to those efforts. The Tennessee Board of Regents moved to require that proposals for new technical associate's degree programs demonstrate the proposed program's workforce relevance and map out how employers would be engaged in program planning and delivery. Although the planning team met quarterly, informal conversations across agencies became routine. According to Ann Thompson, director of workforce development for TNECD, "We broke down the divides and built a team mentality. We drove toward a culture change within state government. Everyone at the table signed on."

While CTE reform was in motion and the pathways approach to engaging employers in high-demand industries was developed at the state and regional levels, Haslam used his 2013 State of the State address and budget to launch the Drive to 55, designed to increase college credential completion so that Tennessee's economy could continue to grow and attract good employers. His leadership—and specific policy actions by the governor and the legislature—improved the environment for pathways implementation. "The governor moved the goalposts for us by focusing so intently on postsecondary success," explained Wrenn. "But since CTE was the only division of the Department of Education that was connected to and focused on postsecondary success, we were well positioned to take advantage."

In 2017, Commissioner McQueen appointed Lyle Ailshie, a longtime school superintendent in Kingsport and Greeneville in northeast Tennessee, deputy commissioner. Ailshie is responsible for both the Division of College, Career and Technical Education (including Pathways Tennessee) and the Teachers and Leaders Division, responsible for improving teacher preparation in the state. This position is an opportunity Ailshie is excited about. "We know that our state will succeed by getting more young people into and through pathways to good jobs in high demand in our state," Ailshie said. "Pathways Tennessee has mobilized some of the most talented Tennessee employers, educators, and civic leaders into partnerships that can make a difference for our students and communities. We are committed to figuring out how we can continue to support this work, align it with other important initiatives, and increase access to good pathways across the state, in cities and towns, large and small."

## ALIGNING PATHWAYS TENNESSEE WITH THE GOVERNOR'S DRIVE TO 55

When Haslam launched the Drive to 55 to increase college degree or certificate attainment from 32 percent to 55 percent of Tennesseans by the year 2025, he emphasized the link between postsecondary credentials and current and future workforce and economic needs: "We want Tennesseans working in Tennessee jobs. We want Tennesseans to have an opportunity to get a good job and for those in the workplace to be able to advance and get an even better job."

Haslam pointed to several areas of weak performance: the more than twenty thousand high school graduates each year who chose not to continue on to college; the nearly 70 percent of new community college students who entered college not ready for college-level work; and the almost one million residents of the state who had some college credits, but no credential. To get from 32 percent to 55 percent of state residents having a college credential, significant progress would be needed for both recent high school graduates and working adults.

According to Richard Rhoda, then-executive director of the Tennessee Higher Education Commission, "[Governor Haslam] got buy-in early on. He named a special advisor for higher education [businessman Randy Boyd].[12] Boyd served for a year, crossing the state meeting with not only educators, but the business community, the nonprofit sector, to talk about the need to increase educational attainment." (See table 2.1.)

The centerpiece of the Drive to 55 initiative is the Tennessee Promise, the scholarship and mentoring program created to provide all Tennessee high school graduates with a guarantee of free tuition and no mandatory fees at any of the state's thirteen community colleges or twenty-seven Tennessee Colleges of Applied Technology. The Promise is a last-dollar scholarship that kicks in after Pell Grants, state HOPE Scholarships, and any other government aid. To be eligible, high school students need to meet a series of milestones in their senior year, including completing the

**TABLE 2.1** Tennessee state initiatives focused on college attainment

| Pathways Tennessee | Aligns with Drive to 55 |
| --- | --- |
| Drive to 55 | Has component initiatives |
| Tennessee Promise | Part of Drive to 55 |
| Tennessee Reconnect | Part of Drive to 55 |
| Labor Education Alignment Program (LEAP) | Part of Drive to 55 |
| Advise TN | Part of Drive to 55 |

Free Application for Federal Student Aid (FAFSA) and attending several college-going mentoring sessions. To remain eligible, students must maintain satisfactory academic progress once enrolled in a postsecondary program and perform at least eight hours of community service each term.

While the Tennessee Promise has received significant attention nationally and has been the inspiration for similar programs in a number of states, there is more to the Drive to 55. There are five pillars: get students ready; get them in; get them through; reconnect adults; and partner with industry. For young people, the state launched Advise TN to fund the provision of additional counseling and college and career advising services for students during their junior and senior years of high school. Advise TN was launched as a pilot, and there are plans to extend the program to additional schools and young people in the years ahead. For adults who want to return to college and earn a credential, regardless of income or past academic performance, the state offers Tennessee Reconnect, which enables adults to attend and earn a certificate free of tuition and mandatory fees at any of the state's community or technical colleges. This last-dollar scholarship for adults ages twenty-five to sixty-four with some college who want to complete credentials also helped drive enrollment in Tennessee Colleges of Applied Technology (TCATs). (Increasing enrollment of youth in TCATs is a focus of Pathways Tennessee.) The Labor Education Alignment Program (LEAP), authorized by the Tennessee legislature in 2013, helped deepen TCAT collaborations with high school CTE programs in high-demand fields.

## Tennessee's Colleges of Applied Technology and Community Colleges

Tennessee's public postsecondary institutions include a flagship research institution (the University of Tennessee), a number of regional four-year state universities, two-year community colleges, and TCATs that specialize in technical certificates and diplomas. The community colleges and TCATs are critically important to the pathways effort. Pathways Tennessee was not created as a high school reform effort but as a system-bridging initiative.

Tennessee's state government is intent on improving the alignment of high school, TCATs and community colleges, and four-year public institutions. Beginning in 2010, there have been significant changes in Tennessee's education policies. The Complete College Tennessee Act of 2010 called for the transition of thirteen locally governed community colleges into a statewide system of coordinated programs and services. The act also called for mutually beneficial relations between the community colleges and TCATs so that community college courses could be offered at TCATs, and TCAT certificates could be offered at the community colleges. Across the state, improved relationships between these two types of institutions are proceeding at different paces, with cooperation and competition both in play as TCATS and community colleges reposition themselves in a changing educational market.

In general, TCATs have traditionally served adult workers looking to upgrade skills or change careers. Their credentials and credits do not transfer to four-year college programs. Community colleges have been geared more toward transfer than technical programs and partnerships with employers. Pathways Tennessee found it easier to partner with TCATs initially, given the potential for alignment between high school CTE and TCAT technical offerings. However, the new Tennessee Promise and Tennessee Reconnect programs are changing some of the incentives and patterns of collaboration at the local level.

In 2016, at Haslam's urging, the state legislature restructured the Tennessee Board of Regents. Four-year schools are no longer under the Board of Regents' authority and will now be independent and locally governed. The Tennessee Board of Regents will focus on TCATs and community colleges and ways to better align their programs, standards, and relationships with K–12 and four-year transfer institutions.

**TCATS.** There are twenty-seven TCATs across the state that offer certificate and diploma programs in over sixty distinct occupational fields. The open entry/open exit programs typically require 2,100 hours of classes, offered in a five-day-a-week, 8:00 a.m. to 3:00 p.m., full-time program. TCATs tend to serve working adults; the average student age is about twenty-seven. High-enrollment programs include: administrative office technology, machine tool technology, practical nursing, welding, and automotive. Because of the program length, occupational focus, and bias toward full-time enrollment, TCATs have a very high success rate: about 80 percent of students complete the program, and about 86 percent of those find employment in their field of study.

However, TCAT capacity is small: only about twenty thousand students enroll annually, about 5 percent of postsecondary enrollment in the state. The state subsidizes more than 50 percent of TCAT costs. It wants to expand TCAT enrollment and has launched new initiatives to encourage increased enrollment, such as Tennessee Promise and LEAP.

**COMMUNITY COLLEGES.** Tennessee's thirteen community colleges serve eighty-seven thousand students annually, about one in four postsecondary students in the state's public and private institutions. The most common majors are liberal arts, the health professions, business, and engineering. Because the state has invested less per student in these institutions than in the TCATs, tuition and fees are a comparatively high $3,800 a year. First-time, full-time students have a six-year graduation rate from their original institution of 28 percent. However, 89 percent of students who do graduate are employed within a year.

Compared to the TCATs, community colleges in Tennessee have been more focused on transfer than on technical programs. However, community college linkages with high schools are becoming stronger as a result of the Tennessee Promise and incentives for dual-enrollment and other EPSOs.

### Accelerating Industry Alignment with LEAP

Another component of Drive to 55 is LEAP. LEAP was not originally a gubernatorial initiative, but has since been folded into Drive to 55. Its origins were in a meeting that Senate Majority Leader Mark Norris (R-Collierville) attended with representatives from TNECD, the multinational firm Unilever, and the TCAT in Tipton County where Unilever was planning to expand operations. Unilever complained that its search for four hundred new employees who could work with robotic machines netted ten thousand applications, but only thirty-five qualified applicants. Norris convened a sidebar conversation among TNECD staff, TCAT representatives, and Unilever about whether the workforce problem could be fixed. He became convinced that the key interests—the employers, the educational institutions, and the state—were not having the right conversations at the right time. Norris and Representative Gerald McCormick of Chattanooga introduced a bill "that would make these people talk with each other," according to his senior policy adviser.

The vehicle for those conversations was a multimillion-dollar grant program that required interested communities to develop a framework for regional partnerships to address the specific skills gaps that local employers experienced. Partners would need to include local TCATs, community colleges, industry, workforce development boards, and K–12 educators—particularly those associated with CTE—in the new framework. In 2014, the first round of grants, totaling $10 million, funded twelve proposals, targeting advanced manufacturing, mechatronics, information technology, and career readiness. Two years later, a second round of $10 million in grants focused on advanced manufacturing and health care. It also prioritized work-based learning for students benefiting from these partnerships: funds in this round could be used to reimburse private employers for up to 50 percent of wages paid as part of a work-based learning program.

For the CTE division and the Pathways Tennessee team, LEAP was a critically important accelerant. The governor's Workforce Subcabinet, composed of commissioners and staff from the state agencies represented on the pathways state leadership team (plus the Tennessee Department of Human Services), was given responsibility for reviewing LEAP proposals and making grants. More importantly, LEAP was a vehicle for convening regional partnerships so the partnerships could secure funding for expensive, sophisticated equipment for their high schools and postsecondary institutions, especially the TCATs. LEAP enabled regions to upgrade their training programs to meet industry needs and to redesign education pathways resulting in credentials and employment in high-demand occupations. Ten of the twelve first-round grants went to stakeholders working directly with Pathways Tennessee.

While they were the most publicized and promoted pieces of the state strategy, the branded elements of Drive to 55—Tennessee Promise, Tennessee Reconnect, LEAP, and Advise TN—were augmented by additional state-level efforts designed to increase educational attainment in Tennessee. The Tennessee Board of Regents took on significant work to simplify and make more transparent transfer pathways in high-volume majors from two- to four-year public institutions.

## SAILS Tackles Developmental Education

State leaders are also tackling remediation, a common barrier to postsecondary completion. Seamless Alignment and Integrated Learning Support (SAILS) is a computer-mediated math program that offers the community college developmental math curriculum to underprepared high school seniors, so they can be ready for college-level work. Created by Chattanooga State Community College for use with its feeder high schools, SAILS is now available across all thirteen community colleges. Over seventeen thousand high school seniors took advantage of SAILS in 2015–2016, about half of those students who had not yet met the state's college-readiness benchmarks.

Although definitive research has not yet been completed, SAILS appears to be contributing to a reduced need for remediation (in combination with the spread of co-requisite remediation strategies in the community colleges): between 2011 and 2015, the percentage of first-time freshman needing remediation in math in Tennessee dropped from 71 percent to 55 percent. Given statewide enthusiasm for the program, a new English skills version has been developed and is being piloted.

In addition, in 2015, the Tennessee Board of Regents implemented a statewide policy of co-requisite remediation through which students in every community college enroll in credit-bearing required courses—as opposed to noncredit developmental education courses—and receive additional learning support. The model reduced costs while simultaneously increasing pass rates in required college courses: from 12 percent to 51 percent in college-level math courses and from 31 percent to 59 percent in college writing courses.[13]

### Dual Enrollment and EPSOs

The state's commitment to promoting dual-enrollment, dual-credit, and other early postsecondary options (EPSOs) statewide was another key component of the overall effort to increase postsecondary enrollment and credential attainment. Tennessee data demonstrated that adding early college credit opportunities in high school narrowed the college enrollment gaps between economically disadvantaged students and their wealthier peers (holding academic performance constant): nearly 75 percent of economically disadvantaged students who took an EPSO enrolled in postsecondary education, higher than the percentage of economically disadvantaged students who did not enroll in an EPSO (42 percent) and non-economically disadvantaged students who did not take an EPSO (66 percent). Researchers also found that students who scored relatively low on the ACT test were more likely to go on to postsecondary education if they had a college course in high school than their peers who did not.[14]

Legislation introduced in 2010 required the state to rationalize and systematize its offerings of EPSOs. In 2016–2017, more than twenty-six thousand Tennessee high school students were dually enrolled in at least one college course, a 57 percent increase from 2011–2012.[15] The state uses lottery funds to subsidize a Dual Enrollment Grant program, which offers eleventh and twelfth graders $500 toward the cost of each of a student's first two community college courses and offers smaller awards for courses beyond the first two. Students who dually enroll at TCATs receive a grant of up to $100 per clock hour. The maximum Dual Enrollment Grant award per student per year is $1,200, and students who dually enroll in more than four courses are subject to dollar-for-dollar reductions in subsequent HOPE Scholarship awards.

## MANY INITIATIVES, ONE STRATEGY

For the Pathways Tennessee team, college attainment and the pathways initiative were part of the same overall strategy. As Casey Wrenn explained, "The Tennessee Promise, dual enrollment and EPSOs, SAILS, and a reduced need for remediation, along with our work raising CTE standards, were all going to increase the odds of students going to college. LEAP, the straightening out of CTE programs of study, and pathways partnerships were going to make it easier for them to find their way to and through college into good careers."

Although Pathways Tennessee fit neatly into Haslam's larger college attainment strategy, he did not brand it publicly as part of Drive to 55. The reason is unclear: perhaps it was because Pathways Tennessee was initiated by the Tennessee Department of Education, rather than the governor's office, or because it was part of a national initiative. Although Mezera and her team would have preferred that Haslam promote pathways more actively, she always felt that the governor's office was highly supportive and a representative of the governor participated actively on the pathways state leadership team. Mezera believed that with or without gubernatorial branding, Pathways Tennessee could be sustained if her team was dogged about staying in the conversation at the state level and maintaining strong cross-agency connections.

So far, she has been proven right. In 2015, the Tennessee Department of Education issued its five-year strategic plan, titled Tennessee Succeeds. In that plan, Pathways Tennessee is not mentioned specifically. But the plan states, "Districts and schools in Tennessee will exemplify excellence and equity such that all students are equipped with the knowledge and skills to successfully embark upon their chosen path in life." One of the five priority areas is "high school and the bridge to postsecondary." The strategies highlighted for the next five years include two pathways priorities: expanding the number of high school students earning early postsecondary credits and industry certifications, particularly in partnership with TCATs, and more robust and effective career and college counseling in middle and high school.

Pathways Tennessee's growth and sustainability has also been aided by timely funding from New Skills for Youth, a national initiative funded by JPMorgan Chase & Co. and led by the Council of Chief State School Officers. In 2016, a planning grant enabled the state to complete regional asset mapping and then put together an action plan for regional expansion and equitable access to pathways programs for underrepresented populations. In 2017, Tennessee was one of ten states nationally to receive a $2 million, three-year New Skills for Youth grant to strengthen its career-focused education programs from middle school through postsecondary credential programs in high-demand fields. This investment has enabled the state to continue to build out the pathways infrastructure at the state and regional levels so that Pathways Tennessee becomes more fully integrated into the state's high school learning model. The investment has also helped accelerate the collection of relevant baseline and progress measures so that Pathways Tennessee will be better positioned to make its case for sustainable support from the state over time.

### Career Forward Task Force

In March 2016, Commissioner McQueen announced the formation of the Career Forward Task Force, charged with exploring ways to improve high school students' academic and workforce readiness and identifying "actionable recommendations that reflect the strong integration of secondary, postsecondary, and workforce readiness into K–14/16 education." Thirty-six task force members representing K–12, higher education, industry, nonprofits, state agencies, local and state elected officials, advocacy groups, parents, and students met six times. They crafted and agreed upon a definition of a "career-ready student": "In Tennessee, career-ready students are those who graduate K–12 education with the knowledge, abilities, and habits to enter and complete postsecondary education without remediation and to seamlessly move into a career that affords them the opportunity to live, work, and sustain a living wage."[16]

Many task force members were active on the pathways state leadership team or with regional pathways partnerships. The task force settled on twenty-three specific recommendations related to incentives, resources, technical assistance, and rules.[17] The recommendations pinpointed state actions that would promote academic-technical pathways for jobs in high demand in particular regions; K–12/postsecondary program alignment at the state and regional levels; work-based learning and incentives for employer participation; early career advising; dual enrollment; and the definition and measurement of employability skills.

The Career Forward Task Force advanced the agenda that the Tennessee Department of Education's College, Career and Technical Education Division and its Pathways Tennessee initiative had been developing since 2012. The point person, handpicked by Commissioner McQueen, was her assistant commissioner for college and CTE, Danielle Mezera.

## REGIONAL IMPLEMENTATION: LESSONS FROM PATHWAYS PIONEERS

Legislation, agency policies, and gubernatorial support have all have been critical to the evolution of Pathways Tennessee. Other states should study Tennessee's aggressive efforts to improve education outcomes and tie them to economic engines across the state.

Ultimately, though, the changes in individual experiences and career trajectories that the state wants to see depend on planning and implementation at the community and regional levels. There is no reform without changes in programs, courses, and students' curricular and extracurricular experiences.

Pathways Tennessee was designed as a statewide effort from the outset, but implementation has been rolling out a few regions at a time. This strategically staggered implementation allows regions with favorable readiness conditions to serve as pilots for the rest of the state, and lessons from their experiences can help other regions leapfrog their predecessors in design and implementation plans and activities.

The experience of the first two regions to begin implementation—Upper Cumberland and Southeast—is instructive. Their early progress underscores four important themes:

- The importance (and difficulty) of building strong regional partnerships
- The critical importance of organization, infrastructure, and venues for regional planning

- The variability of regional priorities and capacity
- The need to balance opportunism with long-term strategy in implementation, so that pathways efforts can get traction, build momentum, and reach target populations

Important lessons can also be drawn on how to structure interactions between the state and regions so that they are mutually strengthening.

In Tennessee's 2012 application for acceptance into the national Pathways to Prosperity Network, Commissioner Huffman identified the southeast and Upper Cumberland regions for initial study and preliminary planning. Both regions, blessed with strong assets in leadership, industry, and postsecondary institutions, were already engaging economic and education leaders on ways to improve career opportunities for young people in high-growth local industries. For example, Huffman convened a CTE summit at Volkswagen's new Chattanooga plant in the heart of the southeast region. The Highlands initiative had also held two economic development summits, bringing together key stakeholders in the Upper Cumberland region around strengthening technical education.

At the same time, the two regions were very different in their histories, populations, urban/rural mix, and industrial bases. A careful mapping of the economic, educational, and collaborative assets of each region, conducted in the summer of 2012 by JFF, identified the strengths and the challenges facing each region. In each community, the process helped to accelerate local action and to identify innovators and institutions with capacity and credibility. The process also highlighted gaps in the educational, economic, and civic infrastructures that would need to be overcome.

## Two Lead Regions: Upper Cumberland and Southeast

*Upper Cumberland* is a predominantly rural region of fourteen counties between Nashville and Knoxville in middle Tennessee. The largest city, Cookeville, has thirty-one thousand residents and is the seat of Putnam County, the largest and fastest-growing community in the region. Some smaller and more rural counties are losing population. Poverty and unemployment rates are higher than the state average. Educational attainment is low: while 84.2 percent of working-age adults have a high school diploma, only 21.9 percent have an associate's degree or higher. There is only one four-year college in the region—Tennessee Technological University (Tennessee Tech)—but there are also four satellite community college campuses and three TCATs. Buoyed by the manufacturing sector, the economy has been picking up. The Highlands Economic Partnership is a strong convener and home for collaborative planning and activity. The region's employment base is primarily made up of smaller firms; there are no significant private funders, though civic leaders hope this is beginning to change. Significant geographic obstacles to regional innovation exist in the sparsely populated and mountainous region.

The *Southeast Tennessee Development District* has a very different profile. Comprising ten counties in Tennessee (and three in Georgia), the region has two significant concentrations of population, industry, and educational resources: the city of Chattanooga and its environs, and the Cleveland Metropolitan Statistical Area further north. The regional population is far more diverse than Upper Cumberland; about a third of Chattanooga's nearly 175,000 residents are African American. The region is in the process of an economic rebirth. Huge new facilities for the European companies Volkswagen and Wacker Polysilicon have spurred secondary growth in industries that supply and support the automotive, chemical, and energy clusters. Foreign investment in the region is five times the state average. Except for Chattanooga and its county, Hamilton, the region's educational attainment is below the state average. But the educational capacity in the region is significant: relatively robust CTE programs across many counties and high schools; eight major two- and four-year colleges and two TCATs; a range of innovative high school models in Hamilton County; and novel partnerships between Wacker and Chattanooga State (Wacker Institute), and between Volkswagen and Hamilton County schools (Volkswagen Academy). The region is fortunate to have five functioning local chambers of commerce and several prominent private foundations with a history of working to improve local educational attainment and quality.

Pathways Tennessee staff selected these two regions as pilot sites for local activities. Using reserve funds available through the federal Carl D.

Perkins Career and Technical Education Act, the state made grants to each region to enable them to plan for the launch of pathways activities in the 2013–2014 school year.

The state required each region to undertake several specific planning activities:

- Select a regional intermediary to coordinate the initiative
- Create a multisector leadership team or council to guide and prioritize collaborative activities
- Establish work groups for each target industry sector to organize stakeholders and build programs beginning in seventh grade and continuing through the end of two- or four-year college
- Prepare regional plans with accountability measures that the intermediary would report on regularly to the state

Pathways Tennessee used Perkins Reserve funds to make grants to regions that included funding for intermediaries and salaries for a group of career coaches who would help sign up schools and students for the newly created pathways. The grants were structured to encourage sustainable investment in pathways efforts over time: the state paid 100 percent of career coaching and other costs in the first year. In successive years, participating districts were required to internalize an increasing percentage of costs in their operating budgets until the state share dropped to zero.

Figure 2.2, created by the state to explain its priorities for the regions, underscores the state planning team's commitment to encouraging local leaders to start from their strengths and to connect the dots strategically across receptive systems, sectors, and communities. Mezera and her team understood that progress had to be incremental and that, in the early going, gains would come from aligning interests and resources and demonstrating value to local leaders who are typically skeptical of help from the state.

The state planning team tried to strike a balance with the regions. According to Mezera, "You have to make clear the structure you want the regions to work with—the guardrails within which they will drive—and you

**FIGURE 2.2** Priorities for the regions

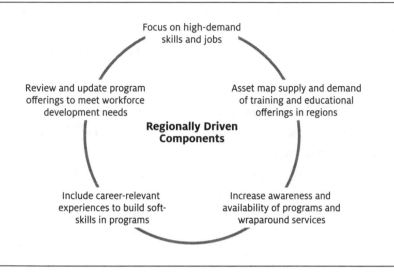

have to give them sufficient guidance so they understand the state's goals. At the same time, though, you have to honor the different ways that regions set their priorities." Policy change and resources from the state would not be sufficient to change long-term behavior on the ground. That had to come from the local conversation and assessment of their own needs. "Everything about pathways is people," said Mezera. "So I focused on working with the point people at the regional intermediaries to drive a common conversation about needs and opportunities, so they would be interested in investing in themselves. The voice from on high was not going to work."

The sensitivity to regional variation and independence was coupled with a commitment by the pathways team to proactively reach out to regional intermediaries and help support the process of regional visioning and strategic planning. Program Director Nick Hansen and Program Manager Ellen Bohle made it clear that they would travel to any region that invited them. Their availability and their respect for local needs made regional leaders more comfortable with top-down aspects of Pathways Tennessee. Regional leaders overcame ingrained skepticism and came to see the state as committed to listening to and learning from them. The state planning team's availability for regional partnerships helped strengthen state-level policy and action as much as it did regional initiatives. The state planning team supported and facilitated regional focus groups, which informed them about regional needs and approaches. Monthly calls between the pathways state planning team and regional intermediaries have become a welcome two-way source of information sharing and strategy development.

**UPPER CUMBERLAND.** In Upper Cumberland, the Highlands Economic Partnership, through its Workforce Development and Education Committee, took the lead in organizing a steering committee for the pathways work, drawing from leaders of school districts, postsecondary institutions, employers, community organizations, and local chambers of commerce. The steering committee set its overall regional goal "to improve the education attainment level and job readiness of our future workforce by enhancing training, education, [and] skill development, and providing work-based learning opportunities to match the needs of targeted industries and existing industry."

Participation was broad and inclusive. According to Tom Brewer, an associate vice president at Tennessee Tech and a Workforce Development and Educational Committee leader, "The organizational chart is my favorite document. It has about 120 names on it. I've never seen anything like that—and I was at General Motors for years. It shows the diversity of the partnership."

A key investment in Upper Cumberland was the funding of five academic career coaches through the state's Perkins Reserve grant: two in Cookeville's Putnam County and one in each of the other three participating counties. The coaches worked with schools and industry to support school participation, starting with career awareness activities in the elementary grades, through exploration in middle school, and engagement and entry into the world of work in the high schools. A lot of the on-the-ground planning for pathways in Upper Cumberland was the result of the coaches' work. Funding for the positions has moved from the state grant into annual school district budgets.

Pathways in health sciences and advanced manufacturing were established, beginning in four counties in the 2013–2014 school year. In the health sciences pathways, about 1,700 seventh and eighth graders were provided career exposure to health science through new curricular modules and attendance at an annual eighth-grade career fair. The health sciences pathways program served 628 students in 2016, with the majority concentrating in nursing. The health sciences group is also working to launch a registered nurse associate's degree program at Volunteer State Community College so that there will be a seamless nursing pathway from TCATs to Volunteer State to Tennessee Tech.

In the pre-engineering/advanced manufacturing pathways, 1,700 seventh graders participated, with about the same number of eighth graders. Mechatronics programs were launched in five high schools in January 2016, enrolling 112 students, with the help of state LEAP program funding for new equipment. "Before the LEAP funding," according to White County Director of Schools Sandra Crouch, "thinking about a mechatronics program was like looking at chocolate from behind glass. We couldn't get there." But LEAP enabled high schools and TCATs to purchase up-to-date equipment and engage employers in curricular development. In the fall of 2016, the pipeline of participating students more than doubled to 251.

For each pathway, a subcommittee assessed employer needs and in-demand jobs. A postsecondary education subgroup developed plans for smooth transitions as well as transfer and articulation agreements where needed. Career exploration modules developed in collaboration with the Tennessee Department of Education are available to seventh graders in participating schools. In the eighth grade, employer-developed tasks are introduced into the curriculum through video.

In addition to these pathways, the Highlands Economic Partnership coordinates a number of programs to improve career preparation:

- An interview boot camp for high school seniors at six area high schools, culminating in a job fair
- A teacher externship program in local industry involving twelve firms and about a hundred teachers

- A speakers bureau that has brought over 130 business and industry speakers to address more than 2,400 students
- A summer bridge program for at-risk rising freshmen
- A creative parental engagement program that is delivered at the workplace rather than the school, which reached over 285 parents in 2016

The Workforce Development and Educational Committee is also a regional lead for the Tennessee Reconnect program. Launched in March 2016, the Upper Cumberland effort advised over seven hundred individuals in its first seven months and helped ninety-five people enroll in postsecondary programs.

**SOUTHEAST.** In 2012, the southeast region looked to be one of the strongest in terms of industry interest and vitality. The region had experienced a large increase in manufacturing and distribution, mainly in automotive, including new capacity in and around Chattanooga from a huge expansion at Volkswagen and Gestamp, as well as investments from other national and international companies, including Whirlpool and Amazon. Chemical and solar energy companies, including Wacker Chemie, joined the Tennessee Valley Authority as leaders in the energy sector. Large, foreign employers, many with experience training young people in their home countries, introduced technology at a rate that increased employers' concern for the pipeline of potential employees in the region. There was a sense that leading employers could be the driver of better alignment between high school CTE and postsecondary providers—and between education and industry.

The Public Education Foundation of Chattanooga (PEF), launched in 1988, developed a robust STEM Innovation Hub program focusing on career options for the city's high school students. PEF sponsored several other relevant programs, including a paid internship program for low-income Chattanooga youth. The hub's dynamic managing director, Tracey Carisch, was at the center of much of this activity. Seeing that PEF had the leadership and capacity to manage new initiatives, the Tennessee

Department of Education approached the organization to gauge its interest in serving in the Pathways Tennessee intermediary role in the southeast region. An agreement was reached, and PEF received a grant from the state's Perkins Reserve funds to build its pathways strategy and plan. The foundation's STEM Innovation Hub became the initial home for Pathways Southeast Tennessee, focusing attention on four contiguous counties: Bradley, Hamilton, Marion, and McMinn. Initial industry targets were manufacturing and information technology. The Leadership Council was co-chaired by the charismatic and dogged Tim Spires, president and CEO of the Chattanooga Regional Manufacturers Association, who was well connected in industry, political, and civic circles regionally and statewide. The other co-chair was Hamilton County Mayor Jim Coppinger, a lifelong Hamilton County resident who served as county fire chief for many years and was a staunch supporter of investment in local economic development and education.

Southeast has made significant progress in the past four years, but it has encountered more obstacles and instability than Upper Cumberland. Over time, the southeast region has evolved a different model of connecting the dots to advance pathways efforts in the region. Volkswagen, Wacker Polysilicon, and Gestamp serve as examples of this model:

- In 2016, *Volkswagen* launched an intensive two-year apprenticeship academy model for high school youth through its Volkswagen Academy. The first cohort of twenty-six CTE students from Hamilton County and other nearby communities currently attends high school on the Volkswagen campus, combining coursework, labs, and employment on the shop floor. The school system houses two instructors on-site.
- *Wacker Polysilicon* is bringing Polytechnic High onto its campus, serving a hundred students.
- *Gestamp*, an assembly and stamping company, moved from purchasing a few industrial robots for CTE programs and training the instructors to designing and getting ready to launch a high school within part of their plant. When Human Resources Director Tony

Cates and others from Gestamp did a site visit to the Southwire plant in Georgia to see its 12 for Life program, in which a high school is co-located with a manufacturing facility operated by high school students, Cates was determined to create something similar at Gestamp. He was amazed to see students doing things he would not trust some of his employees to do. Gestamp opened its own school in fall 2017, run by Hamilton High, an online public high school, that combines four hours of learning with four hours of working.

Southeast manufacturers and schools have also benefited from two LEAP grants: one that enabled the creation of a new mechatronics program at TCAT-Athens in partnership with the McMinn County Schools, and the other targeting Hamilton and Bradley counties.

TCAT leaders in the region see the pathways collaboration as changing their relationship with high schools. According to Jim Barrott, director of TCAT-Chattanooga, "Without Pathways, we wouldn't have improved relations with the high schools. I have improved my communication with CTE directors. I didn't know many of the directors in the outlying counties, but now I do." Barrott then described his vision for the future: "I'd like to see every high school CTE program have a connection to a TCAT program, so that students could complete a third of their program while still in high school and enter the TCAT with credits in hand."

Annie White, the regional project manager for the southeast region, has traveled up and down the pathways counties, working closely with CTE directors and TCAT and community college presidents. Some have gone all in, and some have been less engaged, but progress is evident. Nine high schools have launched advanced manufacturing and/or information technology programs with TCATs in Chattanooga and Athens and with Cleveland and Chattanooga State community colleges. Every semester, the southeast region's career coaches organize plant visits for middle and high school students, industry visits to participating schools, career assessments for middle schoolers, teacher and counselor field trips to industries, and training for CTE directors on the use of the state's pathways tool kit. Recently, White has been working with leading employers to develop a set of criteria for students to meet before graduation to get a work ethic certification on their diplomas. The work ethic seal will certify student mastery of foundational behaviors that employers want in new hires: attendance, appearance, attitude, ambition, acceptance, and accountability.

At the same time, the southeast region has moved more slowly than initially expected in new program development and solidifying regional partnerships. After an initial period, it became clear that the fit with PEF was less than optimal, since PEF's focus was the city of Chattanooga and pathways' was regional. The Chattanooga Regional Manufacturers Association became the new home for pathways in the region, but the association is far better connected to manufacturing than other industries, which has had the effect of narrowing the initiative's scope. In rapid succession, CTE directors and county directors of schools in several of the target counties resigned, were fired, or retired, requiring White to rebuild relationships with key school systems. A shocking blow came to the southeast effort when, in February 2017, Spires died suddenly while hiking in the Tennessee hills he loved, leaving a huge hole in terms of community relationships and leadership.

Today, the footprint of pathways in the region is quite visible. Important questions, however, have arisen about long-term strategy, ability to expand outside manufacturing, the capability of regional CTE programs to upgrade their standards and quality, and the specification of pathways goals and implementation plans. Cleveland State Community College president Bill Seymour said, "We have blurred the lines as to where pathways starts and ends as we pursue our regional interests." White framed it differently: "Pathways operates now as a critical friend. We help identify pain points and ways to deal with them and we help lock into deadlines for action." But she wonders who in education and industry will continue to lead the charge and whether the lead districts will commit to continued investment when state funding for six career coaches winds down this year. The Regional Manufacturers Association has been more of an operational home than a strategic hub for pathways. Dynamics may change when Pathways Southeast Tennessee's home shifts to the regional workforce board in the coming year.

In summary, influence and activity across the region seems less systemic than in Upper Cumberland; pathways is a way to help institutions make connections that then run on their own. The great disparities in district size and capacity in the region—from large city and county systems to very small rural districts—may contribute to the difficulty of designing and implementing a comprehensive regional approach. However, the Tennessee Department of Education's pathways office is supporting a three-year strategic planning process in the southeast and other regions, to be led by the executive committee of southeast's Leadership Council. In the southeast region, one goal is to look at strategies in addition to the career coaches for outreach and implementation support to districts and employers.

## LESSONS FROM PATHWAYS TENNESSEE

Pathways Tennessee has pushed further than most states in developing a statewide policy framework for pathways and promoting significant regional activity on the ground.

Eight of the state's nine economic development regions have put in place partnerships and identified intermediary organizations to coordinate regional efforts. These regions have also launched programs that are changing the learning experience for hundreds of students. This progress is impressive and has been accelerated by the state's commitment to advancing the pathways agenda through state policy and support for local innovation.

At the same time, progress has been uneven. Some regions have yet to establish a viable partnership led by a high-capacity intermediary. Even within more active regions, many districts are not yet engaged. Sustaining momentum in the face of changing district, regional, and state priorities and leadership is a constant challenge. The real test of Pathways Tennessee's potential will come in the next few years, with a gubernatorial change, transitions within state agencies, and ongoing economic ups and downs in the regions.

Important lessons can be drawn from Pathways Tennessee's experience to date—lessons that are relevant for continued growth and improvement within Tennessee as well as for those in other states who are eager to pursue a similar agenda on behalf of their youth. The most salient lessons fall into three categories:

- Lessons for state leaders about policy priorities and support for local innovation
- Lessons for local leaders and partners about infrastructure needs and program design
- Persistent, systemic challenges that still need to be addressed if pathways are to be institutionalized, sustained statewide, and have the desired educational and economic impacts

## Lessons for State Leaders

Tennessee put in place a strong, sophisticated state policy framework for its pathways initiative. Through its Division of College, Career and Technical Education, the state Department of Education has systematically and strategically engaged leaders and staff within key state agencies and offices. Although the team has been bolstered by gubernatorial and legislative support, Mezera and her colleagues decided early on that the launch of and support for Pathways Tennessee had to be treated as a strategic campaign that aligned state- and local-level messaging, alliance building, and resource investments.

**ALIGNMENT ACROSS STATE AGENCIES.** Policy initiatives housed in the CTE division of a state's K–12 education department often have difficulty achieving visibility and avoiding marginalization. Recognizing this, Mezera and her team, with support from the commissioner of education, prioritized building support for the pathways agenda across the many state agencies whose activities pathways could support and advance, including education, labor, economic and community development, the Board of Regents, and the Higher Education Commission. A pathways state planning team of key officials within these departments began meeting soon after the launch of Pathways Tennessee. The group focused initially on goals, language, definitions, and standards that could be agreed on across agencies. By not immediately approaching issues of agency resources and their alignment, the team steered around the usual defensiveness about control of funds that can plague cross-agency collaboration. This approach also facilitated the alignment of vision, language, and standards across state government, embedding pathways definitions and priorities into state agencies beyond the Tennessee Department of Education and its CTE division. Recently, the state Board of Regents and the Department of Education signed a memorandum of understanding to align all industry certifications recognized by the state Department of Education to articulated hours in TCAT programs, deepening the vertical alignment between K–12 and postsecondary systems.

**CROSS-AGENCY STRATEGY AND IMPLEMENTATION.** In Tennessee, the strength of the Department of Education's leadership may also have had a downside because of the imbalance in ownership of pathways within Tennessee government. While other agencies certainly provide advice and align resources to support pathways, the job of supporting local intermediaries and partnerships falls primarily on the education team. Tennessee's Department of Education is the only agency that funds dedicated staff to work full-time on pathways. As a result, in a number of regions, the initial center of gravity in implementation has been in the K–12 districts.

**CONTINUITY OF STATE LEADERSHIP.** Tennessee has benefited in recent years from a remarkably stable political environment. The smooth transition from Democratic governor Bredesen to Republican governor Haslam set a tone of continuity and a bipartisan, depoliticized approach to economic development and educational improvement. Under Haslam, many state agency leaders, particularly at the assistant commissioner level, have stayed in the same job across the governor's two terms. This stability helped pathways steering committee members develop strong interpersonal bonds and engage in long-term planning—something that is uncommon in many state agencies and capitals.

Will this stability be maintained in the coming years? Mezera left her position in the spring of 2017. Because of term limits, Haslam cannot run again. With the election of Republican businessman Bill Lee as governor,

Candice McQueen resigned as commissioner of education in December 2018 to become CEO of the National Institute for Excellence in Teaching. However, there are signs of continuity and commitment to the current agenda. Mezera's replacement is Casey Wrenn, whom Mezera brought with her to the Tennessee Department of Education in 2012. And Lyle Ailshie, a former director of schools with deep understanding of CTE and the college-readiness agenda, has been appointed deputy commissioner.

**VALUE OF GUBERNATORIAL SUPPORT.** Compared to many states, Tennessee's governor has significant authority to implement strong higher education policies and drive cross-agency priorities. In this context, Pathways Tennessee could have benefited from more public support from the outgoing governor. His office sent a representative to Pathway Tennessee's regular steering committee meetings. However, unlike in Delaware, where Governor Jack Markell initiated his state's involvement in the Pathways to Prosperity Network, ran the project initially out of the governor's office, and used the pathways framework and messaging as an umbrella for all of the state's college- and career-readiness and college-completion efforts, Haslam consistently led with the Drive to 55 branding and the marquee Tennessee Promise scholarship. Conversely, Pathways Tennessee was viewed statewide as an important implementation vehicle for reaching the governor's ambitious higher education and workforce quality goals, but it was not generally included in Haslam's topline messaging. This approach was reflected in the limited state funding for pathways, particularly in the initiative's first few years.

**IMPORTANCE OF STATE RESOURCES.** In order to drive significant and lasting local-level change, state policy needs to offer incentives (information, tools, and resources) powerful enough to change the behaviors of institutions and their personnel. Too often, states fail to provide (or underestimate the need for) additional resource investments at the local level, hoping that policy guidance alone will be sufficient to drive behavioral change. The allocation of federal Perkins Reserve grant funds directed toward regional efforts buoyed their ability to build the infrastructure of cross-sector collaboration and planning. In addition, regional intermediaries benefited from the state planning team's advice on using the Perkins Reserve funds to hire regional career coaches to support their partnerships. Higher-capacity intermediaries in Tennessee have tapped other state and private funding streams to pay for new staff and activities. Many won LEAP grants in support of equipment purchases and further partnership development. The Highlands Economic Partnership secured one of the first Tennessee Reconnect grants for improving career pathways for working adults, which has helped deepen the intermediary's overall capacity to maintain strong partnerships. State Department of Education technical assistance, including a playbook for organizing and implementing high-quality, efficient pathways programs and support, has also been an important resource for intermediaries and their partnerships.

**BALANCE OF TOP-DOWN AND BOTTOM-UP APPROACHES.** Pathways strategies require a sensitive balancing of top-down state policy development with bottom-up regional design and implementation so that local needs and conditions can be incorporated in statewide frameworks and strategies. This is not easy to achieve. A state might prioritize grants to regional partnerships but do little to align state policies and guidance to help support regional activity and success. Or a state might put in place a raft of policy directives without making available significant resources, incentives, or technical assistance to strengthen local capacity to act effectively. Tennessee's experience demonstrates the importance and value of aligning local and state action in an interactive and sophisticated way. Local mistrust of the state would have been a more serious obstacle had the state planning team not been thinking about local implementation from the outset. At the same time, too much local flexibility and autonomy can accentuate inefficient implementation strategies and reinforce unevenness and capacity constraints across regions.

## Lessons for Regional Leaders

Regional Pathways Tennessee partnerships that have made progress since the program's 2012 launch have learned a great deal about the kind of capacity, partnership structure, and cross-institutional communication needed to launch, sustain, and expand pathways efforts. From the experience to date, local learning has provided rich lessons in three areas.

**IMPORTANCE OF A HIGH-CAPACITY INTERMEDIARY.** Without a strong, strategic partnership among K–12, higher education, employers, and public officials, little progress can be made in aligning sectors and execution of the pathways agenda. Leadership is critical: at the head of a regional partnership must stand someone (or a small leadership group) who has the broad trust and respect of regional players—and who is not beholden to one narrow interest. Intermediary organization leaders need flexible and diverse skills: strategic, operational, motivational, and entrepreneurial abilities that can be applied as needed. Ultimately, though, heroic individuals are insufficient. A strong, stable, staffed organization is required. Often, chambers of commerce or workforce development organizations step up to take on the role, as has been the case across Tennessee. Sometimes a community college or a sector association steps up. Each possible "home" has pros and cons. In the southeast region, for example, the centrality of the Regional Manufacturers Association has been a boon to pathways efforts in the rapidly growing manufacturing sector, but has made outreach to employers in health care and other industries more difficult. Wherever the pathways partnership is housed, though, attention to funding of staff and activities is important: in Tennessee, the state helped through initial investment from Perkins Reserve funds and then through competitive LEAP grants. How stability is maintained when initial funding wanes can determine whether and how quickly pathways programs grow, plateau, or contract over time.

**SPECIAL ATTENTION TO POSTSECONDARY COMPONENTS AND DESIGN.** Pathways initiatives are built on the premise that secondary and postsecondary curricula, sequences, and standards are aligned and become increasingly seamless. The postsecondary component is critically important, since it is often the actual gateway to quality employment and it is where employer engagement can be most fruitful. However, since first things come first, it is common for the details of the secondary components of pathways to be worked out first, with the intention that postsecondary issues follow.

For various reasons, including the sheer complexity of introducing new pathways or revising existing high school courses into coherent pathways, pathways programs frequently leave the postsecondary components underdeveloped. Additionally, pathways that should be seamless may not even have clearly marked bridges from high school to postsecondary programs for students to cross.

In Tennessee, engagement of postsecondary institutions is uneven across regions and within regions. It is made more complex by the competition and need for better communication and alignment between community colleges and TCATs. In Tennessee and nearly every state pursuing pathways strategies, engaging postsecondary partners early and continuously—and thinking hard about how to fit with the incentive structures facing these institutions—can help accelerate and strengthen implementation of postsecondary pathways components.

**VALUE OF WORK-BASED LEARNING.** It is tempting to think of work-based learning as a nice-to-have component of a pathways program, but Tennessee's experience argues for seeing it as a more central need-to-have element. Work-based learning has proven to be a powerful way to cement and deepen local partnerships between employers and educators. It often becomes the vehicle for employers and educators to sit down and talk through what they think can be learned on the job, how employers can support students at the worksite, and how learning at work should be assessed.

In the southeast region, with its many large transnational employers, work-based learning at Volkswagen, Wacker, and Gestamp became a jumping-off point for ambitious apprenticeship-like programs. In Upper Cumberland, the design of different levels of work-based learning has helped middle and high school leaders set priorities and design a progressive sequence of work-based experiences.

When Tennessee revised its statewide work-based learning policy, regions had to respond and incorporate the new, higher standards into their local activities. At the same time, regional leaders have learned firsthand how difficult it is to provide quality work-based learning experiences at scale—either exploratory experiences for younger students or more ambitious capstone experiences for older ones. One explanation for this is that some regions lack a strong base of employers who can engage older students in intensive experiences. In addition, transportation can be a huge barrier to the expansion of work-based learning, particularly in sparsely populated rural areas.

## Challenges to Address

Several overarching challenges face Tennessee as it continues to build and strengthen its pathways initiative. These challenges are significant: any one of them could limit the ability of Pathways Tennessee to grow, serve students well, and sustain public and political support over time.

**METRICS AND OUTCOMES REPORTING ON THE INITIATIVE, WITH A NEED FOR GREATER CLARITY AND TRANSPARENCY.** Like other large-scale efforts to create new and coherent career pathways opportunities for high school youth, Pathways Tennessee is engaged in building many different local program components at the same time: the partnership and its committees; communication between secondary and postsecondary institutions and between employers in target industries and educational providers; curricular alignment across sectors; the content of the courses that together constitute the pathway; and students' curricular and extracurricular learning in their pathways. Moreover, state policies that promote dual enrollment, free tuition, and reduced remediation in high school can all be considered part of the pathways model. So how are Tennessee policy makers and the public to understand whether Pathways Tennessee is successful; whether it is expanding quickly enough and at a high enough quality; or whether young people's career and educational trajectories are changing in good ways?

Tennessee Tech's Brewer put it this way: "How do we define success? How do we know that we are closing the gap? I came out of General Motors. At the plant, I had to make sixty cars every hour. I knew every hour if we were on target. But education is not a world that works on metrics."

The state has been working incrementally to improve collection and reporting of pathways-related student outcomes, including program expansion metrics, enrollment numbers, and work-based learning and dual-enrollment participation across the state. That is a start, but it is insufficient. Without greater clarity on which outcomes pathways should be evaluated on—what results and for which populations—Pathways Tennessee runs the risk of being unable to make a strong case for continued state support and for scarce resources in leaner times.

The funding competition for JPMorgan Chase & Co.'s New Skills for Youth initiative has helped the state identify a targeted set of accountability metrics and benchmarks for accountability purposes. The state set a baseline using 2016 data and articulated qualitative and quantitative goals for the three years through 2019. Regions will report to the state planning team so that data are held in one place and reported with consistency. To make this system work, greater local capacity for data collection will be needed. In addition, reports must focus not just on easily available data but on useful and meaningful metrics such as educational and economic progress after high school, tracked by academic program, career pathway, EPSO and work-based learning experiences, and population subgroups.

**INEVITABILITY—AND RISKS—OF UNEVEN ECONOMIC VITALITY.** Pathways initiatives are built on the assumption that employers with significant bottlenecks in sub-baccalaureate middle-skill jobs will get involved in shaping curricula and learning goals so that they can benefit from homegrown talent. Employer engagement is central. But what if a region is just too underdeveloped to sustain a strong employer base? Or what if development in a region is uneven, with some counties or communities growing rapidly and others shrinking and depopulating? This is a significant challenge in Tennessee, but Tennessee is not unique. A statewide strategy is necessary for scale and sustainability, but state leaders need to acknowledge at the outset that program implementation within regions is likely to be uneven. At both the state and the regional levels, technical assistance to weaker districts and supports for student transportation could help more robust economic areas generate pathways programs that can benefit students in communities with more limited access to employers and resources. In this way, regional initiatives can be unifying and can avoid exacerbating the uneven opportunities available in different communities in the same region.

**EQUITY AS A DESIGN AND IMPLEMENTATION PRIORITY.** In most communities, manufacturing jobs skew toward men and patient care jobs toward women. Historically, entry-level manufacturing jobs pay higher wages than most frontline health positions. Thus, if pathways initiatives maintain traditional gender patterns in their enrollments, they are likely to reinforce long-standing gender inequities. This can be remedied by the concerted efforts of CTE instructors and school counselors to enroll more women in manufacturing pathways and more men in health programs.

When facing a long history of racial inequities in education, special efforts must be made to ensure that pathways opportunities are broadly accessible across regions and that participation patterns reduce rather than exacerbate racial and ethnic differences. Data analysis presented in the state's successful application for funding from JPMorgan's New Skills for Youth reported that African American students' access to high-quality pathways in Tennessee is more than 20 percentage points below that of other racial demographics. African American students are two times less likely to complete a high-quality pathway and four times less likely to attain early postsecondary credits. Economically disadvantaged students are also less well served: they trail their more affluent peers by 10 percentage points in terms of access to high-quality pathways. Given this dynamic, it is critical that equity be a design criterion from the beginning—as outreach, enrollment, and student supports are built out and then implemented—so that Pathways Tennessee will be more likely to achieve its goal of narrowing existing outcome gaps.

## LOOKING FORWARD

Tennessee was one of the first states to go all in on a statewide approach to implementing the pathways vision.

Tennessee combined an extensive state-level modernization of CTE with support for regional partnerships that bring educators, employers, and civic leaders together to create, strengthen, and publicize clear pathways into high-demand occupations. The combination of state and regional efforts has provided Pathways Tennessee both a coherent systemic approach to change and regional flexibility to pursue economic and educational opportunities that make sense in local contexts.

Pathways Tennessee is benefiting from the state's overall steady commitment to improving college and career readiness and success for youth and adults. The 2017 Tennessee Promise annual report documents increases in the state's already highest-in-the-nation rate of filling out the FAFSA, as well as increases in college-going among high school graduates and in first-time freshman enrollment in Tennessee community colleges and TCATs, the two higher education sectors most directly engaged in Pathways Tennessee.[18]

It remains to be seen whether the momentum for more varied and more effective pathways to postsecondary and career success will continue across the state and its diverse regions after the next gubernatorial election. Also unanswered is whether pathways planners and implementers will address the challenges noted here. But the current moment looks promising. The Tennessee Department of Education has weathered leadership changes, new regional intermediaries are finding their way, and the vision motivating pathways is gaining acceptance across the state.

## CHAPTER 3

# DEVELOPING EQUITABLE PATHWAYS SYSTEMS TO ENSURE POSTSECONDARY SUCCESS

The Great Lakes College and Career Pathways Partnership

*Michael Grady with Kyle Hartung*

As Shayla Sanchez was preparing to enter her freshman year at Palatine High School, her teachers and counselors recommended her for Project Excel, a four-year college and career-readiness program for first-generation college-going, academically promising students. The city of Palatine, Illinois, located an hour northwest of the Chicago Loop, designed Project Excel based on research that shows students need more than just academic content knowledge to thrive in college. Working with grade-level cohorts of about seventy-five students each, Project Excel provides academic support and counseling, builds social-emotional skills and behaviors, and guides students through the often-thorny process of college discovery and application. According to Shayla, "Project Excel helped me discover my interest in medicine and guided me through the courses I needed to complete so I could take three dual-credit courses in my junior and senior years."

Shayla—who also runs track and cross-country, is a member of the photography and student exchange clubs at her school and is deeply involved with her church and community—matriculated in Palatine's demanding Patient Wellness pathway. This pathway is in the health sciences career cluster, one of sixteen available to students in Illinois Township High School District 211, which operates five high schools including Palatine. Her health sciences studies were demanding and culminated in three dual-credit college courses through Harper College in eleventh and twelfth grade, all of which are requirements for numerous postsecondary credentials in the field: medical terminology, anatomy and physiology, and speech. Shayla noted, "It was my experience last year in medical terminology that convinced me to pursue a career in medicine."

With the support of her school and community, Shayla has overcome many of the obstacles that stand in the way of success for first-generation college-bound students: "It's meant so much to me to have support from both Project Excel and all my teachers for these past four years. I've been able to visit colleges and meet college representatives and get help filling out my college applications and FAFSA. And I really needed this help because, as a first-generation college student, my parents don't really know all the steps it takes to get ready for college."

Shayla feels prepared to take the next step in her health sciences studies, when she hopes to attend Loyola University, University of Illinois–Chicago, DePaul University, or one of the other Chicago-area four-year institutions. Shayla's exposure to career options and work-based opportunities in the Patient Wellness pathway, coupled with early college credit aligned to credentials in the health sciences, has provided her with a strong foundation on which to pursue a postsecondary credential and launch a rewarding career in a field of interest to her.

Inspiring stories like this one from the northwest suburbs of Chicago are playing out in communities all over the country as part of a broader movement toward high-quality, career-aligned educational pathways for all young people (see appendix A to learn about the national movement). The following account details how cross-sector partners from four Midwestern communities are leading their respective regions—and the Great Lakes region as a whole—toward a brighter future by building systemic and sustainable infrastructure for high-quality college and career pathway systems. But in this work, one size does not fit all, and pathways systems must build on the strengths of, and be responsive to, local contexts.

While they vary in approach, structure, mission, and membership, these communities are seeking answers to formidable questions facing other states and communities that are pursuing high-quality pathways systems for youth, the most salient of which include:

- How might we build an equitable system of authentic and high-quality learning experiences that avoids the trap of a two-tiered pathway system that privileges some student populations over others?
- How might we create and sustain complex collaborations involving cross-sector partners—K–12, higher education, and industry—that operate in different organizational contexts, with distinct cultures, norms, and incentives?
- How might we transform nascent pathway efforts into durable and coherent systems capable of sustaining changes in leadership, shifting political winds, and resource commitments?

## INTRODUCING THE GREAT LAKES COLLEGE AND CAREER PATHWAYS PARTNERSHIP

In 2015, the Joyce Foundation launched a grant initiative to address the pathways challenge aimed at funding innovations to improve educational and employment outcomes, and to advance equity and economic mobility for the next generation in the Great Lakes region.[1] This grant invited a set of sites—identified for the foundation by MDRC, a nonprofit education and social policy research organization with support from JFF's Pathways to Prosperity team—to propose how they would further improve and expand their pathways systems. While MDRC and JFF explored over ten possible sites in the Great Lakes region, the four sites that they nominated for consideration, and that Joyce invited to participate in this grant, were all affiliated with JFF's Pathways to Prosperity Network—either directly as regional members (Central Ohio and Madison, Wisconsin) or indirectly as regions within a state-level member (the northwest suburbs of Chicago and Rockford, Illinois). Joyce's investment thus launched the Great Lakes College and Career Pathways Partnership (GLCCPP), an initiative committed to expanding and improving the unique approaches to regional college and career pathways systems driven by cross-sector coalitions in these four communities. In order to support these regions in their pathways work, Joyce selected and funded three technical assistance organizations to provide ongoing and coordinated technical assistance, including JFF's Pathways to Prosperity team.

The core challenge the GLCCPP initiative seeks to address is: "America's workforce is experiencing the perfect storm: our workers are lacking the skills needed to grow and strengthen the changing economy, yet the high costs of college as well as lack of opportunity to engage in college and career-based learning is preventing our students from acquiring those skills and getting good jobs."[2]

To this end, GLCCPP has established a desired end result of:

- Greater systematic pathways coherence and access
- Increased numbers of young people—especially low-income youth and students of color—who are ready for and successful in college, careers, and life, as measured by:
  - Early college credit course enrollment and completion (AP and dual enrollment)
  - High school graduation and academic proficiency
  - Postsecondary enrollment with decreased need for remediation
  - Work-based learning participation
  - Pathways enrollment and completion rates
  - Launching a career on a trajectory to earn family-sustaining wages

A high-quality college and career pathways system should be designed with and for the unique needs and strengths of regional economies. Intentional alignment between a region's education and workforce systems ensures that young people gain the competencies and postsecondary credentials necessary to enter careers in high-growth industries that offer high wages and the potential for career advancement. Each of the four partner communities brings unique strengths to GLCCPP, including a compelling vision, dedicated leadership, strong K–12 and postsecondary partnerships, and/or high levels of employer involvement.

At the same time, both research and on-the-ground experience across diverse contexts suggest that high-quality pathways systems share common guiding principles and best practices. Therefore, the California Center for College and Career (ConnectEd), JFF and its Pathways to Prosperity team, and Education Systems Center at Northern Illinois University (EdSystems)—the three technical assistance providers that make up the GLCCPP coordinating team—jointly developed a set of quality indicators to inform the design, implementation, and continuous improvement of pathways systems across and within the four GLCCPP communities.[3] The quality indicators elevate three critical priority areas around which the work of GLCCPP is oriented:

- Leadership and governance
- Secondary-postsecondary alignment
- Work-based learning delivery systems

These indicators also detail how data and metrics, equity and access, communications and messaging, and learning and teaching are priority-spanning considerations for successful pathways design and implementation.

## Approaches to Pathways System-Building Infrastructures

Responding to the pathways challenge requires thoughtful connecting, co-ordinating, collaborating, and convening structures led by high-functioning intermediary organizations. These organizations must effectively lead the shared planning, implementation, and continuous improvement of a community's pathways systems. This is not a recent development, nor is it unique to GLCCPP. The 2011 *Pathways to Prosperity* report highlights the importance of "umbrella infrastructures" to guide the redesign of education and workforce systems and to forge a new "social compact" between American society and its youth. In the Pathways to Prosperity Network, JFF identifies two types of intermediaries: (1) convening intermediaries that connect diverse stakeholders and provide vision and voice to the work, and (2) those specifically focused on brokering youth work-based learning opportunities by bridging employers and educators. While convening and work-based learning intermediaries have distinct roles and functions, they are sometimes led by the same organization and sometimes shared across two or more organizations.

As expected and intended, the four GLCCPP communities employ a range of approaches to intermediary functions and organizations, based on local priorities and partner history. The two Illinois communities use a traditional convening intermediary approach based on principles of shared governance and decision making.

> *Northwest suburbs.* The Northwest Educational Council for Student Success (NECSS) serves as the intermediary for the three school districts that make up the northwest suburbs—Districts 211, 214, and 220.

> *Rockford.* Alignment Rockford is a collective impact organization that aligns community partners and resources to support Rockford Public School students so that they "[graduate] from high school with marketable employment skills and [enroll] in post-secondary education and training," ultimately improving the economic and social well-being of their region.[4] As such, they are convening key partners around the pathways vision and serving as the intermediary for this work.

> *Madison, Wisconsin.* Rather than formally designating an intermediary, Madison unbundles the convening and work-based learning intermediary functions and distributes them across multiple partners from its anchor team, consisting of leaders from the public school system, three local higher education institutions, the City of Madison and the Office of the Mayor, Dane County, the local chamber of commerce, the regional workforce development board, and prominent health-care employers. The main driver of pathways activity in Madison is the Madison Metropolitan School District (MMSD).

*Central Ohio.* Columbus State Community College (CCSC) has steered most of the early work in the Central Ohio region's pathways work and serves as the de facto intermediary connection between employers, K–12 partners, and higher education. The college created an office led by the superintendent of school and community partnerships to serve as the primary convener and coordinator of all pathways work in the region. CCSC also established a new connection to the Central Ohio Compact, a regional coalition of chief executives from education and industry partners that formed in 2011 to increase postsecondary attainment rates of Ohioans.

Through developing and strengthening different approaches to mobilizing diverse stakeholders toward a common pathways goal, GLCCPP is both codifying multiple approaches to this critical intermediary work *and* elevating key learnings across different approaches to it, which will ultimately assist in the spread and scale of pathway systems across the Great Lakes region and nationally.

### Profiles of Exemplary Practice in GLCCPP

Even at this early juncture, the work underway in GLCCPP communities holds valuable lessons for peers in other communities and the broader field of college and career pathways. Both before GLCCPP started and since, cross-sector partners in each of the four communities are seeking answers to questions essential to creating and sustaining equitable systems of pathways to successful adulthood for youth in their regions.

The following sections present profiles that highlight promising examples of new and emerging capacity to provide high-quality pathways experiences to students—especially for historically underrepresented students—and how communities reached strategic decisions aimed at increasing equity and access through enhancing their leadership and governance structures, creating stronger alignment between secondary and postsecondary education, and developing work-based learning delivery systems. These stories both celebrate the promising advances of GLCCPP communities and candidly share the headwinds these partnerships have faced in crafting the new social compact envisioned by the pathways movement.

In the *northwest suburbs of Chicago,* a partnership of secondary, higher education, and industry leaders are building a system of pathways programs of study that is tightly aligned with regional labor market demand. Supported by a high-functioning intermediary organization, the partnership reports a significant increase in dual-credit course enrollment especially for Hispanic students. In the *Madison, Wisconsin,* school district, city, county, higher education, and industry leaders formed an anchor team to engage the Madison community in codesigning a system of personalized pathways in health services. Completing its second full year of pathways implementation, Madison reports promising first-year academic gains for pathways students. *Central Ohio* has set a "North Star goal" of 65 percent adult degree attainment by the year 2025. This regional pathways initiative is aided by fully engaged industry partners and a supportive state education and workforce policy environment. *Rockford, Illinois,* capitalized on an existing career academy infrastructure in its high schools to introduce pathways that are aligned to industry demand, postsecondary programs of study, and student interest. A memorandum of understanding (MOU) between the local community college and the Rockford Public Schools provides a framework for expanding dual-credit course opportunities for Rockford students.

## Expansion of Dual Credit in Northwest Suburbs of Chicago

NECSS is a secondary-postsecondary collaborative whose partners serve students in Chicago's northwest suburbs and include William Rainey Harper Community College, Township High School Districts 211 and 214, and Community Unit School District 220. NECSS is a rapidly emerging national leader in the movement to develop equitable systems of high-quality pathways that prepare students for success in their postsecondary endeavors and beyond. A key element of their college and career pathways systems is to expand opportunities for students to complete early college credit in advanced placement and dual-credit course taking. The following account relates the recent success in increasing the number of students in the northwest suburbs taking courses for early college credit—at little or no cost to students with a priority on participation of low-income youth and students of color.

**EXPANDING DUAL-CREDIT COURSE TAKING.** When President Kenneth Ender arrived to begin his tenure at Harper College in 2010, his first calls were to the local school district superintendents to set up a meeting. The fruit of their discussion was to unite their efforts into what has now become NECSS. After building infrastructure and aligning resources, Harper's provost and the associate superintendents of the school districts were engaged in this process and, subsequently, in bringing their respective teams and instructors on board. By spring 2012, the NECSS intergovernmental agreement had been approved. Its purpose was to provide a framework for offering coordinated college and career-readiness programs and services for high school, college, and adult learners who reside within a member district.

Harper College's associate provost, Brian Knetl, recalled the day in 2014 when the college's provost announced to deans and department chairs that Harper would support an ambitious expansion of early college credit opportunities through dual-enrollment courses in collaboration with the region's high schools. Since the late 1990s, the districts and Harper had offered a limited number of dual-enrollment courses, but the provost's message would set in motion a significant expansion in the number of opportunities high school students could pursue, thus reducing the time and cost they would need to attain a college degree. Knetl recounted the impact of the announcement on the college community: "It was pretty clear the provost's message would make dual credit a significant priority for the college from that point forward." Harper backed up this commitment to dual credit by allocating staff time to this effort, including a dual-credit coordinator and half-time support for a transition adviser.

According to Knetl, Harper College sees its dual-credit commitment as a wise investment, as first-year students arrive better prepared for college-level work. But support for dual credit and pathways in general is also integral to the college's commitment to a stronger region, said Knetl.

"Increasing college and career awareness and readiness to succeed beyond high school is good for our individual institutions, but also preparing our postsecondary youth to experience success whether they enroll at Harper or another college or career training program."

To facilitate dual-credit expansion, Harper developed a proposal review process for the high school partners that wished to have courses approved for dual credit. District leaders submit a request to the Harper dual-credit coordinator to offer a dual-credit course. At the same time, credentials are submitted for potential high school teachers for the college deans' approval. Then a team of high school and college teachers, department chairs, district personnel, and the appropriate dean, along with a NECSS team member, come together to discuss the development of the course. If approved, high school and Harper faculty meet to align instructional content and performance standards. The college and high school also collaborate on professional development to strengthen dual-credit courses.

The heightened commitment to early college credit in the northwest suburbs has sparked significant gains in student participation in both AP and dual-credit courses. Based on data reported by the Illinois State Board of Education Report Card for school years 2015–2016, 2016–2017, and 2017–2018:[5]

- From the three districts, 12,396 sophomores, juniors, and seniors were enrolled in *at least one early college course*. This represents an overall increase of 1,272 students since 2015–2016, or 11.4 percent.
- Fifty-six percent were taking *one or more AP courses*; others were enrolled in one or more dual-credit courses.
- For 2017–2018, over 60 percent of all students in these three grade levels were participating in *at least one college credit-bearing course* as part of their high school program of study.
- District 214 reported the largest number of students enrolled in early college courses (5,862, or 64 percent of all tenth, eleventh, and twelfth graders).
- District 211 showed the fastest rate of growth over the three-year period (+24 percent).

- Most importantly, enrollment gains for black and Hispanic students outpaced others across the three districts, increasing from 2,823 in 2015–2016 to 3,631 in 2017–2018, a three-year gain of 29 percent.
- District 211 reported the largest percentage increase in early college course participation for students of color—from 969 to 1,464, or 51 percent.

The message about the value of early college credit has clearly gotten through to the educators, parents, and students of the northwest suburbs.

**NAVIGATING HEADWINDS.** It's not uncommon for college faculty to raise concerns over efforts to expand dual-credit courses, and Harper College was no exception. The pushback from some professors and department chairs was based on two reservations: (1) a surge in dual-credit courses taught by high school teachers driving down enrollment in on-campus first-year introductory courses at the college; and (2) the appropriateness of college credit-bearing courses being taught off-site where the college would have limited jurisdiction over instructional quality and performance expectations. In reality, the college has experienced no discernible falloff in enrollment due to dual-credit offerings.

The concern over quality control is a more complicated issue. Knetl feels the best way to address concerns in this regard is by building strong professional relationships between college and high school faculty: "I believe the key is that, once we approve a course for dual credit, we need to get the college and high school teaching faculty together to build those professional relationships and shared expectations about teaching and learning standards. Currently, some departments do this very well; others require more support." In its newly approved strategic plan, NECSS has assigned responsibility to a team to ensure that engagement between high school and college instructors is strengthened.

What also strengthened the case for dual credit was the release in 2017 of a report by the Institute for Education Sciences' What Works Clearinghouse (WWC). This WWC intervention report was based on a research synthesis of existing high-quality research studies, largely derived from

JFF-led early college and dual-credit research and initiatives, which together reported solid empirical support for dual enrollment on the following student outcomes: high school academic achievement, high school completion, college access and enrollment, college degree attainment, and college credit accumulation.[6]

**EXPANDING DUAL-CREDIT OFFERINGS.** NECSS has served for ten years as the backbone organization for collaborative education planning related to pathways expansion, including aligned early college credit offerings. Committed to expanding the capacity for preparing the region's youth for successful transition to careers and society, NECSS pursues a mission "to develop programs, share talent and data, and leverage joint resources to ensure that every elementary, high school, and college graduate will have the opportunity to be prepared for a global society, 21st-century careers, and postsecondary readiness/success."[7]

NECSS Vice President and Board Chair Kenya Ayers, a former academic dean at Harper, pointed out that a critical advantage of the NECSS model is its organizational structure. "The NECSS board includes the president of Harper College and superintendents of the three partner districts and myself as chair," she said. "I can't emphasize enough the importance of having the CEOs of these four education organizations setting the strategic vision for the work."

The second level of NECSS leadership structure, the coordinating council, has primary responsibility for executing the NECSS board's vision through a committee structure that governs specific domains such as data, communications, professional development, and student support, among others. The council includes the provost of the college, Harper's vice president for workforce solutions, the associate superintendents of districts 211 and 214, the assistant superintendent of District 220, the regional Education for Employment director, and the NECSS vice president.

Finally, the operational planning of dual credit is the responsibility of the Power of 15 team (refers to the goal of all high school graduates earning fifteen college credits). That team includes the associate provost of the college and instructional leaders from three districts. Knetl explained that one of the keys to the Power of 15 committee is the trust the partners have cultivated over the years: "The four of us have developed a strong bond and good communications practices. As we do our work through NECSS, [we] don't hesitate to pick up the phone and have honest conversations with each other. When issues come up, we try to tackle them right away."

Harper's renewed commitment to dual credit in 2014 dovetailed with the high schools' long-standing effort to design coherent and rigorous pathways of study. Township High School District 214 is the largest high school district in the state of Illinois, serving 12,331 students. Six high schools and one specialized school offer forty-four programs of study across sixteen nationally recognized career clusters. Dan Weidner, director of academic programs and pathways for 214, described the district's underlying philosophy for pathways:

> We're determined to be very intentional about the work and believe it starts by introducing career exploration in the middle grades. We want our students to progress through our early college pathways *with a purpose*; understanding the connections between their possible career interests, their high school program of study and internships, capstone courses where they can earn early college credit, and options available to them after [high school] graduation.

District 214 will soon launch a comprehensive data platform that will carefully monitor student progress across the pathways continuum for the purpose of extending pathway opportunities for students underrepresented in college and quality career credentialing programs. More broadly, NECSS released a data dashboard in the 2018–2019 academic year with input from all four partners. The cross-sector work allows NECSS to provide longitudinal tracking of students. It can also be disaggregated internally by various student types—affording the opportunity to address equity gaps.

Located about twenty-five miles northwest of Chicago, Township District 211 serves twelve thousand students in five high schools and two alternative high schools. Danielle Hauser, 211's director of instructional improvement, reported that the district's sustained focus on equity has yielded important gains in dual-credit enrollment for Hispanic students:

> Three years ago we partnered with Equal Opportunity Schools to close equity enrollment gaps by expanding the enrollment of students in our AP and dual-credit courses. Now we're seeing significant increases in AP enrollment of our Hispanic students relative to their enrollment in our general student population. In fact, District 211 received the AP Honor Roll for the fourth time out of [the] College Board's nine-year history. Regarding our dual-credit courses, District 211 continues to expand enrollment and currently has no equity gaps between student groups.

Andrea Messing-Mathie, former deputy director of EdSystems, one of the technical assistance organizations working with the GLCCPP communities, adds that District 211, through very specific outreach and support, also achieved significant gains in the enrollment of students with disabilities in dual-credit courses.

Unlike its two partner districts, Barrington 220 operates as a unified preK–12 school district with five elementary schools, two middle schools, and a single high school that serves 2,900 students. Currently, 73 percent of District 220 graduates have earned college credit either through AP courses or dual credit. According to Assistant Superintendent for Teaching and Learning John Bruesch, the district aims to increase participation by another 7 and 12 percentage points by 2020. Working with the Equal Opportunity Schools, 220 is using its data to identify systemic barriers to expanding dual-credit opportunities for the remaining 27 percent of its seniors who graduate without college credit. In particular, according to Bruesch, the district is using the review to reveal "what adult issues might be holding us back."

**EXPANDING ACCESS TO EARLY COLLEGE CREDIT.** Looking ahead to the next three to five years, NECSS is targeting a number of priorities specific to expanding its early college career pathway work. First is the commitment to accelerating progress on regional equity goals through increased sharing of strategies and tools across the region. Several partners report important advances in data systems, dashboards, and data utilization practices. The strategic use of comprehensive, disaggregated data could help determine causes of persistent gaps in access to dual-credit courses. Second, Harper College is committed to deepening professional relationships between high school and college faculty to ensure that dual-credit courses in the high schools are high quality and well supported by academic departments at the college. This will include providing high-quality professional development to prepare the next cohort of high school teachers qualified to teach college-level courses. And finally, NECSS will continue to improve the quality of communications to parents and students about the value of college and career pathways, in general, and early college credit course taking, in particular.

Through the collective efforts of NECSS partners, the northwest suburbs are moving into the vanguard of the national movement to create high-quality secondary to postsecondary career pathways. Several key elements have enabled this work and inspired confidence in plans to extend pathways opportunities to serve more students—especially the region's low-income youth and students of color. These include:

- A high-functioning, secondary-postsecondary intermediary organization whose partners are united on a mission of achieving equitable learning opportunities and outcomes for all students.
- A higher education partner committed to work side by side with high school partners to better prepare students for postsecondary success as part of its broader mission to contribute to regional social and economic development.
- High school district leadership committed to building public awareness and support for high-quality pathways, expanding access to dual credit, developing new program designs that are aligned with postsecondary opportunities, and using data to inform continuous improvement.

## Cross-Sector Collaboration to Design and Launch
## Personalized Pathways in Madison

In October 2013, Race to Equity released a baseline report on the extreme racial disparities in Madison and Dane County broadly; in thirty-eight of forty indicators, the region had significantly greater racial disparities for African Americans than the national average. This report was shared at the 2013 YWCA Racial Justice Summit, and it catalyzed self-reflection and an urgency for improving equity in a community that long considered itself to be progressive and inclusive and providing excellent education and career opportunities to its citizens:

> The legacy of slavery and racism, the mismatch between our labor markets and key parts of our workforce, and the fragmentation and underdevelopment of too many of our neighborhoods of color—these are all large and powerful drivers of the vast inequalities that separate white and black Dane County. But they are not the whole story.
>
> The whole story has to include a broader and more forthright evaluation of the composition, priorities, policies, training, and practices of many of the county's majority-dominated institutions, especially those that directly influence the future education, employment, opportunity, status, achievement, security, health, and empowerment of Dane County's growing populations of color.[8]

Facing a situation in which fewer than 60 percent of its African American students were graduating on time from high school, MMSD embarked on a comprehensive review of its secondary school programs and supports. According to Cynthia Green, MMSD's executive director of secondary programs and pathways, "We knew we weren't serving all of our students well in their high school experience, so we wanted to really reconceptualize the high school experience so that all of our students were not only graduating but were on a really clear postsecondary success path." That review and subsequent planning led the district to create a call to action outlining a vision for the redesign of its four comprehensive high schools. This vision included offering a "personalized pathways" option for students in all four of Madison's comprehensive high schools, with a clear lens on equity for all students. This is the story of the first part of Madison's journey to create multiple pathways to support students' successful transition to postsecondary education or training, and launch rewarding careers. This section considers the design and early implementation of Madison's pathways strategy, the pivotal role of community organizations, industry and postsecondary partners, and Madison's vision for pathways expansion.

**A COMMUNITY'S CALL TO ACTION.** In 2014, Madison joined the Pathways to Prosperity Network. With JFF's support and guidance, MMSD and its civic partners responded to the call to action with a communitywide planning and design process. Green recalled the scope of the outreach effort: "We brought in sixty community partners to help develop and design what the new system was going to look like." MMSD invested three years in planning before committing to an initial design for health services pathways across the district, with the vision of expanding to other in-demand industry sectors in the years to come. These pathways admitted their first ninth-grade cohort in the 2017–2018 school year and expanded with a second cohort in 2018–2019. MMSD will continue to add new groups of students until these pathways reach full capacity in the fall of 2020. The district also has plans to launch information technology and communication pathways at three of the high schools in the 2019–2020 school year.

The communitywide coalition created an anchor team of partners to formalize its work to provide intermediary functions supporting pathways. The anchor team consists of four original members: MMSD, the Greater Madison Chamber of Commerce, the Workforce Development Board of South-Central Wisconsin, and Madison Area Technical College. These founding partners played key roles in the initial community outreach and design plan for Madison's personalized pathways. New civic and postsecondary partners subsequently joined the anchor team, including the City of Madison, Dane County, UW Health (a large local health-care provider with ties to the University of Wisconsin), the University of Wisconsin-Madison (UW-Madison), and Edgewood College. According to Jen Wegner, MMSD's director of personalized pathways and career/technical education, the expanded anchor team adds important new capacity to the collaborative and helped to clarify decision-making structures: "We saw it as an opportunity to be more intentional about the role of each member, of the levels and connections between each, and how we all work in the best interest of our students."

The anchor team uses a three-tiered organizational structure to provide intermediary support for personalized pathways:

- The chief executives of the partner organizations make up the executive team, which meets twice a year to set overall goals and strategic priorities for the pathways partnership.
- Senior managers of anchor team organizations make up the action team, through which strategies and work plans are developed to achieve pathways goals.
- Much of the day-to-day implementation work occurs through three subcommittees—Secondary-to-Postsecondary Pathways, Student Supports, and Experiential Learning—each focused on a vital system component for implementing personalized pathways.

**THE DESIGN OF PERSONALIZED PATHWAYS.** At the district level, MMSD, with planning support and guidance from JFF's Pathways to Prosperity team and ConnectEd, reserved a full year for high school faculty to plan how they would adjust their course content and instructional approach to blend in the health services theme. Wegner explained, "We really turned to our best and brightest teachers who were ready and willing to embrace this new way of teaching and learning. We asked them to step up to serve as our pioneers in personalized pathways." MMSD was committed to giving its teachers the time and space to examine how authentic day-to-day teaching and learning would change in the context of the health services theme.

Another aspect of pathways planning and implementation involves collaboration between MMSD teachers and faculty at area colleges. MMSD teachers and Madison College instructors make a regular practice of meeting at least annually to ensure that high school staff align their course content and standards to anticipate the rigor and expectations of college-level work. With a goal of students' preparedness for dual-credit coursework, Wegner highlighted that "those discussions focus on making sure our coursework leading up to those opportunities are solid, and that requires connecting the college faculty with our staff at the K–12 level."

Bridgett Willey, director of UW Health's Allied Health Education and Career Pathways, reflected on some of the work of the Secondary-to-Postsecondary Subcommittee:

> The subcommittee mapped out over sixty academic and career pathways to careers in the health services sciences via the work of our Secondary-to-Postsecondary Subcommittee. We also convened a session that included professors of anatomy, physiology, and sciences from our two- and four-year colleges and universities, teachers from the health services pathway in MMSD, and representatives from industry to brainstorm a list of competencies and skills that every student in the pathway should develop in high school in order to be successful in postsecondary education and training.

While these early conversations between content-area faculty and teachers prioritized secondary to postsecondary alignment in personalized pathways, the prospect of scaling these discussions to include other disciplines is daunting. Schauna Rasmussen, dean of workforce and economic development at Madison College, emphasized this challenge:

> I think the anchor team has produced some really strong plans for alignment and articulation between the high school and college curricula. Where this all gets more challenging is with the implementation of those plans in schools and working with teachers to align their course content and methods to better prepare their students for success in college-level work.

How does the new pathways design change high school teaching and learning on a daily basis? Wegner noted that the first big change is that students in pathways form small learning communities in each of the high schools. "The learning communities consist of pathways teachers and about a hundred students who form a small learning family," she said. "Teachers meet to discuss what's happening in each classroom, connections across classrooms, and supporting all students within the cohort." A typical ninth grader's course schedule has not changed radically. Students still take their regular core academic courses of US history, math, English I, science, physical education, and an elective. Personalized pathways students, however, also take a health science exploration elective in which students are exposed to various careers in the health services field. While the course titles are unchanged, MMSD is challenging all its teachers to infuse core course content with the health services theme through completion of an integrated project in the health sciences field. Green added:

> Our high school teachers are very strong in their content knowledge, but we're really asking them to rethink their instructional delivery. And we're pulling on our anchor partners to help deliver the health sciences professional development to help teachers make authentic connections. UW Health has been really involved and a tremendous asset in connecting our teachers with health services professionals in clinical settings.

Wegner elaborated on Green's point about MMSD's commitment to professional development for pathways:

> A foundational part of our work is elevating for our high school staff connections between the core academic courses and the health services thematic cluster: How does the health services theme connect to English I, our ninth-grade English course? How does it connect to World History, the tenth-grade history course? A key component to our pathways work is experiential learning—but not just for our students, for our high school staff as well.

**COMMUNITY PARTNERS CONTRIBUTE TO STUDENT LEARNING.** In addition to lending their professional expertise to pathways implementation, anchor team partners coordinate to provide experiential learning opportunities that support building career awareness to students enrolled in the health services pathways. UW-Madison, as part of its anchor partner commitment, developed a tour for all ninth-grade pathways students to orient them to the range of career opportunities in the health services field as well as the educational requirements of each. The university also offers a paid, for-credit, health services summer internship for select students on the UW-Madison campus that includes information about admissions and financial aid processes and resources.

As the integrated health system for UW-Madison and operator of six hospitals and eighty-seven outpatient clinics, UW Health is the region's largest employer in the health services sector. UW Health's flagship initiative for MMSD's health services pathways is the Health Occupations and Professions Exploration (HOPE) program, a one-day seminar in which students, working with a college student mentor, learn about the forty-plus career paths in health services. In addition to HOPE, UW Health offers paid summer internships for underrepresented high school students to work in a clinical or nonclinical setting under the supervision of a professional staff member.

As a member of the anchor team, the City of Madison plays a critical intermediary function in providing internships and other experiential learning opportunities for MMSD students. Mayor Paul Soglin has directed city agencies to offer work-based learning opportunities for pathways students and encourages the same from community-based organizations and companies that do business with the city. Wegner summed up the impact of the partners support: "When you're working elbow-to-elbow with partners on the work, there's a shared ownership both across and within our organizations . . . it's no longer just an MMSD thing."

**INDUSTRY STEPS UP TO SUPPORT PATHWAYS STUDENTS.** Working through the Experiential Learning Subcommittee, members of the anchor team established an industry council that meets quarterly to develop career exploration and learning opportunities in the health services field. The council also creates opportunities to share best practices and build partnerships to expand the region's capacity for experiential learning. Willey of UW Health reported on the subcommittee's efforts: "The subcommittee created a communication process and online repository that facilitates sharing new requests for work-based learning as well as opportunities that are currently being offered." Likewise, teams of MMSD teachers are working with industry partners to design integrated project work focused on the health services theme.

Pat Schramm, executive director of the Workforce Development Board of South Central Wisconsin (WDBSCW), another one of the anchor team members, is eager for the health services pathways to extend into the eleventh and twelfth grades. These grade levels are in "the WDBSCW's wheelhouse," and students will be able to take advantage of the WDBSCW's training platform designed to work with students of various skill levels and advance their attainment of industry credentials.[9] According to Schramm, "Our board is laser focused on making sure that the training that we're doing is credential based and that the credential is aligned with formal credentials at our technical college system." The WDB has also sponsored a middle college for eight years where, said Schramm, "we work with seniors in high school who begin their own college experience in September. By the time they graduate as seniors, they have an average of twenty Madison College credits on their transcript." This strategy puts students on a clear trajectory to earn their first postsecondary credential.

**ENCOURAGING RESULTS FROM THE YEAR-ONE REVIEW.** MMSD's research staff recently presented the results from the year-one review of personalized pathways to the school board. While district researchers urge caution, given that this was the first year of implementation, the report presents promising results on student participation and academic performance. About one-fourth of all eligible high school students across the four high schools have elected to enroll in health services pathways. The report notes that personalized pathways have a higher percentage of students of color (69 percent), low-income students (62 percent), and English language learners (43 percent) than the ninth-grade cohort overall (55 percent, 45 percent, and 25 percent, respectively).[10]

Using a propensity score matching design, the evaluation found that more pathways students are on track for graduation than their nonpathways matched peers.[11] Of critical importance—given the original inspiration for pathways, low graduation rates for African American students—the evaluation reports the following positive findings:[12]

- Attendance rates for pathways students identifying as black or African American are higher relative to the comparison group (89 percent vs. 84 percent).
- On-track rates are higher for African American and white students in pathways than their matched nonpathways peers (71 percent vs. 56 percent).
- GPA results for pathways students relative to the comparison group are higher for African American students (2.18 vs. 1.98).
- Pathways students identifying as black or African American had *course failure rates* four percentage points lower than their comparison group peers (13 percent vs. 17 percent).

The report also indicates strong satisfaction with the personalized pathways experience among students, parents, and pathways teachers.

**BUILDING PUBLIC UNDERSTANDING, TEACHER PARTICIPATION, AND COMMUNITY CAPACITY FOR PATHWAYS.** A number of partners see a need for greater communication about the purpose and potential benefits of pathways for all students, whether they plan to pursue a postsecondary credential or directly enter the workforce following graduation. This requires targeted outreach to students, parents, elected officials, community leaders, and school staff who are still unclear or unconvinced about the purpose of pathways. Given the focus on equity, MMSD must be particularly vigilant to convey that (1) personalized pathways are academically rigorous and lead to high-quality postsecondary and career options; and (2) they are *not* replicating the largely race- and class-based tracking into vocational education that was prevalent in the twentieth century. Moreover, pathways is not a program that sits alongside the traditional high school classroom instruction but, rather, represents an intentional shift in how educators make decisions about the way instruction is delivered based on needs of students. MMSD's ongoing commitment to using data on pathways' impact can be useful to any future strategic communications effort.

A second priority that anchor team members identified involves ongoing engagement of teachers and other high school staff as personalized pathways expand to upper-grade levels and new fields of study. Rasmussen of Madison College believes it is necessary for high school personnel to take a more active role in planning. "It may be helpful to have school, not just district, leadership in order to move forward," she said. "Without input and a commitment from leadership and teachers in the high schools, we will continue to have the same conversations." The school district continues to recruit pathways "pioneer teachers" who can serve as ambassadors for the work and expand MMSD's capacity for pathways and dual-credit offerings.

Representatives also expressed concern with the human capital capacity required as personalized pathways in MMSD expands to other sectors and scales to include all four grade levels at each high school. While this is primarily an MMSD personnel challenge, it also has implications for college and industry partners. For example, as the demand for experiential learning opportunities multiplies and increases in complexity in the coming years, so will pressure on UW-Madison, UW Health, the WDB, the Chamber of Commerce, and other key providers. The various anchor partner subcommittees are exploring technological solutions to reduce the reliance on person power as at least part of the solution.

Madison's four comprehensive high schools are now three semesters into the implementation of personalized pathways in the field of health services. The rollout of pathways to ninth and tenth graders has strong participation from both students and staff and has demonstrated positive early student outcomes. Notwithstanding formidable scaling challenges and some limited public reticence, the following factors bode well for the continued expansion of personalized pathways in Madison:

- The anchor team is a formidable assembly of social and political capital that has forged strong and trusting cross-sector working relationships.
- A critical mass exists of support and participation of high school teachers and staff as advocates for the power of personalized pathways for all students.
- Capacity and commitment are growing to gather, interpret, and use data to strengthen the implementation of pathways and to make the case to the broader public that redesigned secondary programs are putting all Madison students on a successful course to attaining postsecondary credentials and rewarding careers.

### Intersection of Education, Industry, and Pathways in Central Ohio

As superintendent of the Reynoldsburg City Schools, Steve Dackin decided to declare war on the senior year. While exaggerating for dramatic effect, Dackin was quite serious about accelerating and improving the transition to college and career, having seen so many students lose momentum at this critical time in their education. He said, "I thought the senior year had become the longest social hour in our culture, both for kids who were university-bound and those who wanted to get started on their careers. I had this harebrained idea that grades 11 and 12 should be integrated with [grades] 13 and 14." For this to work, however, Dackin and the Reynoldsburg schools needed a willing college partner. When Columbus State Community College (CSCC), the largest two-year college serving the Central Ohio region, welcomed David Harrison as its new president in 2010, Dackin made his move: "I gave him about a week to settle in, then called to pitch my idea. I got a call back within twenty-four hours, he was on my high school campus in a week, and the following year we opened eighteen college classrooms on one of my high school campuses."

**UNITY AROUND A VISION TO BOOST ADULT EDUCATIONAL ATTAINMENT.**
That early work in Reynoldsburg City marked the beginning of a sweeping
collaboration among regional colleges, K–12 systems, and employers, with
an eye toward increasing degree and credential attainment in the eleven
counties that make up the Central Ohio region. Given the region's high
density of colleges, universities, and industry, Harrison saw an opportunity to strengthen the talent pipeline to prepare the region's young adults
to enter the workforce and contribute to the region's social and economic
vitality through a coordinated pathways approach. Harrison learned about
the Pathways to Prosperity Network early in his tenure while attending a
Harvard Kennedy School retreat of the Columbus Partnership, an organization of more than seventy CEOs from Columbus's leading businesses
and institutions focused on regional economic development.

The Central Ohio region joined the Pathways to Prosperity Network
in 2013, and JFF had a key role in developing the pathways strategy in
the region. While attending the fall 2013 Pathways to Prosperity Network
Institute, the director of partnerships and shared services for Reynoldsburg City School District worked with the Central Ohio team and JFF
on a proposal for Ohio's Straight A grant initiative—and they were subsequently awarded $14.4 million to design, implement, and scale Path-
ways to Prosperity in districts across the entire region. The following year,
the region received another $7 million from Straight A funds to design a
data system to track pathways progress. In 2015, JFF co-wrote a US Department of Education Investing in Innovation (i3) proposal with and for
CSCC, and CSCC was awarded $11.5 million to scale early college strate-
gies in the region, with the college as the hub for the work. When Dackin
retired from his superintendent post in Reynoldsburg City in 2014, he
joined Columbus State to lead the college's pathways initiative and run the
Central Ohio Compact.

This emphasis on college attainment complemented the momentum
started by the Lumina Foundation's statewide investment in Ohio, among
other cities and states, aimed at increasing the national rate of adult degree
and credential attainment to 60 percent by 2025. The Central Ohio Compact, which formed in 2011, mobilized a coalition of fifty-five education

partners and twenty-five industry partners, to embrace the 60 percent attainment goal as its collective North Star. In turn, the state of Ohio upped the ante by setting its big goal at 65 percent. With Central Ohio's current attainment rate of 44 percent, filling the talent gap will require 1.7 million more young people and adults in the Central Ohio region to attain a high-quality postsecondary certificate or degree by 2025.

To supplement the efforts of the compact, CSCC launched the Workforce Advisory Council (WAC) in 2015 to provide a mechanism for coordinating industry engagement in pathways work. The WAC is a body led by CSCC and comprises the chief talent officers from the twenty-five top employers in the region, representing a wide spectrum of job sectors, including financial services, insurance, health care, law, customer care, logistics and distribution, information technology, hospitality, and education. With the NECSS in Illinois and Madison's anchor team in Madison, the WAC led by CSCC is the third of the intermediary structures profiled in this chapter. Todd Warner, the executive in residence, Workforce Innovation, noted that "by 2015 we had reached an inflection point with our K–12 and college collaboration, and it was time to add the third part of the equation, the employer side."

**AN INDUSTRY-LED PATHWAYS INITIATIVE.** Input from these industry leaders yielded important early benefits for Columbus State students. Having identified a core set of field-specific job competencies, CSCC committed to plan two new academic pathway opportunities, in addition to the wide array that it already offered: (1) a trio of certificated programs in digital technology, and (2) the five-semester modern manufacturing program based on a work-study model that leads to an associate's degree in electromechanical engineering technology. Warner explained how the planning process for digital technology coursework unfolded:

> Based on discussions that started in the WAC meetings, a planning team spun off, led by Nationwide, a *Fortune* 100 company, who offered to be our development partner. The Nationwide-CSCC team spent nine months doing program development in each of three

specialized areas of digital technology: cybersecurity, data analytics, and software development. We basically came up with a menu of competencies our graduates would need to enter each of these fields. Then we stepped back and asked, what courses do we already offer to satisfy those competencies and what new ones do we need to build?

After completing a pilot proof-of-concept phase, the college started enrolling students in the certificate programs in 2017. Of the programs, two are six months in duration, and the third is yearlong.

In an email, Warner described the scope and sequence of the modern manufacturing work-study model:

This is a five-semester program design that combines college curriculum with part-time paid employment at a partner company such as Honda. The students begin two full-time, academically intense semesters of Columbus State coursework. Near the end of the second semester, students and partner companies engage in an interview event designed to match companies with students that have a high potential to succeed within their specific organization. Beginning in the third semester, students are hired by the company through federal work-study funding. Over the course of the next three semesters, students reduce class time to two days per week and begin working at the facility three days per week as paid part-time employees. At the end of the five semesters, students walk away with an electromechanical associate degree, paid work experience, enhanced technical skills, and potential full-time job offers.

The compact made a critical early decision to ask industry to lead the pathways work with competency mapping. This, in turn, challenged the college to review its programs of study to ensure alignment with industry standards. However, to realize a full system alignment for a grade 9–14 pathways vision, CSCC's feeder high schools would need to follow suit by also realigning the design and approach to their secondary pathways.

Has there been progress on that front? Dackin's answer is "yes, no, and maybe." One of the region's definitive yeses is the Dublin City Schools, one of the five Ohio districts currently participating in GLCCPP.

**ONE DISTRICT'S BOLD PLAN FOR PATHWAYS EXPANSION.** Located about twenty miles northwest of downtown Columbus, the Dublin City Schools serve about sixteen thousand students, including about six thousand in three comprehensive high schools. According to the most recent data published in the Ohio School Report Card, 12 percent of the Dublin City students are low income, 9 percent are English learners, and 39 percent are students of color, the majority of those being Asian and Pacific Islanders.

For over twenty years, Dublin City Schools have offered two academy pathways for its high school students, a Teacher Academy and Young Professionals Academy. Craig Heath, Dublin's director of secondary education, recalled the critical choice the Dublin community had to make when faced with projected high school enrollment increase: "We had reached a crossroads about four years ago when we as a community needed to decide what to do about our need to increase capacity for our secondary program. The choice was whether to build a fourth comprehensive high school or pursue a different instructional model for our secondary students."

Dublin City turned to a number of trusted regional partners to assist with data analysis and community engagement for its secondary plan. Heath described the payoff of the district's long-standing relationship with CSCC and the Central Ohio Compact: "The Central Ohio Compact connected us to Columbus 2020, which is our regional economic development agency that does great work in projecting future labor market demand." Columbus 2020's analysts helped inform the planning of Dublin City's expanded array of academies.[13] The result was the addition of four new academies, all closely aligned with the future demand of the region's top employers: biomedical research, business, engineering, and information technology.

In addition to Columbus 2020, Dublin City turned to the Education Service Center of Central Ohio (ESCCO), which provides technical support to the forty-two school districts that make up the region. ESCCO helped Dublin City design and implement an extensive community engagement and consultation process involving over ninety community forums. This allowed the school district to both educate its community about the purpose and benefits of pathways and engage residents and other stakeholders in designing the new system.

In the end, the community opted not to build a fourth comprehensive high school but rather created a dedicated "Emerald Campus," which would house all of the school district's career pathways academies. Heath explains, "We bought a four-story office building that used to be a Verizon call center and completely retrofitted it to meet the needs of our academy programs. It's a very nontraditional setting that doesn't look at all like a school, and that's done purposefully." By consolidating all six pathway academies onto one campus, students take their core academic courses at their home school campuses and travel daily to the Emerald Campus for their pathway academy courses. Heath highlighted how one of the new academies is further deepening its relationship with CSCC: "What's really exciting about our new IT academy is we're working with Columbus State on a sequence of six courses which will allow our students to graduate with one full year of college credit courses toward an associate's degree in IT."

With the opening of the Emerald Campus in school year 2017–2018, Dublin City doubled its pathways academy enrollment to five hundred students. It currently has space and capacity to accommodate a total of a thousand students in its structure, which would constitute about one-third of the total number of juniors and seniors (academies are designed primarily for these grades). Looking to the future, Dublin City officials are considering the purchase of a building adjacent to the Emerald Campus that would allow them to add new pathways academies and expand enrollment.

**OHIO'S FAVORABLE STATE POLICY ENVIRONMENT.** Education and workforce leaders in Central Ohio point to a number of recent state policy initiatives that enable local and regional innovation to take root. According to Dackin, "Ohio has really good state policy when it comes to educational attainment and workforce development; this allows the work to flourish and accelerate and, I really think, puts us ahead of the game in respect to many states." In 2015, ESCCO released a report, *Navigating Central Ohio's College and Career Readiness System.* The report's section on the state policy landscape details several key actions taken by the legislature supportive of scaling a pathways strategy in Central Ohio:[14]

- Ohio's College Credit Plus program has become a vital and effective component of the state's integrated strategies to enhance students' college and career readiness and postsecondary success. Through this program, eligible middle and high school students can take dual-enrollment college courses at no cost to them and earn high school and college credit that appears on both their high school and college transcripts.
- Ohio's updated learning standards are underway, with new high school end-of-course exams to measure subject matter mastery. These new exams and other independent assessments also are being used to measure readiness for college and careers.
- Colleges and universities have come together to develop performance-based funding formulas and Remediation Free Standards. The state has worked with higher education institutions to reevaluate the effectiveness of developmental education programs.
- Since 2012, Ohio's institutions of higher education have complied with statutory requirements to assemble planned pathways that will allow students to complete a traditional bachelor's degree in three years, with many of the plans relying on students' attainment of college credits while in high school.

**EARLY EQUITY GAINS IN CENTRAL OHIO.** In its quest to increase educational attainment, Central Ohio leadership points to recent promising gains in learning opportunities and outcomes for underrepresented students. The

2017 Central Ohio Compact Report reveals that between 2012 and 2015, Columbus State reported:[15]

- A 24 percent decrease in the performance gap between African American and white students
- A 50 percent reduction in the gap between low-income and middle-income students
- A 14 percent increase in credentials awarded to African American students

Still, Central Ohio leaders acknowledge that much challenging work remains to reach the region's North Star of 65 percent degree attainment. Dackin stated that it's imperative that "we continue to engage with our higher education, industry, and K–12 partners, to demonstrate progress to date and to further illustrate that our investment in pathways, student and family supports, and workforce development is all about increasing economic mobility for individuals and the overall vitality of our region."

For Central Ohio to continue these gains, the region must provide every student with individualized supports that strengthen their position to succeed. Both the compact and member districts have invested in supports for high school students to help them build the academic and social-emotional skills needed to succeed in their college and career pursuits. Columbus State's Sherry Minton, who works with K–12 districts developing grades 9–14 pathways, described one approach used for students who don't yet qualify for College Credit Plus courses: "They can build that readiness to take a College Credit Plus course by pursuing an industry-recognized credential while still in high school." That path carries the double benefit of helping students build foundational skills while also earning a credential with value in the labor market that qualifies them for an entry-level position in a high-demand career field.

**ACCELERATING PROGRESS ON DEGREE ATTAINMENT.** What are the main challenges to the full rollout of the pathways work as an engine for reaching Central Ohio's North Star goal of 65 percent degree and credential attainment? First, the region is projecting two countervailing trends. Enrollment in both the K–12 and higher education systems is declining and expected to continue to decline, at least in the near term. At the same time, the region is experiencing growth in the number of employers that need an increasingly skilled workforce. As Warner framed the issue, "We're not going to grow our way out of this supply-demand problem with more students coming through the pipeline; rather, we need to increase the success rates of students already enrolled in our K–16 institutions."

The region is also confronting other challenges to achieving its attainment goal, including the hidden costs of college. Some students find themselves unable to persist in their studies due to lack of access to basic needs such as food, transportation, childcare, and housing. This problem is part of a national trend as more low-income students are enrolling in two- and four-year institutions. Dackin noted that "[w]e are really looking at these barriers that keep students from completing their education and then engaging in workforce."

The Central Ohio region is also facing a shortage of teachers prepared to teach in highly specialized fields, including such popular pathways as IT, health sciences, and engineering. Finally, several regional leaders pointed out that schools and colleges must develop additional support strategies that help strengthen students' social and emotional skills (e.g., resilience, self-advocacy, and academic tenacity). These challenges are preventing some students from powering through the inevitable challenges all students encounter in their first year of college.

The Compact's 65 percent attainment goal is the main driver behind the education and workforce development strategy in the Central Ohio region. And while educational attainment in the region has ticked up in recent years, it is still 20 percentage points shy of the goal. Fortunately, the region has cultivated several cornerstone capacities that provide a civic foundation for further attainment gains in the years ahead:

- The Compact has proved to be an effective vehicle for K–12, postsecondary, and industry collaboration, with strong CEO-level commitments from all three industry sectors key to the region.

- An expanding pool of regional employers is motivated to be part of increasing the productivity of the education and workforce systems and provide experiential and work-based learning opportunities to students.
- Capacity to produce and utilize data from across systems for both diagnostic and continuous improvement purposes is deepening.
- The array of student support strategies aimed especially at underserved and first-generation college students is expanding, aimed to help them overcome barriers to enrollment and completion of degrees and credentials.
- The state policy environment is favorable to continued advances in dual-credit course completion, pathways alignment, work-based learning, and student supports.

## From Career Academies to Aligned College and Career Pathways in Rockford, Illinois

Anisha Grimmett brings a unique perspective and set of professional experiences to her work as executive director of Alignment Rockford, an education support organization—the fourth intermediary discussed among these cases—and key partner in that city's effort to prepare youth for successful transitions to college and the workforce. An engineer by training, Grimmett is applying her twenty-two years as a project management and human resources specialist in the aerospace industry to help design a seamless system of learning for Rockford youth. Her work in the private sector also taught her what it takes for young people to enter and succeed in the workforce: a solid academic foundation, knowledge of rewarding career paths, and work-based experiences for *all* students. And as a graduate of Rockford Public Schools and active member of her community, Grimmett respects the uphill battle many youth face in navigating the path from high school to enter college or the workforce. "As a community, we are accountable for connecting supports systems and resources to create impactful interactions for our students that will help them transition successfully to college and work. We must ensure that these college and work opportunities are accessible and equitable to all students no matter their background," she said.

This story is about one community's effort to marshal the public will and resources to design a system of integrated learning opportunities that prepare its youth for productive and fulfilling adulthoods.

**A SYSTEM OF PATHWAYS TO ENHANCE EDUCATIONAL EQUITY.** Located ninety minutes west of Chicago on the Rock River, Rockford is the third-largest city in the state of Illinois. By the mid-twentieth century, the city had grown to become an important manufacturing center, specializing in the production of heavy machinery and tools. But like other cities in the industrial Midwest, Rockford fell on hard times with the decline of heavy manufacturing and was forced to reinvent its regional economy. Today, the dominant industries of Rockford include the aerospace, automobile, and health-care sectors, which together have stoked demand for a highly skilled workforce in the region.

Rockford Public Schools (RPS) serves twenty-eight thousand students in forty-seven schools, including four comprehensive high schools. The demographic makeup of the enrollment is approximately one-third each of white, African American, and Hispanic students, and over half of all students are economically disadvantaged. In the face of persistently low graduation rates and large achievement gaps, the Rockford community came together in 2010 to plan the redesign of its approach to high school education. The result was a system in which the schools operate four wall-to-wall career academies (meaning that all students are enrolled in an academy) specializing in business, production, public service, and health at each of Rockford's four comprehensive high schools. These academies were designed to support students in exploring a specific career interest, then gaining the secondary academic and work-based experiences needed to pursue those careers after graduation.

The early years of Rockford's pathways work exposed high school students to career options and specialized coursework. Three years into implementation of the academies, when Rockford joined GLCCPP, it endeavored to refine its approach to pathways in each of the academies and create a more seamless system of learning that connects secondary, postsecondary, and industry-sponsored work-based opportunities.

One of the early milestones of this pathways planning process was the community's consensus on defining a discrete and measurable set of skills, knowledge, behaviors, and experiences that constitute the "Profile of a Graduate."[16] Rockford's vision of a successful graduate stands as a helpful framework for the education, civic, and corporate leadership of Rockford to answer the question: what systems, structures, supports, and partnerships are essential to helping our students attain these critical skills and experiences? The profile articulates three dimensions of readiness:

- *College ready.* GPA of 2.8 and a postsecondary plan; dual credit, AP (3 or higher) developmental math/reading completion, C or higher in Algebra 2 or Math 3; or 1080 SAT, 22 ACT
- *Career ready.* Ninety-five percent attendance; 95 percent complete three-course pathway sequence; 100 percent with work-based learning experience; 100 percent co-curricular experience; and 100 percent capstone experience
- *Life ready.* Digital student profile; 100 percent with ten-year plan; 100 percent community service experience; and 100 percent relationship with a trusted adult

For their part of the pathways planning process, RPS district leaders completed a top-to-bottom review of their career academies. According to Bridget French, RPS's executive director of college and career readiness, the review started by revisiting the existing pathway structures within each academy, as well as the embedded course sequences for each:

We developed a rubric to look at each pathway sequence and courses within each to help answer three questions: First, is there a strong workforce demand for graduates of the pathway? To answer that question, we worked with the Department of Labor and our Illinois Department of Employment Security to look at workforce projections. Second, we asked what can we put into place with our college partners and our industry partners to ensure students will earn early college credit or industry certifications? Because 65 percent of our graduates enroll at Rock Valley College, they were obviously key to that part of the analysis. And third, we focused on student demand: Which of the pathways and courses were of interest to our students? We did some internal work with focus groups and student surveys to determine interest levels. We examined our existing pathway sequences using those three filters which led to a tighter and more coherent program of study within each pathway.

In the end, the analysis yielded a revitalized college and career academy structure offering over fourteen pathways in each of Rockford's comprehensive high schools: (1) business, studio arts, modern world languages, and information technology; (2) engineering, manufacturing, industrial and trades technology; (3) human and public services; and (4) health sciences. College and career academies in Rockford function as small learning communities of students and teachers. Ninth grade is devoted to career exploration; students complete a freshman seminar that exposes them to the array of career options and prepares them to select an academy in their sophomore year. That begins a three-course pathway sequence (one course per year) culminating in their junior or senior years with courses that yield either dual credit, articulated credit, or an industry certification in their chosen field of study. In addition to the dedicated pathways courses, the students' core academic studies are thematically infused with the pathways focus. Beyond the enhanced coherence of its pathways system, RPS also added a transitional math course in high school so students can avoid placement in a noncredit-bearing remedial courses in college. The district hopes to add a companion transition course in English language arts in the 2019–2020 school year.

The law and public safety pathway, housed within the Human and Public Service Academy, offers a prototype for a coherent program of study that leads to articulated credit and dual-credit courses for juniors and seniors. Law and public safety is offered to students with a stated interest in the broad career pathway in public safety. These interests include careers such as police officer, attorney, public administrator, emergency medical technician, and firefighter, among others. Following their freshman seminar, sophomores take a course in either criminal law, business, or psychology. Juniors are eligible to take Introduction to Criminal Justice, in which they earn articulated credit at Rock Valley College. In their senior year, students take Introduction to Crime Scene Investigation, which is taught by active or retired police officers certified to teach in the Rockford high schools.

**A RENEWED PARTNERSHIP BETWEEN RPS AND ROCK VALLEY COLLEGE.** Pathways planning provided an opening for reinvigorating the relationship between Rockford Public Schools and Rock Valley College, where nearly two-thirds of RPS graduates enroll postgraduation. The appointment in 2016 of Doug Jensen, Rock Valley's seventh president, further bolstered the secondary-postsecondary link. Throughout his career in higher education administration, Jensen has built partnerships for enriching the social and economic vitality of colleges' surrounding community. This has led to the college's renewed commitment to work with RPS on college- and career-readiness goals connected to employer needs and economic development.

RPS and Rock Valley officials meet regularly to plan how to increase high school student access to Rock Valley–approved dual-credit and articulated credit courses and industry credentials. According to Kelly Cooper, executive director of early college at Rock Valley, enrollment in these courses has been trending upward in recent years:

> Last year we had fifteen sections of dual credit running in our regional high schools. In comparison, this academic year we will have nineteen. Next academic year we will see a more significant increase. This fall we have 242 students participating in our Running Start program that allows students to receive an associate's degree here on campus while completing their high school graduation requirements simultaneously. Furthermore, we have just over 100 students taking one or more dual credit classes on campus outside of the Running Start program this fall.

To facilitate the expansion of dual-credit courses available to Rockford students, the Rock Valley and the RPS district signed an MOU in February 2019. The MOU, entitled "Linking Talent with Opportunity," stipulates the district's and college's respective responsibilities in the dual-credit expansion process. (Table 3.1 shows responsibilities outlined in the MOU.)

This strong statement of institutional commitments is an important resource for supporting students in attaining the goals articulated in Rockford's Profile of a Graduate.

**A PROGRESSION OF WORK-BASED LEARNING OPPORTUNITIES.** Alignment Rockford supplies much of the infrastructure and supports needed to connect Rockford's students with work-based learning opportunities. According to Anisha Grimmett, "What we're striving for is to provide our students with an integrated learning system that connects our schools, our colleges, the community, and regional employers. And a big part of this system is work-based learning." For the past year, Alignment Rockford has designed and piloted a four-year developmental continuum of experiential learning. While enrolled in a freshman career exploration seminar, ninth graders attend a career expo where they have access to over a hundred employers that align to the career academies and pathways. Grimmett said, "We stage our annual expo in a local sports arena and invite most of our major employers

**TABLE 3.1** Shared responsibilities in the dual-credit expansion process, Rockford

| | **Rockford Public Schools** | **Rock Valley College** |
|---|---|---|
| *Logistics* | • Complete an application to offer a dual-credit course at the high school<br>• Ensure that participating students have fulfilled course prerequisites | • Award credit and college transcripts for students who earn credit |
| *Course materials* | • Confirm that approved curriculum and textbooks are being used | • Make all syllabi available |
| *Staff and faculty* | • Verify that high school faculty are properly credentialed to teach a dual-credit course<br>• Enable college faculty to observe classes | • Provide faculty support to high school dual-credit instructors<br>• Host an annual dual-credit orientation meeting for school and district staff |

in the region. Companies set up kiosks and spend the day answering students' questions about career opportunities, entry-level requirements, and what to expect in terms of starting salaries and opportunities for advancement. This event helps our students explore different careers within our community and choose their pathway for their sophomore year."

In sophomore year, every student visits a local company or agency in his or her chosen pathway. "This is a chance for students to continue to home in on their career interests and experience on-site what's expected of employees and what the work environment looks like," explained Grimmett. As juniors, students spend four hours job-shadowing a professional in their field of interest. This includes a tour of the facility and opportunity to follow an employee and experience his or her everyday tasks. Students are allowed time to ask questions of their host and other employees. Finally, in their senior year, students are expected to complete a capstone project as part of an English elective course, a formal internship or apprenticeship, or independently in their chosen career area. These capstone projects connect them to a workforce or community need and helps students develop project management and problem-solving skills.

Alignment Rockford continues to fine-tune and pilot aspects of this work-based strategy in hopes of having the full array of work-based learning opportunities operational in the 2020–2021 school year. On the enormous undertaking entailed in taking this system to scale, Grimmett said, "What keeps me up at night is the prospect of extending these opportunities to all of Rockford's ten thousand high school students and to do that while adhering to the highest standards of quality. To ensure a high standard is met, we are currently designing a platform that will allow us to seamlessly connect students to our community through technology."

**THE SYSTEMIC CAPACITY AND PUBLIC WILL TO PREVAIL.** As Rockford prepares to scale its pathways work, it faces many of the same challenges as peer communities engaged in similar efforts to ensure postsecondary readiness and success for students at scale. With efforts such as content-area specialists providing professional development on how to infuse career academy themes into traditional academic content, district leaders are expanding efforts to secure broader teacher buy-in for pathways. Likewise, continuing the steady expansion of dual-credit courses will require a significant number of teachers to invest the effort needed to become credentialed dual-credit instructors in the school district.

Realizing the vision of Rockford's Profile of a Graduate will require an expansion of dual-credit and similar early college credit offerings. The MOU between RPS and Rock Valley College provides a clear framework and road map for expanding dual-credit capacity. Several RPS leaders urged Rock Valley to revisit some of its course requirements and prerequisites for some pathways. French said, "We just need to make sure, moving forward, that we're doing everything we can to take down any unnecessary barriers to dual-credit access for our students."

As Grimmett said, the prospect of scaling its work-based learning offerings to ten thousand students is daunting for Alignment Rockford's staff of three (who also support a major initiative in early childhood education), and so is building capacity to effectively connect all Rockford high school students with meaningful work-based experiences. Alignment Rockford has hosted a successful ninth-grade career expo for several years. However, the more labor-intensive upper-grades components that involve coordinating site visits, job-shadowing experiences, and work-based internships will require further system building, recruitment, and technology-based solutions to fulfill the needs of twenty-five hundred students per grade.

In the face of these challenges, leaders of Rockford's pathways partnership are buoyed by early wins such as significant progress in increasing pathways participation for special-needs students, who make up 15 percent of Rockford's enrollment. French noted the steps the district took to address this equity priority: "This year we hired an academy coach who focuses solely on ensuring our special-needs students have access to academies and pathways especially as it relates to the work-based learning component. This has really been a game changer for us."

To weather the expected challenges, Rockford will need to rely on its base of new structures and partnerships, renewed collaborations and trust, and steady support from industry and civic leaders. Its strengths for others to consider include:

- Rockford's concerted effort to involve the broader community in the pathways design work will continue to pay dividends. Public support for pathways across stakeholder groups remains high and the community continues to be actively engaged on pathways advisory boards.
- The renewed relationship and collaboration between RPS and Rock Valley College augurs well for the effort to expand dual-credit offerings. The MOU provides a strong framework for further progress. Open lines of communication between the college and district officials will facilitate the ongoing examination of course requirements for specific pathways.
- Alignment Rockford continues to serve as a steady resource for both community outreach and employer engagement. The intermediary has developed, and is now testing, a promising grade-level framework for work-based learning that provides students with graduated exposure to the workplace in their chosen fields of study.

## KEY LESSONS FROM GLCCPP COMMUNITY EFFORTS

What can we learn from these stories about building systems of high-quality college and career pathways in the four GLCCPP communities? First, a focus on equity in access and attainment can improve the quality of education and career preparation for all students, not just a select few. Second, finding common ground across stakeholder groups from K–12, higher education, and industry can create stronger and more seamless connections between education and workforce systems that will ultimately benefit not just students, but also employers and regional economies. Third, nascent efforts can be strengthened and accelerated through intentional and sustained commitment to building a broad-based leadership coalition capable of driving a bold vision for pathways.

Much of this progress has been facilitated through the GLCCPP community of practice. Many times a year, cross-sector stakeholders from the four communities convene to engage in cross-community learning. At these events, pathways leaders share effective strategies, elevate problems of practice, and collaborate to refine approaches that will advance their work designing and implementing high-quality college and career pathways systems. Coupled with ongoing guidance and targeted technical assistance from the GLCCPP coordinating team, the pathways work in these communities has accelerated and deepened in ways not possible had they been working in isolation.

While no one community has fully tackled all of the challenges associated with designing a college and career pathways system at scale for their region, there are many bright spots to be found in their collective work. Theirs are stories of works in progress that surface a number of concrete strategies and replicable approaches—in line with the GLCCPP priority areas of leadership and governance, secondary-postsecondary alignment, and work-based learning delivery systems—from which stakeholders and policy makers in other regions can learn as they collaborate in their own contexts to design pathways to improve outcomes and expand opportunities for young people.

## Leadership and Governance

Establishing the conditions for equity in and access to improved educational and employment outcomes for all youth through college and career pathways requires strong cross-sector partnerships with clearly defined leadership roles and responsibilities. Across GLCCPP communities, executive- and operational-level leaders from a variety of institutions and organizations are accepting responsibility for establishing, communicating, and executing on the vision for pathways. This work has sometimes been led, at least initially, by one institution or stakeholder group leveraging its reach and resources to advance a regional pathways effort. However, the long-term sustainability and scaling of any community's pathways work will hinge on the strength and development of distributed leadership, finding common ground, and early wins for all involved. Such leadership is emerging across the four GLCCPP communities. And all have made progress, albeit differently, to establish or strengthen clear intermediary functions to hold and advance a vision for pathways work. NECSS in Chicago's northwest suburbs, CSCC in Central Ohio, Madison's anchor team, and Alignment Rockford highlight the power of cross-organizational vision setting and collaboration as an essential component in a regional effort to build, scale, and sustain a pathways system.

## Secondary-Postsecondary Alignment

All of the GLCCPP communities are striving to establish strong, collaborative partnerships to design programs of study that span secondary and postsecondary education and that are aligned to regional labor market demand. Over time, such partnerships can pay dividends in the form of increases in labor-market-aligned, early college course taking, especially among students from traditionally underserved backgrounds. Early college involvement plays a critical role in students' college-going identity and increases the likelihood they will enter college, persist to completion, and earn a postsecondary degree or credential.

Early college research suggests that students who earn at least twelve college credits while in high school in both gatekeeper academic courses (i.e., nonremedial English and math) *and* technical courses are better served than those whose early college courses are essentially random (i.e., not taken with specific postsecondary credential requirements in a career field in mind). To address this challenge, the GLCCPP communities are making strides to ensure that students receive individualized supports and guidance to make informed decisions about a sequence of courses that are well aligned to stackable, postsecondary credentials with value in their regional labor market. Critical as well to the long-term success of this aspect of communities' pathways work will be how they attend to the quality of early college credit course offerings, how to best prepare students for college-level work in high school, and how to prepare and credential teachers to be qualified to teach such courses.

## Work-Based Learning Delivery Systems

High-quality college and career pathways need educational and industry stakeholders to collaborate to inform pathways design and develop scalable systems for work-based learning. Although the relationships and structures that enable employers to collaborate with educators on the design, structure, and management of career-focused workplace learning are not always in place, each of the GLCCPP communities has made progress. Their increased commitment and capacity building is establishing regional infrastructure to sustain high-quality work-based learning experiences that can support students' successful transition to the labor market. Ultimately, the promise of work-based learning is that young people will gain access to the unknown black box of the world of working adults and, for many, to forms of social capital crucial to launching a career in occupations with strong career ladders. However, to do this well requires abandoning a traditional and deeply ingrained model of teaching and learning predicated on a belief that we must first *learn about* something before we can *learn to be* something. Work-based learning, done well, inverts this model because it welcomes young people into the social activity of the professional world where, through learning to think like a practitioner and use the tools of a discipline, they begin to learn about the discipline.[17] Put another way, the real challenge to realizing a vision for truly integrated and effective work-based learning in a pathways system is one that is built on an understanding that, for example, we don't learn how to be engineers by studying engineering—we learn how to be engineers by doing things that engineers do.

## THE ROAD AHEAD

Despite our best intentions, our nation continues to struggle with a deep misalignment between what the workforce needs and how young people are prepared for careers; the changing nature of work presents new challenges to this already complex endeavor. Far too many young people continue to fall out of our education and career preparation systems without achieving a postsecondary credential or degree with value in the labor market—a reality that severely limits their ability to succeed in today's rapidly changing economy. This challenge cannot be tackled by any one stakeholder group; it is not a demand-side or a supply-side problem to solve alone. Only through co-design and co-creation by key representatives from the K–12, postsecondary, and workforce sectors can we design strong and integrated systems that can counteract the current deepening and widening of socioeconomic inequities.

The stories in this chapter shed light on ways that four communities across three Great Lakes states are working within and across their communities to address this challenge. Their progress provides insight about how other communities in the Great Lakes region and beyond can move the needle, systematically, to ensure that all young people are prepared to not only meet the current and emerging needs of the workplace, but also find value and meaning in their working lives and fully realize their best possible futures.

The GLCCPP work also suggests that, going forward, pathways efforts will need to double-down on two things. First, stakeholders interested in college and career pathways should focus on designing *durable systems* rather than implementing programs that may come or go or that meet only a short-term need. Pathways cannot be fully realized if they are merely an add-on initiative or a high school reform strategy. Second, in both educational and workplace contexts, it is crucial that the student experience and trajectory through the pathways system is *guided by expectations* rather than the mere provision of opportunities that only some students may take advantage of.

Attending to the systematic integration of secondary, postsecondary, and workforce systems at scale is challenging and ambitious work. Yet, it is work worth doing, and a deep commitment and concerted efforts by more communities to engage in the hard task of designing, implementing, and scaling high-quality college and career pathways systems, like those emerging in each of the GLCCPP communities, may yet lead to increased equity in educational and occupational attainment, and economic advancement for all youth.

How will we know when these efforts to build systems with equity and access as their North Star are paying off? When we see more young people like Shayla realizing their hopes and dreams for a brighter future.

## CHAPTER 4

# BREAKING DOWN WALLS BETWEEN HIGH SCHOOL, COLLEGE, AND THE WORKPLACE

Wonderful Agriculture Career Prep

*Thad Nodine*

It's May 2018 in California's San Joaquin Valley, and the orchards have set their fruit. Almond branches are covered with precious gems: fuzzy, silver-green almond hulls hanging among long, olive-colored leaves. Farther along the road, clusters of young pistachio hulls stand out like jewels, iridescent yellow and green against a sea of foliage. The San Joaquin Valley has been called the most productive agricultural region in the world, and its fruit and nuts are some of its highest-yielding crops.[1] But the real treasures in this valley, as in any rural or urban expanse in America, are its young people—and Wonderful Agriculture Career Prep (Ag Prep) is providing them with opportunities to thrive.

At the southern end of the valley, for example, the 2018 graduating class members of Bakersfield College are taking their seats in Memorial Stadium. College president Sonya Christian welcomes everyone and then asks a group of thirty-two women and men to stand. These students in caps and gowns look younger than their peers. They're wearing a special stole, or sash, over their shoulders, to honor their achievements as students of Ag Prep.

The applause from the other college graduates begins slowly and then gets lively. These are high school students, after all, teenagers. Most are the first in their family to attend college. Most are from low-income families.

Many of their parents work in the fields. These students have not yet received their high school diploma, and they're about to be awarded an associate of science degree for transfer (AS-T) in agriculture business from Bakersfield College. According to Lynda Resnick, vice chair and co-owner, The Wonderful Company, "The Ag Prep partnership has the power to change communities across the Central Valley—and it's replicable to other regions. By increasing the number of college graduates and creating a skilled workforce pipeline, we're working to reduce unemployment and generate local economic growth."

The story of how these teenagers celebrated their college degree before graduating from high school is gripping, and it reaches beyond Bakersfield College. It includes twenty-two students who graduated from Reedley College, near Fresno, and thirty-six students graduating from West Hills College, in Coalinga. It's a tale of students at three public high schools who took a leap of faith in the summer of 2014, when they enrolled as freshmen in a brand-new program called Ag Prep. In the four intervening years, they took advantage of everything that Ag Prep offered and were joined by students at four other high schools and six middle schools. They came to school every summer for college classes. They got up early on Saturdays to visit processing plants, greenhouses, and college campuses. They stayed after school to rewrite essays and help classmates finish projects. As one graduate said, reflecting on his experience, "Ag Prep was really hard, taking the classes, staying up late to study, doing extracurricular activities. So when you hear that gasp from the other college graduates [at commencement] and the cheering from our parents from the stands. And then having us rise up and everyone is looking at us, it's just, you know, like, wow! It was worth it."

This narrative is also about partners in education and business coming together to create fundamental changes in how students experience school in the San Joaquin Valley: raising the bar academically while grounding learning through hands-on, work-based experiences. The public-private partnership spans middle schools, high schools, community colleges, and universities. The design for linking these institutions draws primarily from the early college high school initiative and from career academies.[2] A key aspect that makes Ag Prep cutting edge, however, is that it is led by an industry partner. At the center of the work are The Wonderful Company and its subsidiary, Wonderful Education, which brought together the partnership, developed the Ag Prep design, and continue to manage and provide matching funding for its implementation. Wonderful provides Ag Prep students with extensive work experiences, including job shadowing, mock interviews, and paid internships. College presidents, deans, district superintendents, school principals, and Wonderful Company executives prioritized the work and supported a culture of continuous improvement. Teachers, faculty, coordinators, counselors, and tutors worked together to help students catch up, stay on track, and excel academically and in work-based projects. Ag Prep's achievements include policy changes in Sacramento, in school districts, and in community colleges to remove barriers that prevented large numbers of high school students from enrolling in community college classes. When state grant funding ended, Ag Prep's partners stepped up their investments to sustain the program.

This chapter describes the creation and early development of Ag Prep as a public-private partnership and as an educational model, the ways it supports students through a rigorous academic curriculum integrated with work-based learning, and its vision in serving as an engine of economic opportunity for families and communities in the San Joaquin Valley. This chapter is also a celebration of the abilities and vision of Ag Prep students who are taking on these challenges, breaking through low expectations, gaining awareness of new horizons, and creating their own futures through hard work, perseverance, and a healthy dose of goodwill. As one Ag Prep alum said, "We live in a community where we're considered low income. People don't expect us to do anything other than fieldwork. Ag Prep is proving to everybody that our population here is smart and we're able to accomplish more than we've been told. Our income doesn't define who we're going to be."

Many regional education partnerships in the United States are working to improve student opportunities, create career pathways, and build workforces aligned with local market needs, but not many are led by industry. How many thousands or millions more students, in the valley and beyond, might be ready for easier transitions from high school to college and into the workforce? For those asking what industry can do to help achieve these aims, Ag Prep offers a powerful example. Stewart Resnick, founder and co-owner of The Wonderful Company, commented, "The success of the first Ag Prep cohort is proof that when you pair a great academic program with lots of useful work exposure, students become more motivated and serious about their future. If everyone in the Central Valley had the opportunity to experience high school the way they did, imagine the possibilities."

## HOW AG PREP CAME TOGETHER

### The Context for a Partnership

Several factors contributed to the creation of Ag Prep in the San Joaquin Valley, which extends 240 miles from Stockton in the north to Bakersfield in the south, and 70 miles east to west, from the foothills of the Sierras to the rise of the coast ranges of Central California. Ag Prep serves students in the lower San Joaquin Valley, from Fresno to Bakersfield, an area of over 7,000 square miles—nearly the size of New Jersey.

**DISTRESSED COMMUNITIES AMID PLENTY.** The San Joaquin Valley may be the most productive agricultural region in the world, but it also has high rates of poverty and food insecurity, compared with state and national averages. Its communities also tend to have much lower income levels and educational attainment.[3] About 60 percent of residents in Silicon Valley have a bachelor's degree, compared with 8 percent in San Joaquin Valley.[4]

**AN EVOLVING HIGH-TECH INDUSTRY.** About one in five jobs in the valley is provided by agriculture, making the industry the largest employer. But today's agriculture industry has become much more high-tech, specialized, and innovative, with job openings requiring a high level of technical and professional skills. Many managers from the baby boom generation are retiring, and there are not enough young prospects ready to step into leadership roles.

**PERVASIVE SKILLS GAPS.** Skills gaps have been reported as a national challenge, and the San Joaquin Valley is no exception. In the valley, skills gaps in the agriculture industry are correlated with several factors, including college-going rates that are lower than the state average. Schools and colleges are not preparing enough youth for entry-level career positions in the industry. And the agriculture industry has not marketed itself well as a viable choice for innovative, high-tech work. Many young people seeking college and careers move away from the valley, not knowing that there are dynamic career opportunities near their hometowns. Carole Goldsmith, former president of West Hills College, said, "Farming has changed. Whether you want to contribute to plant research as a scientist, build sustainable food sources for your community, make irrigation more efficient, or specialize in the mechanics of packing plants—that's all agriculture."

**A MICROCOSM OF THE SKILLS GAPS.** The Wonderful Company is one of the largest employers in the Central Valley and one of the largest agricultural companies in the world. Through its many brands (including Wonderful Halos, Wonderful Orchards, Wonderful Pistachios & Almonds, Wonderful Citrus, and POM Wonderful), the company grows, harvests, processes, and distributes healthy foods to consumers across America and around the world. Like other agriculture businesses in the San Joaquin Valley region, Wonderful faces challenges in filling job vacancies. In 2014, when Ag Prep was first implemented, Wonderful estimated:

- The company has about 350 job openings for entry-level skilled positions annually—100 percent of those jobs call for a college certificate or degree (84 percent for a certificate or associate's degree; 16 percent prefer a bachelor's degree).
- Thirty-eight percent of the openings remain unfilled annually due to a lack of qualified applicants (many jobs that are filled go to under-qualified candidates who require substantial training), and there are about a thousand agriculture employers in the region.[5]

Stewart Resnick commented: "As the need for skilled agriculture workers increases, there's a growing demand for more college graduates. Right now, California's Central Valley simply doesn't have the number of skilled workers that companies like ours need."

**A TRACK RECORD IN EDUCATION.** For a quarter century, The Wonderful Company has invested in the communities where it has orchards, processing plants, and other businesses. The company's philanthropic contributions focus on community development, education, and health and wellness programs, and now exceed $50 million annually.[6] Lynda and Stewart Resnick, founders and owners of the company, have guided this work. In education, Wonderful promotes better opportunities for young people in the Central Valley by supporting preschools, charter schools, teacher grants, college scholarships, parent engagement, and Ag Prep. Through these efforts, the company seeks to reduce persistent rates of poverty and unemployment, strengthen communities, and improve workforce skills in the valley.

- In 1994, Wonderful began providing large numbers of college scholarships to students.
- In 1997, the company created Wonderful Education as a grant-making subsidiary to help manage and expand its educational contributions and impacts.
- In 2009, the company founded and began supporting Wonderful College Prep Academy, a charter school in Delano, to increase college-going. The school began as a middle and high school (grades 6 to 12), and now includes an elementary school. The high school offers an early college model integrated with two pathways: liberal arts and agriculture.

In 2013, The Wonderful Company hired Noemi Donoso, an experienced education leader, as vice president in charge of Wonderful Education. Donoso worked with Lynda Resnick to create a plan to respond both to the economic challenges that families and communities were facing in the valley and to the skills gaps that impacted hiring for career jobs at The Wonderful Company specifically and the agriculture industry generally. At the same time, California joined the Pathways to Prosperity Network, a multistate initiative led by Jobs for the Future (JFF) and the Harvard Graduate School of Education to create early college career pathways (see appendix A for a description of the Pathways to Prosperity Network). These pathways provided Donoso with a rough outline to draw from. The result was the creation of a public-private partnership called Ag Prep.

### Creating the Partnerships

In envisioning Ag Prep, the basic idea that Lynda Resnick and Noemi Donoso worked from was to make school more rigorous and relevant for students by breaking down the walls between high school, college, and the workplace. They wanted to give high school students the opportunity to earn college credits (including an associate degree) and gain work skills, free of charge; obtain career experience through paid internships in agriculture; and benefit from other work-based and college-prep opportunities.

To bring the concept to fruition, Resnick and Donoso met individually with community college presidents throughout the San Joaquin Valley. They described the concept as agriculture-themed pathways in high school taught by college professors, with access to industry experts. Colleges would receive state funding for dually enrolled Ag Prep students, greater visibility at high schools in their area, and The Wonderful Company's engagement with professors on industry standards, including externships at orchards and production facilities. In exchange, interested colleges were asked to deliver on two non-negotiables:

- Students would *earn college credits in real time*, so that students could take those credits to any state college or university in California.
- College professors would teach the college courses *on the high school campus*.

The two conditions proved to be nonstarters for most colleges. "These conditions were our entry points for a second meeting," Donoso said. "It was disappointing how few wanted to move forward, but that saved us a lot of time up front."[7]

At the second meeting, Donoso shared a detailed partnership agreement with each college. The document laid out a program model that was tightly defined in two ways: (1) specific services and other inputs that partners would provide, and (2) student outcomes they would achieve. West Hills College had recently opened its Farm of the Future program in agriculture and technology, and its board of trustees was the first to sign on. Reedley College and Bakersfield College became partners as well.

Resnick and Donoso began meeting with superintendents of promising school districts that feed into West Hills, Reedley, or Bakersfield colleges. At the first meetings, they again asked for service commitments, none of which were provided by the high schools at the time:

- A schedule of college courses that would lead to an associate of science degree in ag business, ag mechanics, or plant science for all Ag Prep students, and a master schedule to accommodate ninety-minute college classes
- Mandatory summer sessions for all Ag Prep students to complete college courses
- Mandatory enrollment of all Ag Prep students in the full sequence of A-G courses required for entry into the University of California (UC) or California State University (CSU)

In return, Wonderful Education offered:

- Financial support for a portion of Ag Prep services, support in applying for funding from the California Career Pathways Trust (CCPT), and funding for facility upgrades, which was not allowed with CCPT funds
- A team to launch and manage the partnership
- A commitment to provide industry-aligned work-based learning experiences for Ag Prep students, including coordination of guest speakers, tours of orchards and processing plants, job shadowing, paid internships, and more

As with the colleges, those who accepted these conditions were then offered a partnership agreement. Since Ag Prep's inception, about a dozen district leaders seriously explored an Ag Prep partnership. Some struggled to get buy-in from others in their district. Some were reluctant to make changes to the high school's existing agriculture program, others could not get teacher buy-in for requirements like scheduling, and a few met resistance at the board level. "Having ambitious program inputs and student outcomes quantified in partnership agreements definitely made district stakeholders think twice before signing on," said Donoso. "But it saved everybody time and resources over the long run, because it meant that those who signed on were committed." Matt Navo, former superintendent, Sanger Unified School District, said, "Having a detailed agreement establishes a clear vision and mutual accountability. It creates a strong frame for your partnership and for your ongoing conversations. You have to be courageous to create the vision and to make adjustments within that vision. That's really important."

By the end of 2013, two school districts and a charter school joined the partnership: Avenal High School (of the Reef-Sunset Unified School District) partnered with West Hills College to create a career pathway in plant science; Wonderful College Prep Academy (a public charter school) joined Bakersfield College in developing a career pathway in ag business; and Sanger High School (of the Sanger Unified School District) partnered with Reedley College to create career pathways in plant science and ag mechanics.

According to superintendents and college presidents who joined, the key attraction was the opportunity for students to earn college credits and gain career experience while in high school, which was described as a "game changer" in the valley. They were also intrigued, they said, by the potential impacts that The Wonderful Company could bring to their institutions and communities, not only in financial support but in networking, guidance on workforce issues and industry standards, and technical support.

Ag Prep received grant funding in 2014 from the CCPT ($9.9 million in 2014 and $8.7 million in 2015) to expand its model to include additional public high schools (see figure 4.1). The partnership also includes

**FIGURE 4.1.** Ag Prep partners, 2018

| Agricultural Companies | High Schools |
|---|---|
| • The Wonderful Company and its brands:<br><br>  • Wonderful Halos<br>  • Wonderful Orchards<br>  • Wonderful Pistachios & Almonds<br>  • POM Wonderful<br><br>• AgriLand Farming Company<br>• Fowler Packing<br>• Fresno County Farm Bureau<br>• Kearney Agricultural Research and Extension Center<br>• Olam<br>• Western Agricultural Processors Association | • Avenal High School<br>• Mendota High School<br>• Reedley Middle College High School<br>• Sanger High School<br>• Wasco Union High School<br>• Washington Union High School<br>• Wonderful College Prep Academy (Delano) |
| | **Community Colleges**<br><br>• Bakersfield College<br>• Reedley College<br>• West Hills College |
| **Middle Schools** | **Universities** |
| • American Union Elementary School<br>• Mendota Junior High School<br>• Reef-Sunset Middle School<br>• Thomas Jefferson Middle School<br>• West Fresno Middle School<br>• Wonderful College Prep Academy (Delano) | • Cal Poly Pomona<br>• Cal Poly San Luis Obispo<br>• Cal State Bakersfield<br>• Fresno State University<br>• UC Davis |

feeder middle schools in order to engage younger students in hands-on ag projects in STEM fields (science, technology, engineering, and math).

Among postsecondary institutions, Ag Prep reached beyond its three community colleges to partner with UC and CSU campuses in or near the valley to create a seamless pipeline for Ag Prep graduates. Wonderful has partnered with Cal Poly Pomona, Cal Poly San Luis Obispo, Cal State Bakersfield, Fresno State University, and UC Davis to ensure a smooth transition and supports for Ag Prep students, including making sure that all college credits earned in high school transfer to these universities.

On the industry side, The Wonderful Company is joined by several businesses and agriculture companies in the valley, most of which are involved primarily through job shadowing and paid internship experiences for students. In addition, JFF provides advising, support, and documentation of Ag Prep. Christopher Cabaldon, former president, Linked Learning Alliance, said, "The Ag Prep partnership is the prime example of what industry leadership can look like in education, and it's also a prime example of what regional work involves."

## Aspects That Differentiate the Ag Prep Partnerships

Regional public private partnerships among high schools, community colleges, and industry offer powerful opportunities to address student needs across educational systems and streamline student pathways into the workforce. Because the partnerships bring together institutions with different missions and administrative structures, however, they can be difficult to manage and slow to realize change.[8] The work requires active collaboration among staff and instructors who are already working full-time. Each institution brings to the table its own culture and history, professional standards, and regulatory burdens. Participants must advance and sustain change within their own organizations despite leadership turnover.[9] These kinds of partnerships have been likened to the confluence of multiple rivers: deeper and stronger where they merge, but also rough and difficult to navigate.[10]

There are several characteristics, however, that differentiate Ag Prep from most regional partnerships. One is that Ag Prep is managed by an industry partner, which is not unusual in European vocational education systems but is rare in the United States. As well as creating Ag Prep, Wonderful Education also provides leadership, research, coordination, technical support, networking, and information sharing. In 2018, Wonderful Education included these positions: executive vice president, Ag Prep director, two Ag Prep managers, two Ag Prep associate managers, and an administrative assistant. The Wonderful Company invests over $1.6 million annually in the partnership (not including college scholarships and the middle school programs). Wonderful's share (36 percent) roughly matches the contributions of the high schools (36 percent) and community colleges (29 percent).[11] Wonderful's investment, management, networking, and work-based learning experiences are pivotal to Ag Prep's design and outcomes. Nancy Hoffman, senior adviser, JFF, said, "The commitments that The Wonderful Company is making to Ag Prep are very unusual in the United States. Companies in Europe take on this role frequently, but this is one of the best examples in this country of the role that industry can play in helping to connect schools, colleges, and the workforce."

A second distinctive characteristic is Ag Prep's tight educational design, which is codified in its partnership agreements. Each school and college has a strong role in the partnership and authority over its facilities and students, but each partner agrees to implement the full Ag Prep model, including achieving substantial outcomes for student performance. These outcomes include grade-level performance in math and English, completion of the A-G series of courses required for admission to UC or CSU, and completion of the full range of college courses required for an associate degree. Education programs that are more loosely managed and that allow for substantial interpretation in execution can likely be replicated more quickly than more tightly controlled models like Ag Prep, but "the odds that the quality of the results will suffer are also higher."[12]

A third distinguishing characteristic is Ag Prep's structure for information sharing and capacity building among partners, which includes the following components:

- *Regional collaborative.* School district superintendents, school principals, college presidents and deans, and industry managers meet in person three times a year. Regional collaborative meetings enable the partners to learn from one another, codify best practices, hold themselves accountable, make decisions, and keep the partnership focused on improving outcomes.
- *Pathway Advisory Committees (PACs).* Each of Ag Prep's three career pathways—ag business, ag mechanics, and plant science—has formed a PAC that meets in person three times a year for hands-on meetings about skills development and industry alignment. The participants from industry are midlevel managers, supervisors, engineers, and directors. They are joined by high school teachers, coordinators, and principals and by college faculty, department chairs, and deans.
- *Team coordinator meetings.* Each high school and community college has an Ag Prep coordinator to support student needs. These staff members meet monthly in person for data sharing, training, coordination, and problem solving within and across institutions.
- *Individual coordinator meetings.* The Ag Prep director meets weekly by phone with each high school and college Ag Prep coordinator, and

often with superintendents, principals, and deans. Meetings provide updates on student outcomes and focus on issues to be addressed.

- *Site visits.* The director conducts site visits regularly to each high school, to meet with Ag Prep team members and conduct classroom or other observations, with the purpose of supporting teachers and tracking program development.

Ag Prep's tightly controlled model is not for all school districts or community colleges. Rather, it has attracted those with a strong vision to improve opportunities for students and those with the motivation and persistence to make ambitious changes to students' educational experience. According to Donoso, not every institution can implement every element of the partnership agreement on day one, but each element becomes the basis for an ongoing conversation about how to achieve it.

## AG PREP'S DESIGN

Ag Prep seeks to create a fundamental change in the educational experience, so that more high school students are engaged in a rigorous, relevant curriculum that gives them direct experience in college classes, professional agriculture careers, and work-based learning. The design builds from and deepens two educational approaches: a career academy that features substantial work-based learning and a career-focused, early college model that includes an associate degree.

- Incoming high school students join a cohort of peers and work independently and together to complete one of three agriculture-themed pathways: ag business, ag mechanics, or plant science.
- Each pathway includes a college-prep curriculum (the A-G sequence required at UC and CSU) and a sequence of sixty college credits in high school, which enables students to earn an associate of science degree the summer after graduation (free of charge).
- Students obtain career experience and professional and technical skills through a sequence of project-based activities in school and

professional conferences, job shadowing, mock interviews, and a paid internship at industry sites.

• Students attend summer school every year, to fit in the college schedule. A range of tutoring, supports, and interventions before, during, and after class helps students catch up and excel academically.

Graduates can transfer to a university (with half their college credits completed) or they can go straight into a job fellowship in the agriculture industry (with a salary of $35,000), guaranteed by The Wonderful Company for at least one year. Wonderful also offers scholarships and other supports for those who pursue a bachelor's degree. (See figure 4.2.)

**COHORTS AND SMALL LEARNING COMMUNITIES.** Ag Prep is structured as a school within a school: students enter as a cohort and share a range of experiences together—for example, in summer school, on college campuses, and on job shadows and work internships.[13] They also share the same groups of classes and teams of teachers, which gives them a strong community and support system at their schools. The teachers assigned to Ag Prep meet together to plan instructional strategies and supports, as well as interdisciplinary projects. For students, the sense of community also derives

**FIGURE 4.2** Ag Prep's model

| Career Academy | + | Early College | = | College and Career Success |
|---|---|---|---|---|
| • School-within-a-school structure, with student cohorts and teacher teams | | • Rigorous, relevant curriculum focused on science, tech, and math | | • Associate's degree the summer after high school graduation |
| • Three career pathways in agriculture | | • Completion of A-G course sequence required for UC and CSU | | • Ready for entry into a university as a junior with a scholarship for college |
| • Structured sequence of work-based learning, including interdisciplinary, hands-on projects, job shadows, and guaranteed paid internships | | • 60 college credits while in high school, including an associate's degree in science (AS) | | • One-year skilled work fellowship earning $35,000 |
| | | • Integrated academic and work-based learning | | • Prepared with technical and professional skills for the workplace |
| | | • Intensive student supports | | |

from a shared purpose; work-based projects help students see that what they're learning in class connects to careers and real-world problems. "That makes a difference in terms of motivation and engagement," said Juan Ruiz, principal at Avenal High School. "They know how it all fits together."

**CAREER PATHWAYS IN AGRICULTURE.** The program's agriculture-themed pathways include a structured sequence of high school and college courses, including an associate's degree. The pathways were selected because they are in demand in the Central Valley, they pay well, and they lead to promising careers.

- *Ag business.* Students apply principles of and technical skills in human resources, purchasing, storing, inspecting, marketing, and selling agricultural products. *Average annual income: $75,198 plus benefits.*
- *Ag mechanics.* Students focus on skills, knowledge, and training needed for equipment repair, machine operators, maintenance (for example, welding and plumbing), and general administration. *Average annual income: $56,907 plus benefits.*
- *Plant science.* Students study the theories, principles, and practices involved with the production and management of food and soil conservation, including irrigation and pest management. *Average annual income, $35,350 plus benefits.*[14]

**EARLY COLLEGE CURRICULUM.** All students complete the A-G college prep sequence required for admission to UC or CSU. Ag Prep also integrates a full sequence of college courses and intensive student supports into the high school curriculum.[15] In addition, Ag Prep integrates hands-on projects and other work-based learning that draw from the experiences and work of the San Joaquin Valley. Depending on the high school, students typically take a college course every summer, a college course each semester through sophomore year, and two to three college courses per term during their final two years—leading to an associate's degree in science during the summer after their senior year (see figure 4.3).

**FIGURE 4.3** Sample schedule of college classes at the three founding high schools, by career pathway, 2014–2015

| Grade | Wonderful Academy + Bakersfield CC | Avenal High School + West Hills CC | Sanger High School + Reedley CC | |
|---|---|---|---|---|
| | **Ag Business** | **Plant Science** | **Plant Science** | **Ag Mechanics** |
| *Summer* | • Microsoft Office | • Ag Applications to Computers | • Ag Applications to Computers | • Ag Applications to Computers |
| *9th* | • Nutrition<br>• Spanish 1 | • Health<br>• Spanish 1 | • Health<br>• Spanish 1 | • Health<br>• Spanish 1 |
| *Summer* | • Art Appreciation | • Art Appreciation | • Spanish 2 | • Spanish 2 |
| *10th* | • World History<br>• Ag Sales and Comm.<br>• Ag, Environment, & Society<br>• Intro Ag Business | • Intro Plant Science<br>• Tractor Operation | • Plant Nutrition<br>• Pesticides | • Construction Tech.<br>• Welding 1 |
| *Summer* | • Public Speaking | • Psychology | • Public Speaking | • Physical Education |
| *11th* | • Ag Leadership<br>• Intro Plant Science<br>• Intro Chemistry<br>• U.S. History | • California Water<br>• Weeds and Plants<br>• Communications<br>• U.S. History | • Plant Science<br>• Plant Propagation & Production<br>• Art Appreciation<br>• U.S. History | • Electricity & Hydraulics<br>• Small Engines<br>• Art Appreciation<br>• U.S. History |
| *Summer* | • Ag Internship<br>• American Government | • Ag Internship<br>• American Government | • Ag Internship<br>• American Government | • Ag Internship<br>• American Government |
| *12th* | • Ag Economics<br>• Macro Economics<br>• English Comp.<br>• Intro Literature<br>• Statistics | • Ag Economics<br>• Pest Management<br>• Critical Thinking<br>• Intro Chemistry<br>• Statistics | • Ag Economics<br>• Critical Reasoning<br>• General Chemistry<br>• Statistics | • Ag Economics<br>• Welded Structures<br>• Machinery Tech.<br>• Public Speaking<br>• Statistics |
| *Summer* | • [None] | • Soils<br>• English Comp. | • Soils<br>• English Comp. | • Soils<br>• English Comp. |

*Note:* All Ag Prep students are supported in completing these college courses and thereby earning an associate's degree in science (60 credits).

College courses are taught on high school campuses by partnering with community college instructors, which was one of the "non-negotiables" required by Wonderful, primarily because it removes the challenges of transporting students large distances across the valley to a college campus. High schools provide most of the student supports, including case management, mandatory summer school, mandatory interventions, academic tutoring, and dedicated college and career counseling (done jointly with Wonderful Education). The community colleges select and oversee the college instructors, determine the requirements for certificates and degrees, and ensure the quality of the courses and degree programs, as they would at their own cam puses, but they also work with industry experts from the PACs to strengthen alignment with in-demand industry skills. At many high schools, some of their own teachers with master's degrees meet the community college qualifications and complete the procedures to teach the courses. The colleges also provide their own college students as tutors for the high school students.

One of the challenges that Ag Prep faced—and one of its successes—involved helping to change California's policies on dual enrollment. Before 2016, state law required that community college classes be open to the public. Since Ag Prep offers dual-enrollment classes on high school campuses, this created challenges for the high schools, which face restrictions in whom they can allow on their campuses during the school day. Through the enactment of Assembly Bill 288, the California legislature removed this barrier to dual enrollment and allowed the community colleges to offer closed courses on high school campuses during the regular school day. The bill also relaxed limits on how many community college credits high school students could take and waived college fees for high school students enrolled through college and career pathways such as Ag Prep.

## Involving Middle Schools

**MIDDLE SCHOOL AG-STEM PROGRAM.** Since many students in the San Joaquin Valley begin high school well below grade level, Wonderful expanded to feeder middle schools to strengthen their STEM programming and spark interest in STEM careers among their students. Wonderful supports the schools in providing ag-STEM electives for over nine hundred seventh and eighth graders annually, including student trips to industry sites and science centers. Teachers attend training each year to incorporate work-based learning into their STEM curriculum, including learning-garden units.

**SUMMER CAMPS FOR MIDDLE SCHOOL STUDENTS.** Ag Prep provides weeklong overnight camps on college campuses for rising eighth graders in the areas served by the program's high schools. At the camps, students experience college firsthand by staying in dorms for the week and participating in hands-on activities that feature work-based learning. They visit orchards and processing facilities and talk with field managers and line experts. They witness the power of simulations in surveying and in computer-aided design (CAD). They work with farm machinery and tools, including welding and fabricating. And they see the bigger picture—how the farm operates as a business. From these experiences, they get a firsthand look at a wide range of cutting-edge careers in agriculture.

## Student Enrollment

For outreach for its high school program, Ag Prep targets all students who want to pursue college and career goals while in high school. Participating schools recruit a class of thirty or sixty Ag Prep freshmen annually, based on school capacity, and they collaborate with middle schools to inform potential students about the program. High school staff emphasize the program's rigorous requirements (such as summer school, after-school interventions, college course taking, and work-based learning off-site) to ensure that students and parents understand the challenges involved. Students and parents who are interested must sign a contract committing to the program's requirements.

Ag Prep began enrolling freshmen in fall 2014 at Avenal High School, Sanger High School, and the Wonderful College Prep Academy. Reedley Middle College High School, Wasco Union High School, and Washington Union High School enrolled their first cohorts a year later. Mendota High School launched Ag Prep in fall 2016. Enrollments grow annually as new freshmen enter and existing students progress toward graduation (see table 4.1). When the program is at capacity in 2020, enrollments are expected to reach about 1,440 students. Ag Prep participants reflect the demographics of their high schools.

**TABLE 4.1** Ag Prep high school enrollments, first four years

| 2014–2015 | 2015–2016 | 2016–2017 | 2017–2018 |
|-----------|-----------|-----------|-----------|
| 197 | 475 | 737 | 1,010 |

Source: Wonderful Education.

## Technology-Infused Instruction

Ag Prep provides each student with a laptop, tablet, or other device and integrates computer use into everyday assignments and projects—to prepare every student for twenty-first-century learning and workplace environments. Students develop drafts and presentations online (through Google Docs, YouTube, and other platforms). They share their work with classmates and provide feedback before submitting homework electronically (often, their projects span more than one class or subject). Students also learn to use software appropriate for their agricultural pathways, such as global positioning systems (GPS), CAD, geographic information systems (GIS), analytic software, and surveying. Requiring students to complete their work online gives the high schools another way to track student progress and identify student needs or trouble areas readily in order to provide personalized interventions and supports.

## STUDENT SUPPORTS

A key challenge that Ag Prep high schools face is that most ninth graders begin at the sixth- or seventh-grade level in math or reading, yet they start taking classes right away at grade level and beyond, including college courses. In supporting students, Ag Prep uses a holistic approach that builds on student assets and their interests, identifies early on those who are struggling, provides mandatory interventions to address learning gaps and to support students in challenging classes, and adapts school procedures and systems to better meet their needs. According to Wonderful's Donoso, "High schools need to provide support everywhere, all the time, in everything they do, to all students. It's both a mind-set and a follow-through, to help all students meet high expectations."

Ag Prep's strategies for supporting students feature the following approaches.

**COMMIT TO FUNDAMENTAL CHANGES IN THE SCHOOL EXPERIENCE FOR ALL STUDENTS.** Supporting student success is inherent to Ag Prep's design, including organizing around cohorts of students; creating a mind-set so that all students can meet rigorous academic expectations; implementing a relevant, interdisciplinary curriculum through agriculture pathways; featuring hands-on, work-based learning; and ensuring that teachers and staff are engaged with students and working as a team. In Ag Prep's model, students take the same classes, work together on projects, and give each other encouragement and support. Teachers adopt an asset-based mind-set that all students can succeed in rigorous A-G courses and college classes, and the teachers are actively engaged in planning and strategy sessions with other teachers. The academic curriculum—whether English, math, or science—is integrated with work-based learning both at school and through opportunities in the agriculture industry, with hands-on, interdisciplinary projects that address problems of relevance to the San Joaquin Valley. In job shadowing and internships, students can see that what they're learning in school connects to careers and real-world issues, which motivates and engages them. As one student said, "This program—the activities in the field and at the [processing] plants—it's driven me to learn more and to know more." The entire process requires high schools to redirect resources around supporting student success. (See figure 4.4.)

**FIGURE 4.4** A program design that integrates student supports

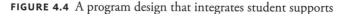

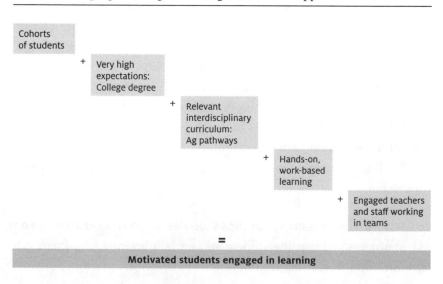

**MONITOR STUDENT PERFORMANCE TENACIOUSLY, ENGAGE WITH STUDENTS DAILY, AND STEP IN QUICKLY TO ADDRESS NEEDS.** At the center of Ag Prep's approach to supporting student success is the creation of an all-embracing case management, tracking, and student engagement process at each high school. Each school has an Ag Prep coordinator (a position funded half by the school and half by Wonderful) who works closely with students to address challenges as they arise and to provide guidance, emotional support, mentoring, and direction. According to Stephanie Bowleg, Avenal's Ag Prep coordinator, "Case management doesn't really explain the full role. For us, it also involves engaging with students as motivator, mentor, and success coach."

Each high school worked several years to develop and refine its own version of this proactive and individualized system. Each school's coordinator interacts daily with students, reviews their records at least weekly, and connects with teachers at least weekly to identify those who are struggling in their classes. They check in with parents, when appropriate. They track student attendance, class participation, homework, test results, and other markers of student progress. They receive technical support from Wonderful Education in setting up systems for tracking student performance. The priority is to identify those who are struggling very early and connect them with interventions.

At one school, for example, the coordinator works with a leadership team—the Ag Prep counselor, math intervention teacher, and English intervention teacher—to determine which team member is in the best position to coach and mentor each struggling student. That team member works one-on-one with the student to set goals and an action plan for personalized tutoring and support, and meets with the student to track performance on weekly objectives.

**PROVIDE MANDATORY, PERSONALIZED SUPPORTS TO ADDRESS LEARNING GAPS.** In monitoring student performance, high schools identify each student's learning and skills gaps and provide personalized supports to address those needs. Because each high school has its own history and context in providing supports, the schools have flexibility in developing or adapting a range of interventions based on the student's needs. The partnership agreements require schools to provide a baseline amount of such services and to meet student progress outcomes that are monitored and shared regularly. If student performance lags, then discussions follow about specific academic support options.

Ag Prep high schools offer peer study groups, one-on-one supports, in-class assistance, after-school study, support classes, adaptive technology, and project-based learning that isolates skills practice. During the summers, students at all the schools are required to attend summer sessions, where they enroll in college classes but also receive individualized support focused on their learning challenges.

A promising approach at some schools has been to create support classes for all students in math and English during the regular school day. Some of these classes use a rotation model with learning stations; the teacher adapts the topics covered in each station based on the students' needs at that time—from supporting their current instruction in their math or English class to addressing their prior learning needs. The stations include:

- *Small-group instruction.* The teacher works with about a third of the class for a third of the class time, providing direct instruction on identified learning issues or in support of the content of their current class.
- *Project-based learning.* Students work either individually or in groups on interdisciplinary projects or other hands-on applications.
- *Adaptive technology.* Students work on a computer, using software applications that assess their learning or skills gaps and lead them through exercises or activities to address them.

Sanger High School has a well-established "pull-out and push-in" schoolwide intervention system that fosters personalized supports. Two intervention teachers are dedicated to Ag Prep, one in English and one in math. The teachers pull targeted students from physical education or an elective class to provide them with tutoring in math or reading. They also provide push-in support by going to math or English classes to work with targeted students individually or in small groups. As one student said, "The intervention teacher was with us during class when our main teacher was in the front teaching. She would be mingling with us to make sure we understood what she was saying. It was helpful." After-school tutoring is mandatory for students who are identified as struggling.

Wonderful College Prep Academy has a robust system of support classes during the day for all Ag Prep students. For freshmen, the school schedule includes two class periods for math and two for English. One math class provides primary instruction, and the second class (with a different teacher) provides individualized support. The same is true for English. At the end of March 2018, for example, the support class in math was focusing its small-group instruction and project-based stations on helping students understand and graph quadratic equations. At the adaptive technology station, students worked on their identified learning gaps, using ALEKS software.

**PROVIDE STRUCTURED SUPPORTS SPECIFIC TO COLLEGE CLASSES FOR ALL STUDENTS.** Ag Prep has found that all of its students need academic supports in college courses. As with its general learning supports, each high school has developed its own approaches to supporting students in college classes, but most embed a high school instructor in the college class with the students. The college classes generally meet less than five days a week. During the off days, the students attend support classes with the high school instructor and/or a college tutor. The support ranges from instruction in college study strategies to hands-on help with homework and test preparation. As one student described, "Every time we have a college class, we have another class just for support. So right now we're taking Art Appreciation, which is a lot of notes and a lot of writing. And we have another two-hour class just on the assignments of that class."

One high school embeds tutors with its students in the college classes; the students meet with the tutors outside of class to receive additional support. Another high school has experimented with providing a college class online, with students attending a support class at the school with a high school instructor. For all the high schools, community colleges have agreed (in their partnership agreements) to provide peer tutors on the high school campuses from among their own college students.

**BE PERSISTENT AND RELENTLESS IN ADAPTING EXISTING SYSTEMS TO MEET STUDENTS' NEEDS.** Engaging students in high school classes, college classes, and work-based learning requires flexibility and persistence in adapting existing school procedures and systems. There are no easy answers for how to schedule the school day to provide sufficient support and interventions. Ag Prep partnership agreements require schools to accommodate longer college-course periods into their class scheduling, and most Ag Prep high schools have adopted block schedules. Some schools are also adopting a longer school day or are providing mandatory tutoring for targeted students before or after school and on weekends. Additional logistics are required to support job shadowing and internships off-site, as described in the next section.

## WORK-BASED LEARNING

Work-based learning is integral to Ag Prep's efforts to transform education. Students work in teams—within and across classes—to complete hands-on, interdisciplinary projects that feature real-world problem solving. They also participate in a structured series of work experiences in industry settings that introduce them to a range of career experiences. These work experiences enable them to apply and deepen the skills they learn in school. As students engage in these diverse opportunities, the distinction between the classroom and the outside world begins to fade. As one student said, "Every time they give us a project, we have a hands-on experience associated with it—like when we did the bee project, we went to see a bee farm, so we got to see how it works."

Work-based learning programs can help students make informed career choices; positively impact college enrollment; develop students' professional and employability skills; and increase their appreciation for the variety of occupations within specific fields, in this case, agriculture.[16] Ag

Prep has found that, via work-based learning, students also try out new skills, apply academic concepts to practical challenges, model successful workplace behaviors, perform tasks in authentic settings, work with and challenge their peers, network with professionals, and make presentations as a professional to other professionals. Work-based learning is one of the best ways to make the school curriculum come alive for students, and it is also one of the most effective ways to learn.

### Skills Mapping to Align Classrooms and the Workplace

One of the first steps that Ag Prep took in connecting classrooms to ag workplaces was to initiate a skills-mapping process. Skills mapping seeks to identify key skills required in the workplace in order to better align the educational curriculum with labor market demand. The process, which was facilitated by JFF, began in fall 2014 by creating a Pathway Advisory Committee for each of Ag Prep's three pathways—ag business, ag mechanics, and plant science. PAC participants included:

- *High schools.* Ag instructors, science instructors, program coordinators, and principals
- *Community colleges.* Ag faculty, department chairs, and deans
- *Wonderful Company.* Managers, supervisors, engineers, directors, and vice presidents of operations

Each of the three PACs engaged in a series of conversations that yielded changes in high schools, colleges, and industry. Each committee collected job descriptions for entry-level, midskilled career positions and syllabi and learning outcomes for pertinent courses. From these materials, JFF created a comprehensive list of industry skills, from which the PACs selected and provided feedback on a maximum of ten top technical and professional skills for each pathway. The committees found that the technical skills vary significantly by pathway, but the professional skills for the workplace—from communication and organization to safety and work etiquette—are common across the three pathways.[17] The results also confirmed the importance of twenty-first-century skills in the workplace, including problem solving, communication, technological literacy, teamwork, organization and analyzing, and scientific and numerical literacy.

The PACs have since simplified the skills maps. Teachers and faculty have used them to adjust and enliven instructional activities (see figure 4.5). They have also been used by Wonderful Education staff and Wonderful Company managers to identify the skills that students gain in job shadowing, internships, and other work-based experiences.

## Interdisciplinary, Work-Based Projects

At Ag Prep, each student works with teams of peers every semester to complete an interdisciplinary, work-based project. Teams of teachers at each school design the projects for each grade level. The primary purpose is to engage students in investigating and responding to an authentic problem that spans academic disciplines and engages the physical world. The students' responses might include proposing a solution, designing an

**FIGURE 4.5** Sample interdisciplinary projects and skills map alignment

| School | Project Title | Technical Skills |
|---|---|---|
| *Avenal High School* | GMOs, yes or no? | **Skills map: Plant Science**<br>1. Applying principles and techniques for growth, fertility, and nutrition of plants and plant products.<br>5. Writing and reviewing reports for plant production and management.<br>7. Using computers/technology to benefit plant production and management. |
| *Reedley Middle College High School* | How do you craft an effective pitch to a potential investor? | **Skills map: Ag Business**<br>1. Using math to analyze and present business information, solve problems, and make decisions.<br>5. Making good business decisions in light of the global market and economy.<br>6. Using the principles of agribusiness to purchase or sell products and services. |
| *Sanger High School* | How can you power a small-scale farming system using alternative energy? | **Skills map: Ag Mechanics**<br>2. Troubleshooting equipment and systems.<br>8. Modifying and fabricating parts and equipment.<br>9. Applying math to practical situations or problems.<br>10. Using technology to make work more effective and efficient. |

experiment, creating a prototype, or otherwise acting to address the challenge. Projects include a hands-on field experience and conclude with a showcase event in which students present their findings in a professional setting, using multiple formats that include writing, calculations, and media. The projects:

- *Are problem-based and team-oriented.* Through planning, experimentation, and analysis, the teams develop and test a workable solution.
- *Feature a hands-on field application.* Projects involve a practical experience in the field or lab tailored to the student's pathway.
- *Are interdisciplinary.* The projects include more than one academic discipline, which in turn requires time for teachers to work together to design the project and integrate it into instruction.
- *Are college and career focused.* Projects align with the scope and sequence of each participating high school course, while addressing college and career standards. This includes identifying professional and technical skills that the projects address.

An Ag Prep student commented, "The projects make the classes really fun. We're also learning what matters."

A secondary purpose of the interdisciplinary projects is to provide routine, ongoing opportunities for teachers to work in teams to integrate work-based learning into the curriculum. Ag Prep emphasizes the following pedagogical components in the projects:

- *An engaging launch.* Ag Prep teachers work together to design project launches that are intriguing for students and that introduce them to the key question that they will be examining. At one high school, for example, the ninth-grade cohort met in a common room, and each table of students had to guess which major crops in the valley use the most water. They were then introduced to the guiding question of their projects: How do we meet the irrigation needs of the Central Valley's top-producing crops with limited impact on natural water supplies?

- *Clear teacher roles.* Each teacher participating in the interdisciplinary project takes responsibility for communicating broadly with students about the project—including the academic standards and professional skills students will learn. Each teacher also oversees and grades project deliverables related to their own course. An English class might focus on research and writing, with results presented in a report, newsletter, PowerPoint presentation, or website. A social studies or history class might explore the historical, cultural, or economic context of a topic. Math might include computations, statistical analysis, and theory.

- *Hands-on field application.* Interdisciplinary projects include hands-on experiences in the field or in a lab as part of the students' investigation of a problem. At Washington Union, for example, students visited a field or orchard to gather soil samples and talk with soil experts on-site; they also had their samples analyzed by a professional lab. At Sanger High School, students coordinated across the ag mechanics and plant science pathways to test water usage using various hydroponic systems; the ag mechanics students built the systems, and the plant science students managed the experiments. At Wonderful College Prep Academy in Delano, teams of students developed a business plan based on their earlier efforts to grow a nutritious food crop without soil. The business plan drew from student participation in a professional agriculture conference and in job shadowing at The Wonderful Company, and the students pitched their plans to business professionals at a job fair. An Ag Prep student said, "We started by researching what needs to be in a nursery and running your own business. I learned how long it would take to make a real business, make it work, and budget everything correctly. It's just so much, what it would actually take!"

- *Support for students in managing the project.* Student teams need autonomy in addressing project challenges, but they also need basic instruction in project management, breaking up functions by role, internal reporting and deadlines, and strategies for peer accountability. Common approaches can include the use of process-oriented assignments such as early mockups or drafts. Some teachers have students post their major steps or benchmarks on the classroom wall or electronically. As students check off each task, they learn to pace their work and monitor progress on their own. To help students prepare for the showcase event, teachers have them practice a variety of presentation formats in advance.

- *The showcase event.* Students demonstrate their mastery through a showcase presentation in a semipublic forum. Some teams organize two events, one for other classes during school hours and a grand showcase for a broader audience in the evening. During the first event, presenters can field questions and receive feedback, to help them prepare for the final showcase. Typically, the project teams invite members of the local industry, the community, the district office, and school administration, teachers, faculty, parents, and other students. When possible, the student teams manage event planning, including invitations, parking, signage, and greeting of guests. They can also manage technical aspects of the presentation. Steven Rizzo, Ag Prep coordinator, Washington Union High School, said, "I've seen so much growth in these students. Two years ago, when they had to make a presentation to their peers, some students were crying. Now they're talking into a microphone to a roomful of adults."

Many teachers do not have experience incorporating work-based learning into their classrooms, and many have not worked with other teachers to develop projects across subjects. The following planning time and professional development is provided to instructors to support the interdisciplinary projects:

- *Several days of training (end of spring or early summer).* For teachers participating in interdisciplinary projects for the first time, Ag Prep offers a few days of training to discuss the role of project-based learning in relation to their students and their discipline.
- *A few days of preplanning (August and December).* Teachers also need dedicated time before the semester begins to plan their projects

across disciplines and consider their impacts on their own classrooms. Working together, teachers determine the processes students will go through, the outcomes the teachers expect, and the standards and skills to address.

* *Planning time during the semester.* Ag Prep schools schedule common planning time weekly for teachers to address issues associated with their students. Throughout the year, teachers use portions of this time to plan the projects.

Claudia Robedo, math instructor, Mendota High School, said, "Now, instead of me focusing on just my math department, I'm collaborating with English and science teachers. The students are seeing the connection—that there is math in health classes, and there is English as well."

## Professional Experiences in the Ag Industry

Ag Prep's work-based learning opportunities are grounded in a highly structured sequence of experiences in the agriculture industry. The sequence prepares students for work by increasing the complexity of their interactions with ag professionals over their four years of high school. The scaffolding also prepares the professionals at Wonderful and its industry partners by increasing their interactions with high school students over time, so that managers and line staff are prepared to supervise young people during the students' internships. This sequence, which was developed, revised, and tested over several years, could serve as a national model for student development of workplace knowledge and experience. (See figure 4.6.) The sequence features:

* *Industry conventions.* All Ag Prep freshmen participate in an agriculture industry conference, where they ask questions of and begin to network with ag professionals.
* *Career expo.* Sophomores learn about various career options from industry experts and have the opportunity to engage in an on-the-job simulation or hands-on project.

**FIGURE 4.6** Work-based learning sequence

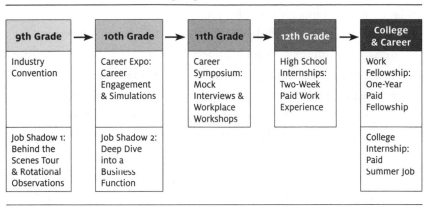

- *Job shadows.* Freshmen participate in a behind-the-scenes tour of a professional workplace in groups of about ten, including observations of a variety of office, production, and field settings. As sophomores, students participate in a deep-dive workplace experience, in which they are assigned to and observe a midlevel manager during his or her normal business day.
- *Mock interviews.* Juniors practice their interview skills in mock interviews and receive real-time feedback from a professional in the industry.
- *High school internships.* Rising seniors experience a highly structured, paid, two-week internship opportunity. They practice their technical and professional skills, apply their Ag Prep coursework, and gain experience as a young professional.
- *The Wonderful Company work fellowship.* Ag Prep graduates who complete all program requirements and decide not to enroll in a university immediately can qualify for a one-year professional job fellowship with The Wonderful Company. The fellowship provides valuable work experience, with an income of $35,000.
- *Wonderful college scholarship.* Based on the first cohort of students who graduated in 2018, about 80 percent of Ag Prep graduates enroll in a university immediately after high school. Wonderful

provides university scholarships ranging from $4,000 to $6,000 annually, depending on the college.

- *College internship.* Wonderful plans to offer summer job internships to Ag Prep alumni who are pursuing four-year degrees in agriculture and are in good standing at their university. These paid internships will be during the summer after their junior year in college.
- *Job placement and career fair.* Wonderful Education is also developing plans for a job placement and career fair event for Ag Prep alumni at four-year universities, during their senior year. The event offers an opportunity for The Wonderful Company and its brands to recruit Ag Prep alumni as they transition from college and into the workforce.

## Job Shadowing

Ag Prep's two industry components that require the most planning and coordination are the job-shadowing and internship experiences. Job shadowing helps students learn about careers in agriculture by empowering them, in their freshman year, to observe a variety of workplaces in small groups of about ten students. In tenth grade, they shadow a midlevel employee throughout the workday. For this activity, each host employee is paired with no more than two students so that each student can engage extensively with the employee while witnessing the activities and tasks associated with the job.

Most Ag Prep students have no professional role models in their lives. By introducing students to a variety of roles and activities in the ag industry, job shadowing:

- *Helps students see the connections between the skills they're learning in school and those needed in a professional workplace.* Whether on the plant floor, at a greenhouse, or in finance meetings, students can see how knowledge and skills are applied in a fast-paced work setting. In many cases, the students who are struggling academically are the most inspired by job shadowing and other work-based learning; that inspiration helps motivate them to advance academically.

- *Broadens horizons and informs students about ag careers and opportunities.* Most high school students have little or no experience with the everyday tasks associated with specific careers, yet they are beginning to make career choices through their course selections. Through their two different job-shadowing experiences, students expand their knowledge of career options and gain experience in the first steps of networking. They also begin to picture themselves in a professional job. (See the sidebar "Student Perspectives on Their Job-Shadowing Experiences.")

Wonderful Education's first steps in creating Ag Prep's job-shadowing program was to build on the relationships it had developed through the PACs. From the skills maps, staff also identified several professional skills that job shadowing could help to augment in the high school curriculum, including:

- *Work readiness.* Work ethic (high levels of effort and perseverance) and a positive attitude toward work
- *Teamwork.* Working well with others and promoting a collaborative environment
- *Leadership.* Motivating and directing people as they work, inspiring others to feel invested in the company's accomplishments

---

### Student Perspectives on Their Job-Shadowing Experiences, 2015–2016

I thought that agriculture was picking grapes and working machines. But then she [turned on] her computer and all these numbers came up . . . I never knew there was that part to agriculture.

This motivated me to think more about the major I'm going into, and to learn more about jobs before I make my final choice.

I learned about truth and integrity. You have to be honest on prices and other things in sales. Being accurate about your numbers is everything.

I saw how important it is to be organized and prepared for the next day. You've got to be detail-oriented.

I saw that you can't just trust that something got done. You have to make sure. You have to have follow-through and quality control.

**COORDINATING THE JOB-SHADOWING PROGRAM.** After skills mapping, Wonderful Education set up a process to engage with its company and school partners to (1) solidify their commitments to a job-shadowing program, (2) prepare host employees and students for the experience, and (3) follow up with the hosts and students afterward. The program was piloted in 2015–2016 as a one-day experience for students. Based on its popularity and impacts, it was expanded to include an experience for freshmen and for sophomores. According to Derek Cruz, former principal, Washington Union High School, "Ag Prep is making education more relevant for our students. Combine that with the college credits that they earn, and this is a game changer. It influences their lives."

**SOLIDIFYING COMMITMENTS.** Wonderful Education staff meet at least annually with executive leadership at The Wonderful Company and partnering businesses to confirm their commitment to the shadowing experience, and more frequently with supervisors (in most cases, the human resources directors) to set specific goals and address logistics. The skills maps have been helpful in establishing a common language for these discussions. Choosing specific skills to address during the job-shadowing experience helps the company supervisors decide which employees to select for job shadowing—that is, those who best exhibit the skills identified and who are most appropriate for interacting with high school students. Host employees are selected at midlevel positions, such as managers, directors, analysts, and crew leaders. Wonderful Education staff also meet with principals and other high school leaders to explain the job-shadowing goals, confirm their commitment, and receive their guidance.

At Ag Prep, each job-shadowing event is an intensive and transformative daylong experience for students and their hosts. The day is highly structured, yet the shadowing experience is personalized, based on the hosts' job routines (see figure 4.7). Boxed lunches are provided; dining together offers a further opportunity for professional networking. Each host employee is assigned two students for the day. Ideally, about ten to twenty students and five to ten employees participate in each session.

**FIGURE 4.7** Typical job- shadow schedule

| 8:15 a.m. | Students arrive at job shadow site |
|---|---|
| 8:30 a.m. | Welcome, overview, safety briefing, host introduction |
| 10:00 a.m. | Morning job shadowing |
| 12:00 p.m. | Lunch with hosts |
| 12:45 p.m. | Afternoon job shadowing |
| 2:30 p.m. | Debrief activity |
| 3:00 p.m. | Bus departs for school |

**PREPARING HOSTS AND STUDENTS.** Wonderful Education staff meet with host employees about a week before the event to review the job-shadowing goals and design, answer questions, and gather information about each employee. Employees discuss the specific skills they will be addressing. Staff members meet with students at the schools several days in advance to explain the upcoming experience, conduct safety training, answer questions, share links to reading material about the company, and provide information about the host employees. The students participate in role-playing to prepare them for success in a work environment: practicing a firm handshake, making direct eye contact, and asking appropriate questions.

Wonderful Education works with teachers to pair students with employees, based on the student's ag pathway and interests, and the personal and professional information that employees shared about themselves. The pairings also depend on hosts who are available.

In both the company and school settings, Ag Prep has found it crucial to explain that job shadowing is neither a PowerPoint presentation nor a field trip. In particular:

- *Ag Prep encourages employees not to vary their day significantly.* Employees tend to think of their own days as routine, and they may want to spice things up for students. However, the activities they do routinely are precisely the ones that students need and want to see.

- *Ag Prep works with students in advance to prepare questions for industry hosts.* Many students are intimidated by the prospect of conversing with a professional for several hours. However, asking questions and engaging in conversation one-on-one is precisely the experience that is transformative for students.

**FOLLOWING UP WITH STUDENTS AND EMPLOYEES.** During the debriefing at the end of the day, students reflect on their experience. Afterward, they write a thank-you card to their host employee, and they submit a personal narrative of five hundred to a thousand words online about the impact of the experience on their future plans. Each employee provides written comments on the participation and skills exhibited by their students. Employees have responded favorably to their experiences with students. According to Sonya Carrillo, financial analyst at Wonderful Citrus, "It's infectious when you get to show students their options. It energizes everybody." Jared Lorraine, director of continuous improvement and food safety, Wonderful Citrus, commented, "We give them an opportunity to see their potential future. That's priceless. We also hope that one day they'll be interested in working for us."

## Paid Work Internships

During the summer before senior year, students who are academically on track participate in a two-week paid internship (eighty hours) at a professional site in the agriculture industry. The internships go deeper than job shadowing in giving students experience in collaborating and networking with professional adults, and in applying technical and professional skills in a work environment. Several key features, taken together, place Ag Prep's internship program among the best models that are evolving in the United States. The internships are:

- Aligned with rigorous academics
- Built into a sequence of work-based learning
- Part of a career-focused structure for learning and motivation
- Managed by industry
- The product of a partnership across schools, colleges, universities, and industry

By providing paid internships, The Wonderful Company lets students know that their knowledge and skills are valuable, and that their contributions at work add to company productivity. This is in line with national best practices around youth employment and work-based learning.[18] In addition, providing paid internships makes the program more equitable in serving low-income families, since young people in families that experience economic distress need to earn money during the summers. Ag Prep students can also receive college credit for their internship. David East, superintendent, Reef-Sunset Unified School District, said, "This is a game changer for a lot of reasons, particularly The Wonderful Company's commitment for internships and jobs. There's no better way to get kids involved than experience and a paycheck."

The objectives of the internships are to:

- *Apply learning from the classroom.* Students develop industry-specific content knowledge and skills in their high school and college classes. As interns, they learn the value of these competencies as they apply them in the workplace.
- *Promote learning through problem solving and other work experience.* Supervisors assign tasks and responsibilities that require students to learn new systems and solve real challenges, whether on the phone, in meetings or presentations, in a lab or greenhouse, at a warehouse, or in an orchard.
- *Introduce students to collaboration and networking with professionals.* Students work with and develop professional relationships with supervisors who can give them guidance and support. These opportunities help interns build their social capital and professional networks.
- *Expand and deepen understanding of agriculture.* Interns gain direct experience in a fast-paced field that includes a wide range of careers, from human resources and business management to resource management and plant science.

Beyond these goals, Ag Prep is also finding that the internships offer students something bigger and broader: the opportunity to see beyond their own horizons regarding college and career goals. This is consistent with research findings suggesting that, particularly for students who are first in their family to attend college, internships can transform their aspirations about becoming a professional and can help them build the social capital they will need to navigate the labor market as adults.[19] Reflecting on her internship experience, an Ag Prep student said, "Now I have the experience of having to talk to adults who are professionals, so I won't be as nervous when I'm interviewing for my next job. The internship gives you practice as to how to act in a professional workplace."

At Ag Prep, students are encouraged to maintain contact with their internship supervisor and to include him or her as a reference on their résumés. An Ag Prep student said, "These past weeks [as an intern] were amazing, the amount of teamwork that goes on across the different departments. I plan to go to a four-year university for a plant science degree."

Ag Prep's internship program is entering its third year. When the program is at full capacity, it will serve up to 330 students from seven high schools. In 2018, internships were provided at seventeen sites throughout the San Joaquin Valley by The Wonderful Company and its brands (including Wonderful Citrus, Wonderful Orchards, Wonderful Pistachios and Almonds, and POM Wonderful), AgriLand Farming Company, the California Cotton Ginners and Growers Association, Fowler Packing, the Fresno County Farm Bureau, the Kearney Agricultural Research and Extension Center (KARE), and Olam. (See figure 4.8.)

The logistics of providing hundreds of high school students with valuable job experiences at seventeen job sites across the San Joaquin Valley are challenging. In many cases, travel to the job takes more than an hour. Limited access to transportation and a full schedule of high school and college coursework during the school year means that for most students, an after-school internship is not practical. The option of having internships on Saturdays during the school year is not feasible for supervisors; nor would working once a week on weekends immerse students in an active and fast-paced job environment. For these combined reasons, Ag Prep gives students an immersive, full-time work experience for two weeks, with cohorts of students rotating throughout the summer.

**FIGURE 4.8** Ag Prep internships by the numbers, 2018

| |
|---|
| 175 students participated in the program and completed their internships |
| 95 supervisors oversaw the students (75 percent are from Wonderful or its brands and 25 percent are from partner companies) |
| 17 job sites participated, from Fresno to McKittrick, a span of 110 miles |
| 10 Wonderful brands and Ag partners provided internships |
| 6 high schools participated (there were no rising seniors in the seventh Ag Prep high school) |
| 4 counties were represented |

Because two weeks is a short time frame, Wonderful Education works to ensure that the internships are productive and useful for students and supervisors. This includes building the internships into a framework of work-based learning and aligned coursework, so that students have appropriate technical and professional skills for a successful job experience. It also includes providing clarity on roles among education and industry partners; preparation for students and supervisors; and a structured, supported internship experience. Rob Yraceburu, president, Wonderful Orchards, said, "The biggest benefit I saw with our own orchard supervisors having student interns was that it inspired them to step up to the plate. They've gained more confidence in their leadership skills and really taken the opportunity to support and guide the students. These have the potential to be lifelong mentoring opportunities."

**STRONG PARTNERSHIP WITH CLEAR ROLES.** The internships would not be possible without strong coordination and clear roles among several of these key partners.

- *The Wonderful Company and its industry partners* provide supervisors who directly oversee the interns, as well as access for interns to meetings, other employees, computer systems, and business unit infrastructure, as appropriate. The Wonderful Company pays wages for the interns.

- *Wonderful Education* designs and manages the internship program and serves as liaison between the industry business units and the high schools.
- *The partnering schools,* which include the seven high schools and three community colleges that implement Ag Prep programs, help students master the technical and professional knowledge and skills needed to succeed in a professional workplace. The high schools also help deliver the initial internship training, plan and coordinate logistics, pay for student transportation, and facilitate intern-supervisor matching.
- *The Foundation for California Community Colleges* (FCCC), a nonprofit organization, partners with Wonderful Education to serve as the legal employer of record for the internship program. This partnership relieves companies of the administrative burdens of providing human resources and all payroll services for interns. FCCC charges a 15 percent program management fee, plus $100 per student for onboarding.

**TRANSPORTATION.** In rural communities like those in the Central Valley, many students live far from each other, from schools, and from their internship site. As a result, transportation to and from work-based learning experiences can be expensive and a logistical challenge for students and for programs. For all Ag Prep students, the high schools provide and pay for buses from the schools to the jobs. The buses drop students at multiple sites along their routes, so many students are up at 5 a.m. and on the bus for over an hour to get to work on time.

**STUDENT PREPARATION.** Students participate in a series of activities to prepare them for their internships.

- *Symposium.* Near the end of spring semester, Wonderful Education provides a full-day symposium at Wonderful College Prep Academy for all eleventh graders eligible for the internship. At these leadership and professional development events, students rotate through workshops where they learn about and practice professional competencies that they need to demonstrate on day one of their internship. They also draft their résumé and participate in a mock interview process. For the interviews, students meet one-on-one with an industry professional, answer questions about their career interests, and receive feedback about their performance. These are skills that the students have worked on since ninth grade.

- *Student matching.* In preparation for their mock interview, students identify their career interests in relation to a range of internship sites available. Wonderful Education uses these data to help match students with the supervisors and business units. Other factors are also considered, including transportation from high schools, the number of supervisors and business units available, and the uncertainty of students about their interests.

- *Orientation.* Wonderful Education provides a two-hour orientation for students and their families a few weeks before the internship. Typically held in the evening at the high school, these events cover internship logistics and workplace safety. Students also learn who they will be working with and complete a professional assessment activity, during which they reflect on their experiences and rate themselves on a range of employability skills. After their internship, students rate themselves on these same skills, as part of their self-evaluation. One student said, "I was able to see the importance of communication, time management, and personal responsibility in the workplace. Everyone says communication is important, but I wasn't able to understand that until I saw it myself."

**SUPERVISOR TRAINING.** Wonderful Education advises business units to hold student interns to the same expectations as other employees, but supervisors need support in understanding the complexities of working with high school students. Wonderful Education's training, offered in a variety of formats, gives brief introductions to the following elements of the supervisor's role.

- *Physical and emotional safety.* What concerns and needs do sixteen- and seventeen-year-olds have in a professional workplace, and what do they need to know about boundaries and limitations on their behavior?
- *Technical and professional skill building.* Wonderful Education introduces supervisors to the skills maps in Ag Prep's three pathways and asks them to identify the skills that each task will strengthen for interns.
- *Professional relationships.* The existence of a single caring adult can make a substantial difference in youths' vision of their own opportunities, which in turn brings significant responsibilities for supervisors in modeling professional behavior.
- *Youth agency and voice.* Meaningful internships give youth substantive tasks, including opportunities to make choices, have a voice in planning or organizing, and otherwise reveal leadership.

Sandra Caldwell, former president, Reedley College, commented, "Others talk about the value of paid internships, but The Wonderful Company understood why they're important to these students in the Central Valley, and so they made the investment. Creating an internship program that reaches across the Valley was a huge challenge, and they stepped up and addressed that challenge."

**PUTTING IT TOGETHER: A STRUCTURED, SUPPORTED INTERNSHIP EXPERIENCE.** For sixteen- and seventeen-year-olds, a first work experience in a professional setting is exciting, but it can also be intimidating and confusing. Ag Prep's structured internship helps ensure that students can make the most of their two-week experience. Ag Prep also recognizes the power of individualized supports, particularly for young people who are engaging in the world of work for the first time.

- *Student orientation at the business unit.* Business units provide safety training and safety gear for interns on their first day. Wonderful Education encourages each unit to provide the same orientation offered to other employees, but without the sections that are not pertinent for interns, such as health and retirement benefits.

- *Internship work plans.* Supervisors develop work plans that iden- tify the tasks that interns will complete daily and the corresponding technical or professional skills (from the skills maps) associated with those tasks.[20] The work plans serve as a daily schedule for supervisors and students. Linking the tasks to the skills maps encourages super- visors to give students meaningful tasks and helps students under- stand why they are working on these tasks and how the tasks build on knowledge from the classroom.

- *On-site support.* Through its trainings, Wonderful Education builds relationships in advance of each internship and draws on those rela- tionships to maintain open communication and support while stu- dents are at a job site. Challenges on the job can range from logistical questions about wages or transportation to job performance, behav- ioral issues, and interpersonal dynamics. The Wonderful Education team is equipped to navigate these situations, in partnership with su- pervisors and students.

- *Final presentations.* During the internships, Wonderful Education gives the interns a PowerPoint template to use on their final day, when each student makes a business presentation that describes his or her personal interests, college and career goals, the tasks they per- formed, the technical and professional skills they applied, and the overall lessons they learned from the experience. Students present in a conference room to their supervisors, business unit colleagues, Wonderful Education staff, and other interns. The students field questions at the event. (See the sidebar "Students' Comments During Their Internship Presentations" on the next page.)

## OUTCOMES FOR AG PREP'S FIRST COHORT

Ag Prep students are proving to be outstanding learners in the classroom, supportive team members to their classmates, and skilled professionals in

**Students' Comments During
Their Internship Presentations**

In the greenhouse, I used skills from my integrated pest management class and my plant science class. That helped in understanding pest behaviors.

I learned how to reproduce plants through mist propagation.

I learned how the greenhouse works, how automation functions with the sensors for moisture and temperature.

I worked with the customer service department to take orders, identify how much they wanted of a particular item, and how much we had in inventory.

We collected water samples and tested them for e. coli. We entered the information into the computer.

I understood the process of what the sales team does, and all the emailed tasks they have to follow through on.

We had to communicate with our supervisor immediately if we found a pest, or something we weren't sure about. Then she would pull together a team of co-workers to problem solve. It was great to see that teamwork.

the workplace. Even as Ag Prep has been refining its processes and structures during its inaugural years, its first students have achieved remarkable outcomes (see the sidebars "Ag Prep's Outcomes: Full Freshman Cohort" and "Ag Prep's Outcomes: First Graduating Class"). As David Krause, president of Wonderful Citrus, said, "What impressed me most is the quality, hard work, and maturity level of the students. These kids are engaged and committed. They're just the kind of dedicated people we're looking for to be a part of our team."

## What Do Students Say About Their Experiences?

Ag Prep's academic expectations are considerable; the program requires students and parents to commit to its requirements before they can join the program. So why did about sixty rising ninth graders at each of Ag Prep's founding high schools take a risk and join this fledgling program back in fall 2014? And what are their perceptions after participating?

## AG PREP'S OUTCOMES: Full Freshman Cohort

Ag Prep's first cohort of high school students entered as freshmen in fall 2014 at Avenal High School, Sanger High School, and the Wonderful College Prep Academy. Ag Prep's students begin taking a college course each semester during freshman year, and their college load doubles or triples during their junior and senior years. By the end of tenth grade, those who are missing more than two college classes or A-G college-prep classes are withdrawn from the program so that the rigorous college requirements do not prevent them from graduating from high school on time, or otherwise diminish their chances of getting into a four-year college. Their participation in Ag Prep during their first two years, however, appears to improve their college readiness. Based on 197 freshmen who joined Ag Prep in fall 2014:

- **Ninety-one percent graduated from high school** within four years. For comparison, the graduation rates for Fresno, Kern, and Kings counties (where Ag Prep is located) are 81 percent, 85 percent, and 83 percent, respectively.[21]
- **Eighty-one percent graduated with all A-G courses** required for admission to UC or CSU. The share of graduates completing this course sequence for Fresno, Kern, and Kings counties are 44 percent, 35 percent, and 34 percent, respectively.[22]
- **Eighty-one percent graduated with at least nine units of college credits.** Two-thirds (66 percent) graduated with at least one year of college credits. In California, 8 percent of community college students begin taking college courses in high school. Students who earn college credits in high school are much more likely to earn college degrees.[23]

*Source*: Wonderful Education.

**WERE THE STUDENTS DRAWN TO WORK-BASED LEARNING?** In describing why they chose Ag Prep, none of the students talked about the structure of the program. At the time, they hadn't experienced high school or college. They didn't know what hands-on, project-based learning was. After participating for several years, however, many students in focus groups described the work-based components as their favorite aspects of Ag Prep:

"What makes this [project-based learning] different is the process. I really liked this not just because it's hands-on, but [also] because it's like an insight into your future."

"After going to a lab, I realized that I can use math in my everyday job—and English, because if you're behind a desk all day you communicate with people and you write."

## AG PREP'S OUTCOMES: First Graduating Class

Of the 197 freshmen who joined Ag Prep in fall 2014, 124 graduated from Ag Prep in June 2018. These graduates completed the A-G sequence of college prep courses for UC and CSU, and Ag Prep's work-based learning sequence, including a paid internship. Almost all graduates completed the full high school and college course sequence required by one of Ag Prep's pathways. Of the 124 Ag Prep graduates:

- **Seventy-three percent earned an associate's of science degree** the summer after high school graduation. Very few high schools—in California or nationally—offer early college programs that include an associate's degree.
- **Eighty percent enrolled in a four-year university** in fall 2018, and most entered as juniors. In Fresno, Kern, and Kings counties, less than 20 percent of graduates enroll in a public four-year university right after high school.[24]
- **Seventy-six** are enrolled at a CSU campus, twenty-one at UC, and two at private nonprofit universities.
- **Fifty-three** are planning to major in agriculture or an ag-related field.
- **Two** Ag Prep graduates were awarded a full-time job fellowship at The Wonderful Company, with a salary of $35,000, guaranteed for at least one year.

*Source*: Wonderful Education.

"Being in an internship shows you; it actually *shows* you. It's not just something that you're told or you see through research. It's something you live."

"The internship motivated me to continue striving for my academic goals because, at the end, all the hard work pays off."

**WHEN THEY JOINED AG PREP, WERE THEY CONSIDERING THE AGRICULTURE INDUSTRY AS A CAREER?** A few students described a long-term interest in agriculture. Most, however, emphasized that they were *not* interested in the industry before they joined Ag Prep. This, too, changed for them in high school. As they worked in teams to study and solve problems in business, health, science, and technology, and as they interacted with ag professionals through their job shadowing and internship, they saw firsthand the scope and diversity of careers in an industry that was all around them in the valley. For example, students reported:

"At first, I didn't want to be in Ag Prep because they said agriculture and, like, basically my parents work in the fields for a living, I didn't want to do that. But this opened my eyes. Agriculture is much more than what people think."

"The program changed my perspective on agriculture. It isn't just about crops and stuff. It's a whole lot more."

"[Job shadowing] was life-changing. I went in there thinking I never want to do a job that involves agriculture, but after I job shadowed Alejandra, it really opened my mind that I could do what she's doing."

**DO EIGHTH GRADERS CARE MUCH ABOUT COLLEGE AND CAREERS?** In the San Joaquin Valley, they do. In describing themselves when they were eighth graders, several alumni from the first cohort said they were "lost" or "chilling" or "a procrastinator." When they joined Ag Prep, they did not fully understand what they were getting into; none of their older friends had been through such a program. But they also said that they understood from the start that Ag Prep would give them a head start on college, which would impact their whole families:

"Coming here and knowing they would pay for college classes? It took a load off my parents."

"None of my family members have been to college. I want to do that for my younger brothers and sisters so they can see that anything is possible."

"I'm a first-generation [college student], so I want to set the bar as high as possible and let my sisters know the sky's the limit. I want to leave that legacy to them, and let them know that they can do whatever they set their mind to do."

**WHAT WAS IT LIKE FOR THEM TO GRADUATE FROM COLLEGE?** Because college commencements occur in May, Ag Prep's first cohort of students had the rare honor of celebrating their college commencement before graduating from high school in June. For many students, the enormity of their accomplishments did not sink in when they were congratulated as college graduates and alumni, an experience they described later as "surreal" and "unforgettable." Their achievement hit home only afterward, when they were surrounded by their families on the stadium turf. According to an alum from Sanger High School who received his associate's degree from Reedley College, "It was only then . . . that I realized what I accomplished. Seeing the look on my parents' faces made it worthwhile." An Avenal High School student who graduated from West Hill College said, "My mom always smiles . . . My dad is old school, very strict. That's just the tough life." But at her college graduation, she said, her father was "giggling."

**HOW DO THESE STUDENTS DESCRIBE AG PREP?** In focus groups, Ag Prep graduates used these words to describe their experiences in the program: "Incredible." "Phenomenal." "Unforgettable." "A blessing." "I'm speechless." According to one alum, "This was the best choice I ever made. Right now I'm taking, at Bakersfield College, Stats and English B1B. Those are the last two classes I need so that I can get my degree."

## BUILDING ON PROGRAM SUCCESS

Ag Prep's early results suggest that this model can produce remarkable outcomes for students. Ag Prep's combination of work-based learning, college course-taking, and intensive supports appears to be helping students:

- connect their schoolwork to real-world problems and solutions,
- succeed in college-prep classes and college courses,
- gain important technical and professional career skills,
- excel in a professional workplace,
- earn an associate degree while in high school, and
- achieve outstanding college-going rates to universities.

Ag Prep also appears to be helping students exceed the expectations of others. As Superintendent David East of Reef-Sunset Unified School

District said, "At the beginning, a common narrative was, 'These kids can't do college-level work.' Well, we don't hear that anymore, because these students are succeeding in college." Lynda Resnick of The Wonderful Company, said, "Our first Ag Prep graduating class are the pioneers of a new way to look at high school and college education. They are living, breathing inspirations of what's possible when smart kids are given a fair and equal opportunity."

### Growth and Sustainability

Evidence of Ag Prep's success can also be traced to its growth and sustainability. The program has expanded to six middle schools, seven high schools, three community colleges, five universities, and several agricultural companies. Based on current plans, the program will reach capacity in 2020, serving about 1,440 high school students. In terms of sustainability, Ag Prep is funded on a shared-cost model, with high schools, community colleges, and The Wonderful Company investing roughly a third each for the program, per high school program. Substantial grant support from the CCPT helped to defray some initial start-up and expansion costs. When that state support ended, each of the schools doubled down on their own investments, as did Wonderful, to continue offering Ag Prep to students.

### Impacts and Expansion Among School and College Partners

Ag Prep's design is also impacting school and college partners, as they borrow from program components to improve outcomes for all their students.

**HIGH SCHOOL PARTNERS.** Avenal High School, Sanger High School, Washington Union High School, and the Wonderful College Prep Academy are expanding their college course offerings for other students on campus. Wonderful College Prep Academy, for example, changed its graduation requirements so that every graduate must now earn at least one year of college credits. At Avenal High School, the Ag Prep coordinator reports that graduation rates have jumped, attendance is up, and suspensions are down for the school as a whole, since Ag Prep has been implemented. In addition:

- *College for all.* Avenal changed its master schedule, so that all students can now enroll in college classes. The school is now partnering with West Hills College to offer college classes during the school day, as part of students' regular schedule.
- *A-G for all.* Before Ag Prep, Avenal did not offer the full A-G course sequence required for admission at UC and CSU. Now every Avenal High School student is required to enroll in A-G courses. In four years, the campus has increased the share of its students completing the A-G sequence from 0 percent to 37 percent.[25]
- *More career pathways.* Drawing from its experiences with The Wonderful Company, Avenal has created two additional career pathways that integrate college courses and technical training into the high school schedule: the Waste Management Environmental Science Academy and the Health and Medical Occupations Academy. East, of Reef-Sunset, said, "We just got our graduation data, and we had the highest graduation rate in Kings County, higher than the state average. We did that while increasing our graduation requirements. Ag Prep is a key leverage point for all of that."

**COLLEGE PARTNERS.** At the college level, the Ag Prep model also appears to be leading to broader changes. For example, both West Hills College and Reedley College developed an ag science technology degree as an upgrade to their traditional ag mechanics program, based on feedback from industry experts on the PAC. At Bakersfield College, working with Ag Prep has led to a "culture shift" in which college administrators and faculty are better prepared to understand the needs of this generation of students, according to Sonya Christian.

- *Working with high schools.* Bakersfield used to see outreach as an opportunity to enroll high school students in existing courses and programs, Christian said. Now the college works with high schools in a more structured way to develop a sequence of courses in a pathway or several pathways that meets the needs of high school students. College staff meet with groups of students at their high school to do prescreening and develop their education plans. "That intentionality and structure," Christian said, "was influenced by our experiences with Ag Prep."

- *Faculty engagement.* For faculty familiar with teaching at the college, driving to Delano and teaching college classes at a high school was a major change. "But they came back," Christian said, "and gave presentations about how bright and capable these students are, and how they can meet the learning outcomes. That's faculty talking to other faculty to build an understanding, and it has shifted the outlook of our departments."

- *Working with industry.* Ag Prep also gave the college a clear model for how to engage with industry, Christian said. This includes the structuring of industry roles in providing work-based learning through job shadowing, summer camps, and internships. The college has already transferred this approach to other fields, including industrial automation and music.

## Student Persistence

Even as cohorts of Ag Prep students are making outstanding gains, challenges remain in helping every student thrive academically. Ninth graders enter Ag Prep well behind grade level in English and math, and Ag Prep provides substantial supports to help them catch up and excel in high school and college courses. According to Donoso, "Ag Prep's number-one focus currently is to continue to increase student success so that students stay on track to complete all of their college-prep and college courses— with the goal to achieve a program completion rate of 75 percent within the next two years."

## Life After High School for Ag Prep College Goers

Among Ag Prep's first graduating cohort who earned an associate's degree, 98 percent chose to pursue a bachelor's degree right after high school.[26] The

Wonderful Company awarded these students college scholarships of $4,000 to $6,000 annually, depending on the college, to help cover fees and other costs. According to Caldwell, formerly of Reedley College, "That's a huge success, unparalleled, the high number of students enrolling in universities. Ag Prep has shown these students and families the power of education, that a bachelor's degree is attainable for them, and that they deserve their place at a university campus. This is how you create generational change." An Ag Prep alum commented, "My parents weren't so strong about me going to college due to the financial situation. But this program really opened their eyes to see that with education all things are possible."

To support these Ag Prep scholars, Wonderful Education took the following actions.

- *Partnerships.* Wonderful partnered with Cal State Bakersfield, Fresno State, Cal Poly Pomona, Cal Poly San Luis Obispo, and UC Davis to ensure a smooth transition and supports for Ag Prep students, including making sure that all college credits earned in high school transfer to the university.
- *Case manager.* Fifty-one Ag Prep alumni enrolled at Fresno State University in fall 2018. The Wonderful Company and the university are splitting the costs of a case manager at Fresno State dedicated to supporting these students.
- *College success specialist.* Every Ag Prep scholar is assigned a college specialist who provides weekly support through the first year of college and then ongoing support until they earn their degree.

Wonderful Education is also developing new programs to keep Ag Prep alumni connected with workforce opportunities in the San Joaquin Valley, including at The Wonderful Company and its many brands:

- *Postsecondary internship.* Many Ag Prep graduates are enrolling in universities as juniors, so they will have only one summer during college; the following summer they will be seeking their first postcollege job. For Ag Prep alumni who are pursuing a bachelor's degree in agriculture and are in good standing at their university, The Wonderful Company plans to offer them a paid job internship during the summer after their junior year.

- *Alumni career specialist.* Wonderful Education is creating a position to support career and work-based learning opportunities for Ag Prep alumni in the field of agriculture, from the day they graduate from Ag Prep, through their university experience, and into the workforce.
- *Job placement and career fair.* Wonderful Education is also developing plans for job placement and a career fair for Ag Prep alumni at four-year universities, during their senior year. The event offers an opportunity for The Wonderful Company and its brands to recruit Ag Prep alumni as they transition into the workforce. One alum said, "I see myself graduating from the university, and I think I may be coming back here because we've had a lot of support from different people. I feel that the only way to pay it back is to give back."

## IMPLICATIONS FOR EMPLOYERS, SCHOOLS, AND COLLEGES

A key characteristic that makes Ag Prep a cutting-edge education partnership is that an industry partner leads and manages it. Many of the district superintendents and college presidents interviewed said that The Wonderful Company's commitment to and leadership of Ag Prep was critical to their institution's participation in the program. They also said, however, that it was not the potential funding that made the difference in agreeing to participate in the program. Rather, interviewees pointed to other potential benefits that Wonderful brought to the table, particularly networking among industry partners, technical assistance regarding innovations in the field, expert guidance in aligning coursework with industry standards, and the opportunities the program offered their students, particularly access to professional workplaces and paid internships for seniors.

Beyond Ag Prep's grant funding from the CCPT, the bulk of the program is paid for through standard per-pupil funding at the K–12 schools and the community colleges, including for dual-enrollment programs. The Wonderful Company contributes about a third of ongoing program costs, primarily to pay Wonderful Education staff to manage the program and its work-based learning components. The fact that the schools and colleges decided to continue Ag Prep after grant funding was completed attests to their view of the program's value and sustainability. The school and college partners not only have reallocated their own dollars to the program, but also have committed additional administrative, counseling, and support services and staff, and replicated the program's components as part of their overall practices. The Wonderful Company's leadership, Ag Prep's program design, and the program's shared-cost model offer a powerful and sustainable framework for schools and colleges.

The Wonderful Company, for its part, has doubled down on its investments through ongoing support and management of the program, while also creating new supports for Ag Prep graduates, through university scholarships, counseling services, and work internships. Wonderful plans to build on the learning and success of Ag Prep by sharing the model for employer replication in other industries. Wonderful is also launching an ag apprenticeship model with two high schools in the San Joaquin Valley. The six-year apprenticeship program will include a high school diploma, an AS degree in ag science technology, and a two-year paid apprenticeship.

Not every region has an industry leader willing to step in and invest its own staff and dollars in an initiative such as Ag Prep. Nor is every company in a position to make these kinds of investments. But for those industry partners wondering what they can do to work with their local education institutions to help expand student opportunities and build a future workforce aligned with regional labor market needs, the priorities that The Wonderful Company has established through Ag Prep are compelling. These include taking a strong role as an employer in insisting on comprehensive strategies: to change the educational experience for students; to incorporate work-based learning and professional experiences as part of school; to align high school and college coursework; to share strategies and progress toward clear objectives for student outcomes; and to develop a student support system that tracks student progress tenaciously and steps in quickly to provide persistent, holistic, and individualized interventions.

In its Master Plan for Higher Education of 1960, California created separate education systems at the K–12, community college, and university levels. This Ag Prep partnership presents a model for creating cohesion across the education systems and into the workforce in the San Joaquin Valley, to facilitate student transitions from middle school through high school graduation into colleges and universities, and from college into the job market. Ag Prep's outcomes for its first graduating class; its expansion to schools, colleges, and universities in the San Joaquin Valley; and the sustainability of its shared-cost model attest to the power of this public-private partnership to transform education and serve as an engine of opportunity for students and families in the San Joaquin Valley.

## CHAPTER 5

# BUILDING A STEM EARLY COLLEGE

## Marlborough High School and Its College and Industry Partners

*Katie Bayerl with Anna O'Connor*

On a cold day in January, the Marlborough High School cafeteria crackles with excitement. Ninth graders cluster around project tables, describing their imaginative designs for accessible playground rides. There is a motorized octopus merry-go-round, a space shuttle–themed clubhouse, and a monkey-bar maze strung among 3D-printed trees. Students tell visitors how these projects evolved through research, planning, and trial and error. They worked on the projects all semester, and today, as they present their ideas to guests from local companies at the Ninth-Grade Expo, they are poised, prepared, and ready to discuss the creative decisions and teamwork that got them to the end product.

Marlborough High School enrolls just under eleven hundred students from a small, industrial community in Massachusetts. Historically, Marlborough has had a relatively suburban feel, and high school graduates could count on plentiful jobs in the manufacturing and service sectors. But the labor market has changed over the past two decades, with lower-skill jobs replaced by a booming high-tech sector. At the same time, the city has experienced a significant demographic shift. Both sets of changes put a new kind of pressure on the high school. To position its increasingly high-need student population for success in a demanding new job market, district leaders knew they had to do something different.

In 2011, the district launched an integrated science, technology, engineering, and math (STEM) program in the middle and high schools with support from a federal Race to the Top grant. A few years later, in 2014, the district joined the national Pathways to Prosperity Network. With support from a multiyear federal Youth CareerConnect (YCC) grant and strategic implementation guidance from JFF's Pathways to Prosperity team, the district expanded the emerging STEM program into college and career pathways in grades 9 through 12.

While the YCC grant focuses on grades 9 through 12, leaders in Marlborough intentionally expanded the early college STEM-focused career pathway model, with the goal of creating a seamless continuum for grades 6 through 14. The Pathways to Prosperity team encouraged leaders in Marlborough to make employers and postsecondary educators equal partners in the process of developing these pathways, from conception through implementation.

This case study provides an in-depth look at Marlborough's innovative approach to designing and developing the K–12 components of college and career pathways as part of the YCC grant. In just six years, the Marlborough STEM partners have successfully transformed the learning experience for over seven hundred young people in grades 6 through 12 with rigorous interdisciplinary projects, thoughtfully scaffolded career-focused learning, and early college coursework aligned with postsecondary programs of study. Students will graduate from high school with substantial college credit, transferable skills, and a clear sense of their career options. They will be well prepared to continue in pathways that lead to and through postsecondary education and on to careers.

The early outcomes have been impressive. (See the sidebar "Impressive Early Outcomes.") STEM program participants' reading and math proficiency rates far exceed those of their peers, as do their high school graduation and college enrollment rates. Longer-term outcomes such as college

> ### Impressive Early Outcomes
>
> Marlborough's STEM Early College students are already outpacing their peers on several important measures of college and career readiness.
>
> - One hundred percent reached proficiency in English language arts in 2016, compared with 79 percent of peers.
> - Ninety-two percent achieved math proficiency in 2016, compared with 57 percent of peers.
> - Ninety-two percent of sophomores passed the ACCUPLACER college placement test in 2016.
> - One hundred percent of the students in the last two STEM cohorts have graduated, compared with schoolwide graduation rates of 86 percent in 2015 and 89 percent in 2016.
> - Ninety-seven percent of the students in the STEM class of 2016 enrolled in college; 63 percent matriculated into postsecondary STEM pathways.
>
> *Source*: Marlborough High School, 2017.

completion and employment rates are yet to be seen, but the results to date make it a model worth watching.

This chapter will help practitioners and policy leaders understand what pathways look like within a high school, highlighting robust K–12 components of college and career pathways. It describes the core features of Marlborough's STEM Early College program, identifying major lessons learned, trade-offs and midcourse adjustments, key roles and cost considerations, and the work that lies ahead.

## A DISTRICT AND COMMUNITY IN TRANSITION

Ten years ago, Marlborough High School operated like any other large US high school. Students took seven classes a day, individually slotted into a complex master schedule that included general education, honors core courses, and a slew of electives in everything from health to accounting. The four-year graduation rate hovered near 82 percent; about 78 percent of Marlborough High School graduates went on to college.[1]

These outcomes weren't necessarily concerning. In the recent past, young people in Boston's MetroWest region could access decent-paying jobs with or without a postsecondary education, but since the early 2000s, the job market has changed dramatically. A booming high-tech sector— led by large employers like Dow Chemical, Raytheon, and Hologic—began to seek entry-level employees who had completed some postsecondary education and who could think critically, manage complex technology, and collaboratively solve problems.

At the same time, Marlborough experienced a demographic shift. A growing community of immigrants brought diversity to the city. Some households also struggled financially due to the changing economy. Today, students in Marlborough speak twenty-nine languages at home.[2] Nearly 36 percent are economically disadvantaged. (See table 5.1.)

Marlborough High School principal Daniel Riley explained that, for him, these simultaneous shifts created an "increased sense of responsibility to get kids on a path to the middle class." With a growing number of students who would be first in their families to attend college or who lacked documentation necessary to access college financial aid, Riley was eager to design a high school experience that would allow students to complete some postsecondary training and gain the skills needed to obtain family-supporting jobs. A challenge is that students of color, English language learners, and students from low-income families are currently underrepresented in the STEM program. Riley and other leaders

**TABLE 5.1** A rapidly changing district

| School year | Percentage of economically disadvantaged students | Percentage of students with a first language other than English |
|---|---|---|
| 2005–2006 | 26% | 21% |
| 2011–2012 | 40% | 31% |
| 2017–2018 | 36% | 47% |

*Source*: Massachusetts Department of Elementary and Secondary Education, School and District Profiles, Selected Populations Report (District), Marlborough.[3]

in Marlborough are proactively developing strategies, such as changing recruitment tactics and expanding enrollment, to address this issue.

## REIMAGINING MARLBOROUGH'S EDUCATION SYSTEM

A Race to the Top grant was the initial catalyst for Marlborough's new grades 6 through 10 STEM program, launched in the fall of 2011 with technical assistance from JFF. Two years later, Marlborough joined with JFF and other partners in an application for a US Department of Labor YCC grant to scale up innovative high school models geared toward regional labor market needs. The US Department of Labor awarded JFF's Pathways to Prosperity team a four-and-a-half-year YCC grant to scale innovative pathways. Marlborough STEM Early College High School was chosen as one of three demonstration sites in Massachusetts. (The two other sites are West Springfield High School and Brockton High School.) The YCC grant outlined six core elements of program design, including integrated academic and career-focused learning, employer engagement, individualized career and academic counseling, work-based learning and exposure to the world of work, program sustainability, and program performance and outcomes. These elements closely align with the Pathways to Prosperity Network's core strategies (see appendix A for more on the network's strategy).

The grant was ambitious in scope, as were the goals of local leaders. They planned to overhaul the secondary school experience, embedding rigorous STEM curricula, career exposure, and college coursework in a nonselective program that would prepare a significant portion of the school population for a demanding labor market. The bold design was matched by a cross-sector governance structure—with school leaders, the regional workforce development board, employers, and local colleges jointly responsible for designing and managing the program.

Now entering its eighth year of operation, the program has evolved in scope and depth each year, adding more expansive employer partnerships and more ambitious dual-enrollment options to its core STEM academic program. (See table 5.2.)

**TABLE 5.2** Marlborough STEM Early College cross-sector partners

| Key Partners | Description |
|---|---|
| *Marlborough High School* | Marlborough High School in Marlborough, Massachusetts, launched a STEM-focused early college program to prepare students for college and careers. |
| *Quinsigamond Community College (QCC)* | QCC is a two-year postsecondary institution in Worcester, Massachusetts, that offers Marlborough High School students opportunities to earn college credits. |
| *Partnerships for a Skilled Workforce (PSW)* | PSW is a workforce development board in Marlborough, Massachusetts, that serves as an intermediary, engaging employers to offer workplace experiences for students in the Metro Southwest area of Massachusetts, including students at Marlborough High School. |
| *Marlborough STEM Leadership Steering Committee* | The committee, which includes representatives from Marlborough High School, QCC, and PSW, ensures alignment of curricula with industry requirements and helps build the partnerships needed to offer various career-focused learning opportunities. Local employers represented on the committee include UMass Memorial–Marlborough Hospital, Boston Scientific, Dow Chemical, Raytheon, and Geisel Software, among many others. |

## LAYING A CAREER-READY FOUNDATION (GRADES 6 THROUGH 10)

The foundation of Marlborough's STEM model is its grade 6 through 10 curriculum, which immerses students in career-focused learning and dynamic, real-world projects. (See table 5.3.) This innovative approach to teaching and learning has been shaped in close collaboration with Partnerships for a Skilled Workforce (PSW), JFF, and a dedicated group of local employers.

Students can join the STEM program at the end of fifth grade or at the start of high school. Seats are awarded by lottery, with priority given to those from underrepresented populations (e.g., students of color, English language learners, and members of economically disadvantaged families). The program is designed to engage students in collaborative, complex learning that helps them develop skills associated with postsecondary success and needed in the twenty-first-century workplace. Students have frequent opportunities to interact with STEM professionals and to reflect

**TABLE 5.3** STEM Early College: At a glance

Marlborough's STEM Early College program demonstrates best practices in college and career learning, including the notable features listed.

| Grade | 6th | 7th | 8th | 9th | 10th | 11th | 12th |
|---|---|---|---|---|---|---|---|
| *STEM-specific small learning communities* | • | • | • | • | • | | |
| *Cross-disciplinary project-based learning* | • | • | • | • | • | | |
| *Honors-level core curricula* | | | | • | • | | |
| *Industry-aligned college courses* | | | | | | • | • |
| *Carefully staged career exposure activities* | | | | • | • | | |
| *Internships and work-based projects* | | | | | | • | • |
| *Individual development plans to guide progress* | | | | • | • | • | • |

regularly on their learning experiences and interests, and then use that information to identify their career interests and select a more specialized pathway for grades 11 and 12.

The program is both deeply practical and engaging. Ninth grader Tess le Duc explained the difference between the STEM curriculum and a typical high school course of study: "They just learn the basics, but we're learning how you can change the world."

When asked about their projects or their future plans, STEM students speak with a degree of self-awareness, specificity, and enthusiasm not typical for their age, and Principal Riley confirmed that is one of the goals of the program: "We want to create passion that stays with them."

Former PSW Director of Youth Careers Kelley French echoed his sentiment: "If we can go in there and teach them about these careers, instead of just the academics, that excitement might allow them to get through a class that's more difficult than they expected because they want to be a scientist or they want to be a chemist. It's the inspiration of what they're seeing out in real life: what it really means to have a career, what it really means to love what you want to do."

What is perhaps most striking is how widespread the STEM culture is. While most of Marlborough's STEM students enter the program in middle school, about 20 percent enter in ninth grade. "We see some pretty instant results in a change in behavior," Riley said. "There's more self-efficacy. They just have a stronger vision for themselves and why all of this is important."

What exactly has the Marlborough team put in place to generate this transformation? Students and staff point to five core features of the design of the high school's STEM program.

**SMALL LEARNING COMMUNITIES.** Marlborough faculty members attribute a large part of their students' success to the support the students receive in small learning communities. The high school STEM program serves seventy-five to eighty students per grade level. Students in grades 9 and 10 are assigned to a team of five teachers (English, math, science, history, and engineering) and take their four core classes and the engineering elective within that small learning community. On most days, they follow the school's regular bell schedule, mixing with the rest of the school population during lunch and an additional elective.

The STEM teachers meet daily, with common planning time counting as one of two official contractual duties. They use the time to plan project-based learning days, complementary lessons, and support for students who need it.

"A lot of kids are coming into the program at different maturity and ability levels," said science teacher Stephanie Gill. "The interventions that are required to keep them functioning at a level where they can do projects and complete their content is heavy sometimes. That wouldn't be possible if we didn't have the time together."

The strong relationships that staff members and students form with one another help prevent students from disengaging or falling behind. Gill said she thinks those relationships help foster a sense of confidence and efficacy among the students. "Ninth and tenth grades are really a big adjustment. You get dumped in ninth grade with kids who maybe weren't in your middle school team, and now you have to partner with them and do a presentation in front of twenty people you don't know — all of those things are really stressful," Gill described. "The STEM kids have been through it. They know their peers. There is way less anxiety."

**PROJECT-BASED LEARNING.** Twice a semester, the schoolwide schedule breaks for an extended learning day. Non-STEM students spend the time on field trips and in study halls. For those in the STEM program, the time is dedicated to project-based learning (PBL) that is designed to simulate the workplace by exposing students to real-word issues and professional roles. STEM teachers create additional opportunities for project-based learning by freeing up their own class periods roughly twice a month. On those additional PBL days, they allow students to rotate among classrooms based on where they are in their projects and what sort of support they need. In total, STEM students spend about 10 percent of their core academic time working on interdisciplinary projects.

Each semester, high school students are assigned a major project. (In middle school, students take on one major project per year.) Students work in small teams to devise a unique solution to a complex, multistage problem, such as an energy-efficient system for a tourist destination or a playground experience that is engaging and accessible for kids with disabilities. Students find these hands-on projects both fun and meaningful. They are further motivated by the freedom they have to think creatively and by the ownership they have over their projects.

Teachers serve primarily as facilitators and resources. They introduce students to each phase of the project and specific requirements (such as keeping a design journal) and then students are responsible for divvying up roles (e.g., chief executive, chief financial officer, and marketing director) and determining how to use their time. This requires teachers to engage in a fair bit of planning as they lay out the project steps; it also requires them to have a lot of trust in what ninth-grade math teacher Heather Kohn calls "organized chaos."

On any given day, students may be investigating topics online, using the robotics lab to build a component, testing a model, or getting feedback from industry professionals. Because team members' schedules vary, they may not all be in the same room at the same time, so they have to communicate and make plans with one another—just as they would in a real-life work environment. They receive grades as a team and for their individual contributions.

Students and staff alike speak about how transformative these projects are. Tenth-grader Miguel said:

> We're learning a lot about ourselves and how we work within deadlines and within groups. We're refining our skills, so we're prepared for college when those deadlines come. [Adults who are pursuing careers] really like to focus on higher thinking, [asking questions like], "How could you reshape this so that it changes something in the world?" I think it's going to be really helpful that I've already started changing my mind-set.

Riley noted that students who have participated in project-based learning stand out from their peers: "They think outside the box more. They're better at critical thinking. They're better at being creative because they're presented with some challenging interdisciplinary projects that require them to be just that. They're better collaborators because they're constantly working on teams." Kohn said, "The best part about this is I don't know the answers to all of these questions. That was hard the first year because students would come up and be like, 'Tell us about bridges,' and I'd say, 'I don't know about bridges, but we'll learn together.'"

**HONORS CURRICULUM.** STEM students take an all-honors curriculum regardless of their starting places. Teachers find that, with support from teachers and peers who know them well, students rise to the expectations. The curriculum that students explore in their four core classes is not necessarily different from what other honors students at Marlborough High School study. In fact, the STEM teachers typically teach one or two sections with the general school population in addition to their work with the STEM students. They use largely the same lesson plans (based on the

Massachusetts Curriculum Frameworks) for both sets of students. (See table 5.4.)

The primary difference between STEM honors classes and traditional honors classes is that STEM teachers often find ways to complement one another's lessons—for example, deliberately sequencing how and when students explore slope in math and velocity in physics (the same concept) or linking a history unit on ancient civilizations with a related study of mythology in English.

The STEM faculty members all volunteered for their positions, and while they didn't receive training in a common type of pedagogy for their core classes, they have learned best practices from one another and from their experiences with project-based learning. They've become better teachers as a result, often integrating mini-projects and collaborative learning into regular lessons. Math teacher Kohn said, "I couldn't imagine teaching a different way at this point. It all feels so natural. If you took this away from me, I'd say, 'What am I going to do with all this time?'"

The teachers notice that they can push their STEM students to think harder—and more independently—than they can with traditional honors students. According to physics teacher Scott Brown, "The STEM students are able to work in groups and work through things. With the non-STEM

**TABLE 5.4** Standard schedule for Marlborough Public Schools ninth-grade STEM student

| Course Title | Length |
| --- | --- |
| Honors Intro to Physics | Full Year |
| Honors Freshman English | Full Year |
| Honors World History 2 | Full Year |
| Honors Algebra 1 | Full Year |
| World/Classical Language | Full Year |
| Honors Engineering (CAD)/Architecture | Half Year |
| Honors Electricity/Electronics/Robotics | Half Year |
| Wellness 9 | Half Year |
| Art Foundation (STEAM) | Half Year |
| STEM Project 9 | Full Year—Meets once per cycle |

students, you tell them, 'Go,' and they're lost. They don't know what to do in a group. They're always asking after every little step they do: 'Is this right? Is this right?' The STEM students are just able to get into a group and work through things without a lot of input from teachers."

Riley said he is proud of the transformation he sees in STEM students: "Outside of STEM, if you're in an honors environment, you have to be a very driven student who will go home and do all your math problems without a lot of prodding." Typically, about 20 to 25 percent of Marlborough students fit that description, but the STEM program turns middle-tier students into high achievers. Entering ninth grade, about 75 percent of STEM students are at a level that would place them in the school's college prep course sequence, which is less academically demanding than honors. When they finish, the percentage has flipped, with almost 80 percent entering honors or AP-level classes in eleventh grade. (See the sidebar "Spotlight: Mission to Mars Design Challenge.")

**CAREER EXPLORATION AND EXPOSURE.** STEM students have opportunities to interact with local employers and to become deeply familiar with career opportunities related to their interests. Career exploration activities vary, ranging from employers providing feedback on student projects to mentoring youth during the school day and sharing their career experiences during panel discussions. These activities prepare students for work-based learning, which JFF defines as programs that help students develop skills, knowledge, and readiness for work through meaningful job tasks in the workplace that support entry or advancement in a particular career field. Career exploration and exposure activities are rolled out in stages: by the time they graduate, STEM students are approaching their next steps with a clear sense of where they are headed and why.

In ninth grade, the activities focus on careers and self-awareness. Students take interest and aptitude surveys at the start of the year, and each term they explore a different high-growth sector (computer science/information technology, engineering/advanced manufacturing, and health/biotechnology) by selecting from a trove of online videos that introduce them to opportunities in each field. After viewing each video, students

**SPOTLIGHT: Mission to Mars Design Challenge**

A popular recent project in Marlborough's STEM Early College program was the Mars Colony Design Challenge. Tenth graders spent a semester designing a prototype for a piece of technology (a transporter, a wind turbine, or a biosphere) that could be used on Mars. They then developed plans for an entire colony that could support a thousand inhabitants.

Teachers divided the project into stages, with assignments touching on every discipline. Students conducted research on historical settlements and examined modern-day urban systems (e.g., police departments and hospitals) for lessons that could be applied to a settlement on Mars. Then they developed detailed floor plans, analyzed materials used to build NASA spacecraft and equipment, and designed and tested their own 3D prototypes. They even created a company logo and a brochure for their exploration company. Students were required to keep detailed engineering journals throughout the project. As a final step, they presented their plans and prototypes at a special exposition where seventy guest professionals voted on the best project.

Kimberly Votruba-Matook of UMass Memorial–Marlborough Hospital attended the showcase and was impressed by "the drive and creativity of STEM students who are involved in designing real-world solutions." "These teams learn to integrate new knowledge, question together, set goals, and take responsibility for outcomes," Votruba-Matook said.

write a personal reflection, evaluating their level of interest and noting other relevant pieces of information, such as the skills required and typical salaries for various roles. These reflections count toward their project-based learning grades.[4]

Ninth graders also have opportunities to interact with local employers who come to the school to participate in panel discussions and to meet with students on project-based learning days. Freshmen visit local companies, too. Site visits typically involve a company tour, a lunch conversation with staff, and a hands-on demonstration or problem-solving activity. According to ninth grader Igor, after a visit to Dow Chemical, "It was the best field trip I've ever had. It was so interesting to see how they make everything, like chips and processors. I learned a lot, and I would love another chance to go. Working at Dow is what I want to do someday." By the end of ninth grade, students are ready to select an industry that they would like to investigate further.

In tenth grade, the focus shifts to career mentoring, which allows students to explore careers of interest in more depth while building transferable workplace skills. Through a series of one-on-one and small-group interactions, students have extended conversations with professionals in which they practice professional skills, such as listening and speaking clearly, that they'll need in any career. Mentors typically visit on project-based learning days, circulating among students to offer feedback on design problems, answer technical questions, and have conversations about professional or employability skills they use every day—for example, managing friction in groups.

During the first one-on-one mentoring session, the mentors introduce the topic of employability skills. In the second session, mentors explain their careers and talk about their employers, sharing the aspects of their work that they find most inspiring and satisfying; students then have time to ask questions. During the third mentoring visit, students deliver their own elevator pitches—describing their work interests and goals to their mentors—and then receive feedback. The fourth mentoring visit is organized as a mock interview. Through these structured conversations, students practice crucial social and networking skills, while seeing how the skills apply to the work of a real professional.

By the end of tenth grade, STEM students are ready to apply for summer internships, participate in job shadowing, and engage in informational interviews. While they may select a different industry area from those of their mentors for their eleventh-grade career pathway, they approach their next steps with much greater understanding of themselves, their possible interests, and how to interact in a workplace.

STEM Career Specialist Laura Bilazarian Purutyan sees an immediate impact from these different interactions. She recalled a time when students had designed an outdoor classroom and a guest employer posed a helpful question about weather. The students adjusted their design before the final presentation based on that feedback. "Talking to someone who does this for a career helped them ask better questions," Purutyan said, "and they realized talking about work can really be fun."

**INDIVIDUAL DEVELOPMENT PLAN.** The final feature weaves the STEM experiences together, helping students take control of their own trajectories. At the start of ninth grade, students create individual development plans (IDPs) in Naviance, a college and career readiness software program that helps students reflect, explore interests, and set future goals. Ninth graders meet with the STEM counselor and career specialist during a series of lunch sessions in which they become familiar with the purpose of the IDP and discuss mini-assignments that will fold into their project-based learning grades.

In ninth grade, the assignments include quizzes, aptitude tests, learning preference surveys, and reflections on what the students are learning about different industries. In tenth grade, students use Naviance to create résumés, career vision statements, and visual portfolios that become tools they can use in conversations with potential employers. Students continue to use their IDPs in grades 11 and 12 as they select early college pathways, determine which dual-enrollment courses they will take, plan for and reflect on work-based experiences, and make decisions about college.

The IDP becomes a sharable collection of data that drives conversations with guidance counselors and families about course selection, internship applications, and postsecondary school plans. The IDP changes counseling conversations from a simple review of courses to a "student-driven, dynamic process," said STEM Counselor Elizabeth Kennedy DeHoratius. By empowering students to make big-picture decisions and consider their interests holistically, the IDP positions them to set goals that they are passionate about and that they will persevere to achieve.

## STEM EARLY COLLEGE PATHWAYS (GRADES 11 THROUGH 12)

Beginning in eleventh grade, Marlborough students can elect into one of six early college pathways through which they may accumulate twelve or more college credits toward a degree in a designated field.

### Developing Degree-Specific Course Trajectories

College credits are granted by Quinsigamond Community College (QCC), the school's primary postsecondary partner. Currently, ninety-five students are dually enrolled in pathway courses. Most are students who participated in the STEM program in grades 9 and 10, but the STEM pathways are open to all students who elect in and pass the ACCUPLACER test, which the Massachusetts public college system uses to determine readiness for credit-bearing coursework. (Students can take a summer bridge course if they need additional support to meet the ACCUPLACER cutoff.) Recently, Marlborough High School and QCC jointly created a high school math class that qualifies students—if they pass—to enroll in a college-level math course without needing to take ACCUPLACER.

Marlborough's approach to dual enrollment has evolved significantly since the early college pathways were first established in 2014. The design has become both more elaborate—to serve a range of needs and postsecondary aspirations—and more sustainable. Five design features are particularly noteworthy.

**COLLEGE COURSES TAUGHT AT THE HIGH SCHOOL.** Pathways students take college credit–bearing courses at the high school from teachers who have earned adjunct faculty status at QCC. The classes occur during the school day and can be taken as part of a regular course load. There is a two-week break in the winter to align the courses with fifteen-week college semesters.

Initially, pathways students dually enrolled in courses at a local four-year institution, but the per-pupil cost wasn't sustainable. Riley and his team then tried hosting visiting lecturers on the high school campus, but those classes didn't sync with the rest of the schedule. They then tried offering online courses, but that option was a tough sell for students who had other commitments at home and work and had trouble meeting online deadlines on top of a full day of high school classes.

In the fall of 2016, the school launched a new model, with high school teachers—who are also adjunct faculty at the college—teaching the courses. So far, the results are strong: 94 percent of students enrolled in college classes in the first semester progressed to the second semester.

Existing Marlborough faculty had to apply to teach the college courses and submit their résumés and transcripts (indicating a subject-area master's degree) in order to be eligible. The college classes are part of their regular high school course load and are assigned like any other class. The early college teachers are not embedded in the STEM program or a small learning community. They receive support directly from the college faculty and staff, including on-campus training in using Blackboard technology, the faculty portal, and an early alert system for students. Teachers receive a stipend for the training time, which goes beyond their contractually required professional development as high school teachers. The college supplies each teacher with a syllabus and a mentor to answer questions.

The first year involved a lot of work, as the early college teachers fleshed out sometimes skeletal syllabi with lessons and supplemental materials to help students fill in background knowledge. Teachers also designed group work to keep students engaged. (See figure 5.1.)

**FIGURE 5.1** The evolution of the dual-enrollment plan

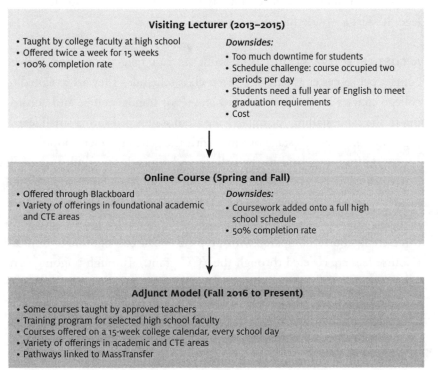

**Visiting Lecturer (2013–2015)**

- Taught by college faculty at high school
- Offered twice a week for 15 weeks
- 100% completion rate

*Downsides:*
- Too much downtime for students
- Schedule challenge: course occupied two periods per day
- Students need a full year of English to meet graduation requirements
- Cost

**Online Course (Spring and Fall)**

- Offered through Blackboard
- Variety of offerings in foundational academic and CTE areas

*Downsides:*
- Coursework added onto a full high school schedule
- 50% completion rate

**Adjunct Model (Fall 2016 to Present)**

- Some courses taught by approved teachers
- Training program for selected high school faculty
- Courses offered on a 15-week college calendar, every school day
- Variety of offerings in academic and CTE areas
- Pathways linked to MassTransfer

It's a much heavier load for students, too. Karen Bento, who teaches College Composition 1 and 2, covers far more territory than she does with her other eleventh graders and assigns more reading and multiple papers. Students meet for the same number of hours as they would on a college campus, which was part of the agreement with the college.

For the most part, students have stepped up to the challenge. Only three of the seventy-five students enrolled in English Composition 1 had to withdraw; the remaining students passed and moved on to Composition 2. Bento elaborated: "I think most students aren't aware of their own capabilities and that they can really succeed in a college class. A lot of students in my class said they worked really hard and they weren't sure if they'd be able to do it, but then they had a sense of accomplishment and pride that they were able to take a college class while they were still in high school."

Information technology teacher Sharon Mattingly agreed: "I think it builds hope. It's so wonderful for them to say, 'I have a college course in my pocket. I did it.' We have so many who may not be able to afford college. It's just a wonderful opportunity."

**A COST-EFFECTIVE STRUCTURE.** Students can take up to two college courses per semester as part of a seven-class schedule. They are assigned to college courses as they would be to an AP or honors course and according to the same staffing formula. They are not grouped into a small learning community at this stage but mix with the general student population.

Aside from fees paid to the college and stipends for faculty training, the courses cost the same as any other high school class. Using high school faculty eliminates the primary cost for the college, allowing it to discount its per-credit fee. Marlborough High School pays $450 per student for a three-credit course, compared with a typical course cost of $900 to $1,000. (Course fees are covered through the YCC grant.) Through ongoing conversations, Marlborough has helped QCC develop a fee structure with further discounted fees of $100 per student for a three-credit course taught at a high school. That is the rate the college has begun to roll out with other schools in the region. When Marlborough's YCC grant expires, the school will shift to that reduced fee structure. (See figure 5.2.)

**FIGURE 5.2** Sample pathway: 2018 associate's degree in computer systems engineering technology—Computer support option

| Summer 1 | 11th Grade | Summer 2 | 12th Grade |
|---|---|---|---|
| Intro to Microcomputer Applications (online) | Composition I (fall) | Advanced Microcomputer Applications (online) | Introductory Sociology—Principles |
| IT Help Desk Concepts (online) | Composition II (spring) | | Introduction to Psychology |
| | College Algebra (fall) | | Speech Communication Skills |
| | Introduction to Programming with C++ (spring) | | Technical and Workplace Writing |
| | Mobile Operating Systems | | IT Security Foundations |
| | Windows Client Operating Systems | | Computer Hardware and Support |
| | Networking Technologies | | Windows Server Operating Systems |
| | Internetworking Principals and Protocols | | Unix Operating Systems |
| | | | Cooperative Work Experience and Seminar |

☐ College Courses Taught at QCC    ☐ College Courses Taught at Marlborough High School

**DIFFERENTIATED PATHWAYS.** The ultimate goal is for all students to be on pathways to college completion by the time they finish high school. Students will have different career interests, with some better aligned to a two-year degree and others to a four-year degree. Some students may choose to go directly into the workforce, particularly those who, due to their documentation status, cannot qualify for many types of college financial aid. The staff considered all of these students when designing pathways.

The school has taken four industry clusters—engineering, computer science, biotechnology, and information technology—and developed pathways within each that serve varied goals. A student who is aiming for a four-year degree in computer science—to become a coder or programmer, for instance—can get a jump start by taking up to twelve foundational credits. Meanwhile, a student who wants to go directly into a well-paying job in the computer industry can complete an associate's degree in information technology during high school. (This pathway includes summer coursework and a split day on the college campus in grades 11 and 12.) A student who wants to join the workforce immediately after graduating from high school also has an option to earn college credits that culminate with an industry-recognized certificate such as a CNC Technologies Certificate (twenty-four credits), a help-desk technician certificate (seventeen credits), or an emergency medical technician certificate (twenty-three credits).

All college courses are part of the Massachusetts Transfer Block, which allows seamless transfer from a two-year school to a four-year state college. A student who starts a biotech program in high school could go to QCC to complete a two-year biotech program and then transfer to a public four-year university, entering as a junior. Or the student could go straight to a public four-year institution, with the credits earned in high school counting toward a degree. Students who opt for a private college will be treated like any other transfer student; their courses would be honored according to the school's own policy.

No matter which pathway students choose, they will have completed enough foundational courses to reduce the total cost and the time required for a college degree. Students who don't enroll in college immediately after high school will have options available should they decide to return to school at a later point in their careers.

**CAREFULLY SELECTED COURSES.** The scope and sequence for each pathway have been carefully crafted, with an emphasis on foundational courses, like English composition and college math, that can count toward core high school graduation requirements, and that students will need to move into advanced coursework. The staff have backward-mapped each pathway, making accommodations where needed. For example, a yearlong version of college math ensures that students who need extra support are ready for college calculus, the starting point for most STEM degrees and one that can be an obstacle for many students. Marlborough graduates will have overcome crucial hurdles before finishing high school.

Where possible, Riley and the team have integrated industry-specific courses, but some courses—like college-level engineering—are simply not realistic because of the equipment or staffing requirements. "We're at the phase of early college where we're parsing out what's appropriate to do in high school and what needs to lead to something more in college," he said.

Sometimes a particular pathway is just too steep to compress into four years. For example, offering students an opportunity to earn an associate's degree in computer science would require more math than can fit in four years of high school. Instead, the computer science pathway provides a solid foundation in core coursework that will give students momentum toward a degree.

Pathways students are encouraged to supplement college courses with AP courses and other electives that are relevant to their career interests, and those options are delineated for each pathway as well. (See figure 5.3.)

**FIGURE 5.3** Sample pathway: Heath care (nursing)

| 11th Grade | | 12th Grade | |
|---|---|---|---|
| *Semester 1* | *Semester 2* | *Semester 1* | *Semester 2* |
| Composition 1 | Composition 2 | Intro to Psychology | Intro to Sociology |
| AP Biology (recommended) | AP Biology (recommended) | Anatomy and Physiology 1 (recommended) | Anatomy and Physiology 2 (recommended) |

☐ College courses taught at Marlborough High School    ☐ High school courses

**CAREER EXPLORATION AND WORK-BASED LEARNING EXPERIENCES.** Building from the career exploration and exposure activities offered in grades 6 through 10, early college pathway students participate in additional learning experiences that deepen their knowledge of their selected fields. This piece of the STEM Early College program is in an earlier stage of development.

STEM career specialist Purutyan matches students and employers. She also works closely with local employers to shape experiences that add value for both students and the company or organization.

Work-based learning may take the form of paid internships. (Some industries, such as health care, restrict the term "internship" to formal graduate-level roles; in those cases, the school uses the preferred terminology of the employer.) Other work-based learning experiences are shorter term—a two-week job-shadow experience or a one-week project based at a work site. All of the programs give students a meaningful perspective about what it is like to work in a particular field while providing them with résumé-building experience. In the summer of 2017, thirty students participated in internships.

It has been a challenge to get employers onboard for this more intensive level of involvement. Purutyan explains that she and her colleagues at PSW are working with employers to "identify innovative ways for employers to engage." It could be a community problem that students work on solving as a mini-project, or it could be an observational experience. Dow Chemical is one of the employers that has been leading the way: last year, two students investigated environmental safety and crafted recommendations on how customer communication could be improved. More recently, a group of students created a STEM curriculum kit that Dow staff can use to teach chemistry to second graders.

## Bridging the High School–Postsecondary Divide

Marlborough isn't the first high school in Massachusetts to attempt an early college design. Others tried and faced significant obstacles, and for Marlborough, the postsecondary partnership was initially challenging. Early on,

Marlborough High School had a dual-enrollment agreement with Framingham State University, a four-year institution, but the fixed per course cost was unsustainable for classes with smaller enrollments. That partnership shifted to a less intensive collaboration focused on college exposure activities, while Riley and his team worked with Quinsigamond Community College to craft a new dual-enrollment design.

The partnership with QCC took some negotiation. Initially, QCC was hesitant because past experiments with dual enrollment had been unsuccessful. In addition, the faculty union raised concerns about staffing for dual-enrollment courses. Such tension is common across the country in dual-enrollment models that rely on high school teachers to teach college courses. In recent years, postsecondary faculty have become increasingly concerned about a broader shift in faculty hiring practices and the increase in contingent faculty positions at many colleges and universities. In the case of QCC, the union issued a cease-and-desist letter to high schools seeking to offer community college courses with their own faculty, even though the faculty of two-year colleges and high schools belong to the same umbrella union—the Massachusetts Teachers Association.

However, Riley made a convincing case to the president of QCC, noting that Marlborough High School would not supplant faculty or cannibalize the existing student population. Instead, it would create a new population of students that the college couldn't currently reach. By outsourcing classes, the college would eliminate its largest costs (staffing and overhead) while securing a new revenue stream through credit fees.

QCC was further motivated by its mission, which is well aligned with Marlborough High School's. As the public two-year postsecondary option for the region, QCC is also facing new demands from local industries that need graduates prepared for complex STEM careers, and the college feels a particular responsibility to reach first-generation college students for whom community college is an important step toward the middle class. Partnering with Marlborough High School to put more underrepresented youth on a path to college (including many who would likely matriculate at QCC) aligns with the college's mission.

Ultimately, the QCC administration decided to proceed, and Marlborough High School agreed to a detailed memorandum of understanding that would ensure that all courses met New England Association of Schools and Colleges standards for course rigor, faculty hiring and training, and supervision and evaluation.

Christina Hebert came on board as QCC's manager of K–12 educational partnerships in 2014 and has been a central figure in the implementation of Marlborough's early college program. As a first step, she met with all of the deans to address concerns that some had voiced about rigor and to discuss how early college courses adhere to college standards and syllabi. She has also helped the deans engage faculty as mentors.

Hebert troubleshoots with the registrar and is in frequent contact with school staff to ensure that logistics are running smoothly. She is a regular participant in the STEM Early College Leadership Committee, a group of dedicated individuals that contribute to all curriculum design efforts and ensure alignment of pathways with industry credentials. At the college, she has her own advisory board, made up of representatives from different departments, to ensure that communication is flowing across the college.

The STEM counselor at the high school plays a key role. Elizabeth DeHoratius was originally brought on as a part-time counselor for the grades 9 and 10 STEM classes; her hours and responsibilities have increased as the early college part of the program has grown. She now coordinates the dual-enrollment program with QCC, helping students select their pathways courses and serving as a link between the two institutions as they reconcile schedules and processes. (See the sidebar "Aliyah: A Student on the Move.")

QCC's successful partnership with Marlborough High School helped inspire broader engagement with the early college approach. In 2016, QCC's president convened a regional institute to discuss developing a more robust and standardized early college model for central Massachusetts. Representatives of about forty school districts attended, and a subset of those attendees have begun working on developing pathways in manufacturing, information technology, and health care. The eventual goal is to develop fifteen to twenty degree pathways for the region.

## ALIYAH: A Student on the Move

Aliyah Nisbett is in her senior year at Marlborough High School. A Marlborough native, Aliyah joined the STEM program as a sixth grader when her mother, a nurse, learned of the opportunity. Aliyah had been a middle-of-the-road student until that point; she worked hard but didn't always have a clear sense of purpose. Her experience in STEM has dramatically changed that.

Aliyah described her STEM experience as "eye opening," especially in her sophomore year. That was when she took an engineering class and had her first experience using AutoCAD, an advanced design system. Her group created a retractable grabber to assist paraplegic athletes. "I was like, wow, this is something I can really feel passionate about," she said. "This is something I can do well." She loved how the tools allowed her to use her imagination to solve real-world problems and became excited about the prospect of a career in mechanical engineering or biotechnology.

Work-based learning experiences have deepened that interest. During the summer after sophomore year, Aliyah participated in a program at Raytheon, where she saw real engineers using the same design tools she used in her STEM classes. "We could relate because we know how to use that program," she said.

The following summer, Aliyah and a classmate researched engineering pathways and created a website, an app, and a series of workshops designed to inspire self-awareness in their peers and to help fellow students use online tools and networking to investigate career options. Aliyah and her classmates planned to pilot the career exploration program with the Marlborough High School staff. That same summer, Aliyah served as the team leader for a project at Boston Scientific, where she and four other students designed, tested, and delivered a STEM exploration activity for three hundred children for Bring Your Child to Work Day. The activity they devised, called "Build a Boat," exposed six- to nine-year-olds to the engineering design process. It proved to be very popular.

In fall 2016, Aliyah was invited through JFF to go to North Carolina to hear President Obama speak to student leaders about the importance of education and leadership. Describing the experience as "uplifting," Aliyah recalled that the president spoke about being a role model: "It really changed my perspective on a lot of things, like education. Today's generation is creating what's going to be next."

Aliyah is now a STEM ambassador for incoming students at the high school, paying forward what she has learned. As she looks ahead, her sights are set on four-year engineering programs; Worcester Polytechnic Institute, Stanford, Northeastern, and UCLA are among her top choices. She is hopeful about her prospects: "I feel like STEM gives you a lot of exposure to new things. As STEM students, you already have that step ahead of other people."

## A MODEL BUILT ON RELATIONSHIPS

Marlborough's STEM Early College design fits largely within existing staffing and scheduling structures while providing a markedly different experience for students. The biggest departure from how traditional high schools operate is in the roles played by community partners. Several of these entities and individuals have been core to the design, oversight, and day-to-day implementation of STEM learning.

### Workforce Intermediary Partner

Partnerships for a Skilled Workforce (PSW), the regional workforce development board, has been deeply involved in developing the STEM program from almost the beginning. PSW's engagement as a core partner began shortly after the arrival of Race to the Top funds, and the workforce board played a key role in developing the Youth CareerConnect proposal that has fueled the program's growth. PSW brings important staff capacity and expertise in career development practices and regional labor market needs to the table. The director of PSW's Youth Careers Initiative and PSW's full-time, school-based STEM coordinator have taken the lead on all employer engagement activities, and PSW consultants provide additional support in curriculum development and public communications. (See the sidebar "Spotlight: A New Kind of Workforce Partnership.")

### Shared Leadership

Riley and French co-convene the STEM Leadership Steering Committee, a group of seventeen individuals representing the district, higher education, and every major industry sector. The committee meets three times per year at the school to provide oversight and input on program implementation. The members have been important thought leaders, helping identify the most important workforce skills to integrate into the STEM curriculum, deepening educators' understanding of the skill needs in each sector, and helping to engage a broad base of employers. The committee has also played a vital role in solving design challenges, using the varied areas of expertise of its members to examine each problem from every angle.

**SPOTLIGHT: A New Kind of Workforce Partnership**

Partnerships for a Skilled Workforce serves as the workforce development board for the Metro Southwest region of Massachusetts. It has a thirty-year history of forging links between employers and public institutions to solve local workforce needs.

Before 2012, PSW's role at Marlborough High School had focused largely on work placement for individual students and career development activities that happened outside the core curriculum. Kelley French, the former director of PSW's Youth Careers Initiative, had been a career liaison at the school and dreamed of the day when career-focused learning could become part of the school day. With the arrival of Race to the Top support, she saw an opportunity to help Principal Daniel Riley and his team deepen the STEM curriculum with employer involvement in career exploration and exposure activities and internships.

She is proud of the model they've built together. "It has all the components [of a successful career-focused learning program]. You have school leadership buy-in. You're teaching young people how to think about careers, learn soft skills, and work together—all of these things we keep hearing employers say they need," French said. "We're able to look at where the jobs are going to be and think about how to best fill the gap that employers are telling us about. And we're educating young people about all of it."

French sees the work that Marlborough High School and PSW are doing as especially important in a high-need community like Marlborough, "You're leveling the playing field so that all these students are graduating with a set of skills that will really help them move forward in life."

## Engaged Employers

Currently, about two hundred local employers, representing an array of companies, nonprofits, and public entities, partner with Marlborough High School. As described earlier, Marlborough offers several tiers of involvement. Career exploration activities are accessible to most employers and include panel discussions, career fairs, project feedback days, and mentoring visits during project-based learning days. At the next tier, partners host workplace visits during which students may tour their facilities, speak with employees, and participate in hands-on activities.

In the upper tier, the most committed employers, of which there are currently twelve, host work-based learning programs at their facilities. These include paid summer internships, multiday or multiweek projects, and job shadowing. Getting employers onboard for this level of involvement has been one of the toughest challenges and has required creative planning to design programs suited to varied industries. PSW has developed an internship tool kit so companies can see what's possible and co-design work-based learning programs that make sense for their industries.

Employers don't sign formal memoranda of understanding with the school, but instead adhere to a set of written expectations and agree to name a contact at the company (usually a human resources or technical manager) to serve as a point person and employee liaison. Individual employees are invited to join the Marlborough STEM Leadership Steering Committee. In the 2014–2015 school year, this committee created the STEM Speakers Bureau, a clearinghouse of individuals who volunteer to participate in panels and project fairs and serve as career mentors.

Career mentoring is an area that has been refined over time. School staffers have found that some industry visitors were so advanced in their careers that they had trouble relating to high school. This past year, PSW recruited younger mentors and asked them to shift their focus from talking about their specific careers to the professional skills that all young people need. Personal job experiences tend to arise organically. "We've found that we have to train the employers," noted Purutyan, "because some come in thinking we want their expertise, and what we want is for them to be able to engage and excite a student, to help them find what they love so they will persevere." Students and employers have responded well to this shift in focus. (See the sidebar "Spotlight: Work-Based Learning at UMass Memorial–Marlborough Hospital.")

## Linchpin Staff

Three grant-funded roles provide critical coordination and management functions. The first is French, who devoted 30 percent of her time to the partnership during the intensive launch and has phased down to 20 percent in the final year of the YCC grant. French played an important management role, convening the steering committee and working on the design and refinement of career-focused learning activities.

## SPOTLIGHT: Work-Based Learning at UMass Memorial–Marlborough Hospital

UMass Memorial–Marlborough Hospital is among the most deeply committed employers participating in Marlborough High School's STEM Early College program. As a nonprofit health-care provider, the hospital has long provided community education to address health needs. It took some time to design a work-based learning structure that would serve the skill development needs of high school students without compromising patient care or privacy guidelines.

For the past two years, the hospital has hosted a small group of students for the month of July; students spend a total of thirty-two hours at the hospital, exploring service areas like orthopedics/sports medicine and mental/behavioral health. Students begin by gaining a bird's-eye view of the hospital through interviews with the hospital's senior leaders. They then take a deep dive into a particular service area, speaking to experts at all levels of care. For last year's mental health project, they interviewed the director of the behavioral health unit, the hospital's chief psychologist, and several social workers, case managers, and staff in the emergency department.

Kimberly Votruba-Matook, the hospital's marketing and development coordinator, worked with two of her colleagues to coordinate the interviews, handle program logistics, and support students as they developed a community project using what they had learned. "That's the creative piece," Votruba-Matook said. "The ideas they come up with are just phenomenal."

The first summer, students planned a sports injury prevention training program for all school athletes. More recently, students planned a week of activities to raise awareness and break down stigmas around mental health. They designed a "little bag of happiness" for fellow students, with everyday objects as tactile aids to help maintain a positive outlook—like a paper clip to "hold things together" and a penny for luck. The hospital's chief executive officer loved the concept and admired the students' passion, and agreed to purchase enough supplies to distribute gift bags to all thirteen hundred high school students and faculty members.

The program requires significant investment of time on the part of staff leaders at the hospital, but Votruba-Matook has seen a substantial payoff for all involved. "It's been an opportunity for caregivers from all different departments and clinical units to connect with our youth and our city in a meaningful way," she said. "They get to provide their expertise, and that then manifests in this really wonderful idea."

Votruba-Matook, who participated in the school's STEM Leadership Steering Committee, is hopeful that this model can be scaled to other industries and beyond the life of the current grant.

A second crucial role is Purutyan, a PSW employee who is based full-time at the school. Purutyan is the primary person in charge of employer outreach; she solicits and maintains contacts within local companies, finding ways to connect the partnership to their goals (for example, showing General Electric how the school can help it develop a strong pipeline of female scientists). Purutyan uses a tool kit that PSW developed to help make the case to employers and to suggest partnership activities that might suit their capacity. She then provides the training they need to interact with students.

Purutyan coordinates all career development activities at the school. She works with students to find internships, helps educators understand how to integrate industry information and resources into the curriculum, and teaches students, teachers, and parents about the labor market. Given the packed high school curriculum, she has to be creative with time, using lunches, project-based learning periods, and weekly career tables to supply the information and support students' needs.

It's a big role, so developing systems to manage the workflow has been important. For each Project Expo, for example, Purutyan schedules emails sent to judges. She has developed similar tools and schedules for other recurring tasks.

A third critical role is that of STEM Counselor DeHoratius, whose part-time position is also grant funded. DeHoratius takes the lead on IDPs, working closely with Purutyan to introduce students to Naviance and helping teacher teams develop assignments that help students identify their career interests. She trained older STEM students to serve as IDP ambassadors for newer students and helps students at every stage access additional support as needed. (See the sidebar "Miguel: Open to Possibilities.")

## CHALLENGES, COST, AND SUSTAINABILITY

Marlborough High School and its partners have charted new territory in many ways. It has been a path that has involved some stumbling and a lot of persistence and creativity.

## MIGUEL: Open to Possibilities

Tenth-grader Miguel Lopez becomes animated when he talks about his experiences in Marlborough's STEM program. He claims that he used to be shy, but after five years working on projects with peers and having extended conversations with career mentors, his old reserve has been replaced by confidence and enthusiasm.

Born and raised in Marlborough, Miguel set his sights on college and career independence early. His mother and stepfather, who never attended college, made education a top priority for their three children. When Miguel initially heard about the STEM program as a fifth grader, he was enticed by the promise of a free laptop. He and his parents quickly realized the program would open important doors. "It gives you opportunities you wouldn't usually get," Miguel explained. "I think it gives you an extra edge."

One of those advantages is access to career-relevant internships, something he's seen his older brother struggle to find without the support of the STEM program. Miguel is also excited about the opportunity to earn college credits and certification as a Level 1 programmer in robotics. He said one of the biggest advantages is project-based learning, where there is always room to "take it a step further and do something really amazing." Projects have taught him a lot about collaboration and helped him develop skills he knows he will need in the future. "You have to know how to compromise, how to delegate tasks, how to pick roles within the group," he said.

Miguel originally had his sights set on a career in medicine, but after taking classes in robotics and AutoCAD, he "started realizing, this is something that interests me. These areas are so flexible, and you can use them in so many different careers." Seeing a lot of options in the rapidly changing technology field, he's now leaning toward a four-year degree in computer science. "I want to use the skills we're practicing now to innovate even more," said Miguel. "I'm still very open to a lot of things."

The partners benefited from technical assistance from JFF, which has over a decade of experience supporting the development of innovative early college and career-driven school designs nationally. Perhaps most important to the Marlborough success story, Marlborough High School's Riley and PSW's French had a clear vision that they were determined to execute, and they brought on staff who were similarly invested and willing to think outside the box to solve challenges as they cropped up.

### Addressing Design Challenges

One of the biggest design challenges that the Marlborough team encountered has already been discussed: setting up a sustainable dual-enrollment

model. After several attempts, Marlborough High School and Quinsigamond Community College have identified an effective and affordable way
to deliver college courses, one that meets college standards and is already
informing other schools and the state. Other design challenges remain,
however. Currently, school staff and partners are grappling with the following issues.

**EXPANDING PAID INTERNSHIPS.** Engaging employers to offer internships
is a common challenge that college and career pathways programs face.
Hosting an internship program requires significant employer investment
and can be daunting for employers that are new to working with high
schools. While PSW has developed effective, mutually beneficial approaches
with several of the most committed employer partners, only seven of thirty
eligible students secured paid experiences last summer. (Five of twenty-
five did so the summer before.) The STEM career counselor and faculty
have adopted creative strategies, such as designing paid experiences that
take place on the high school campus, where students complete a product for an employer or a project for the school. While this isn't the ideal
model, the partners are hesitant to ask for too much too quickly from employers and may need to build relationships over time. With support from
the STEM Leadership Steering Committee, they are still considering options and opportunities.

**DWINDLING INTEREST IN MENTORING.** Very few eleventh graders volunteered to participate in a second year of career mentoring. The STEM
program leaders believe this may be a developmental issue. Students have
been in highly structured, small learning communities since sixth grade;
eleventh grade is when they have more opportunities to choose how they
spend their time. They have a clearer understanding of their career interests and may prefer to network and find an adult mentor with whom they
make a genuine connection instead of being assigned to a mentor. Staff are
responding to this challenge by considering other ways to generate mentor
matches, including through work experiences.

**DUAL-ENROLLMENT RECRUITMENT AND RETENTION.** While student interest remains high in grades 6 through 10, the district has faced participation challenges with dual-enrollment classes. Some eleventh-grade students have been unable to enroll in their intended dual-enrollment courses because of scheduling conflicts, and about ten students didn't pass the ACCUPLACER test that would make them eligible to take Composition 1, the first course in the sequence for most pathways. Enrollment in the new information technology pathway was especially disappointing: only two of the fourteen students recruited signed on. There may be a combination of factors at play—including how the school communicates the value of these courses relative to other advanced course options. The school may also need to figure out a way to set up support systems to keep students engaged in their selected pathways after they leave the intensive support of their small learning communities after tenth grade. While the high school ideally hopes to retain students in the college and career pathways they select, it would be helpful to clearly convey that even if they don't stay in the pathway, dual-enrollment classes are a win-win because they give students a chance to earn college elective credit.

**EQUITY.** Equity is another challenge that leaders in Marlborough are grappling with. Previously, about one-third of middle school students were enrolled in the STEM learning community, which had a large waiting list. STEM students were receiving more instructional time and much more interdisciplinary learning, and their outcomes were very strong. The program had become so popular that the city's more affluent families were signing up their children in large numbers; even with a lottery system that provided preference to underserved groups, high-needs groups were significantly underrepresented (see table 5.5). Students of color are currently underrepresented in the program: just under one-third of STEM students are Latino, whereas Latinos account for nearly half of all Marlborough High School students. The Marlborough team has worked to recruit and enroll students representative of the student population, reserving priority spots for students of color, English language learners, and young people

**TABLE 5.5** Demographics

|  | STEM Program (grades 9 through 12) | Marlborough High School (all students, grades 9 through 12) |
|---|---|---|
| Total Enrolled | 292 | 1,051 |
| Male | 53% | 51% |
| Female | 47% | 49% |
| Latino | 32% | 49% |
| African American | 5% | 3% |
| Special Education | 5% | 14% |
| English Language Learners | 3% | 16% |
| Economically Disadvantaged | 40% | 54% |

Source: Marlborough High School.

from economically disadvantaged families. This school year, the district expanded the program to all students in the middle and high schools, making it the default experience for every student. Given the high demand, Marlborough leaders viewed this expansion of the program as the only fair thing to do.

## A Surprisingly Lean Budget

Given the tangible impact on students, it's surprising how little Marlborough's STEM program actually costs. That is largely because the bulk of programming falls within traditional school structures. STEM students attend school for the same number of hours as their peers and stick to a very similar schedule; most of their classes follow the same state-approved curriculum. High school faculty who teach dual-enrollment courses work according to the same union contract as other Marlborough faculty. As a result, the STEM program is largely budget neutral, with a few exceptions, particularly during the start-up phase.

Federal grant funding was critical during the planning and launch phase. Two large federal grants covered, among other things, curriculum development, professional development for teachers, and strategic equipment purchases. Equipment included 3D printers, lab hoods, state-of-the-art industrial robots, lasers, videoconferencing equipment, a CNC router (a computer numerical control cutting machine), software, and a van to transport students to their job placements and the community college campus. The grants also covered the three important staff positions previously discussed.

In total, Marlborough High School received approximately $1.3 million in federal grant support from YCC. Its intermediary partner, PSW, received an additional $540,000 over four and a half years. Marlborough High School allocated the majority of its budget (53 percent) to equipment purchases. The remainder was allocated to other costs, such as professional development, teacher stipends, and transportation (19 percent); supplies (11 percent); personnel (14 percent); and staff travel (3 percent).

## Sustainability

Looking ahead at the sunset of federal funding, Riley and his team aren't especially worried. The state has already begun to show greater investment in helping schools with equipment upgrades, which Riley likes to think was influenced by a visit that the state education secretary made to Marlborough, where he saw what students can do with advanced STEM equipment. The state is also increasingly committed to expanding early college models, which Riley hopes will create a sustainable source of funding for dual-enrollment courses.

The school and PSW will need to find a way to cover program management and coordination roles beyond the start-up phase. They are currently considering ways to braid multiple funding sources, such as allocating $40,000 for early college programming (tuition, resources, and other supplemental expenses) from the district's fiscal allowance, building staffing roles into the district budget, and applying for the competitive Massachusetts Early College Designation, which, if awarded, could bring in an additional $140,000.

## GOING TO SCALE . . . AND BEYOND

In just a few years, the district has rolled out an impressive new model for middle and high school education.[5]

The grades 6 through 10 program of study—with its focus on rigorous, interdisciplinary projects and STEM career exposure—has been transformative, and the grades 11 through 12 college and career pathways, while still evolving, are thoughtfully structured and likely to further improve outcomes. Now the district is taking this model to scale.

Beginning in 2016, all fifth to eighth graders were integrated into a slightly revamped STEAM (the A is for "arts") model. District leaders decided to expand the STEM concept to STEAM to incorporate a broader set of interests for young students who are still discovering their passions, and to enable students to explore a greater range of skills and ways of thinking. Now, all three small learning communities participate in project-based learning, with middle schoolers rotating through sixty-day cycles in instructional technology, engineering, and visual arts.

A similar expansion is underway at the high school. Last fall, all incoming ninth graders joined a small learning community with a career-related theme. The high school overhaul is a response to the difference Riley was seeing between STEM and non-STEM students—STEM students were more engaged and clearer about their purpose as students—as well as a marked difference in teachers' sense of efficacy and job satisfaction. "The teachers who aren't involved in these small learning communities are trying to bear the weight of so many student issues and needs," he explained. "It's really overwhelming. They don't feel students know why they're here on a deeper level. They don't feel like they have the support of anyone beyond themselves."

The small learning communities structure has made a significant difference for both students and adults, and the focus on relevant, career-oriented learning has created a culture of positive learning and purpose. It's a model that school leaders are ready to try schoolwide, with houses organized by three career themes: STEM, business, and arts and humanities. It's a big move, and one that will require buy-in from many more staff members.

(In the past, STEM teachers had all volunteered to join the program and retention was very high.) The school—and the district—will have new lessons to share from this experience in the next year or two.

Meanwhile, Marlborough High School has begun to attract attention from educators beyond the city. The school has become a regular destination for leaders of other districts and state officials interested in innovative college and career pathways. In March 2017, the Massachusetts Departments of Higher Education and Elementary and Secondary Education highlighted Marlborough High School at a meeting that helped set the agenda for establishing high-quality early college partnerships across the state. Riley spoke to a group of over 250 stakeholders about the lessons learned in his district, noting that, across the state, there is a "real sense of urgency" about the need to address the gap between postsecondary completion rates and the skills and credentials required by employers for viable middle-class jobs. Riley concluded his address: "This type of innovative program is exactly what we need to keep up with the changing trends in our communities."

# PATHWAYS TO PROSPERITY NETWORK

More than half of young Americans reach their mid-twenties without the skills and credentials needed for success in today's demanding economy. Yet 65 percent of jobs, especially in high-demand STEM fields, will require postsecondary credentials by 2020. In 2012, Jobs for the Future (JFF) and the Harvard Graduate School of Education (HGSE), in collaboration with five states, launched the Pathways to Prosperity Network to reenvision how our education system—from K–12 through college—partners with employers and prepares our young people for success. Today, the Pathways Network has fifteen members, a mix of states, metropolitan regions, and urban communities. The network seeks to ensure that many more young people complete high school, attain a first postsecondary credential with currency in the labor market, and launch careers while leaving open the prospect of further education.

The **core elements** of college and career pathways systems include:

**Secondary and postsecondary alignment and integration.** College and career pathways span grades 9–14, intentionally aligning and integrating rigorous academic, career-focused curricula and work-based learning with local labor market demands.

**Career information and advising.** Starting in middle school, students learn about postsecondary and career options through real-world, developmentally appropriate activities.

**Education-industry partnerships.** Business and industry leaders collaborate with educators to design curricula and offer a continuum of work-based learning opportunities such as job shadows and internships that expose students to the world of work.

**Intermediary development and capacity building.** Local or regional organizations provide staffing, infrastructure, and capacity to support pathways work.

**Effective leadership and enabling policies.** States enact legislation and policies that advance college and career pathways, provide sustainable funding to districts and community colleges, and offer financial incentives to support work-based learning opportunities.

# LIST OF INTERVIEWEES

The contributors would like to thank the dozens of people who took time from their busy schedules for the interviews that made this book possible. We are grateful for their insights and work.

Note: Titles and organizations are reflective of their positions at the time of the interview.

## DELAWARE PATHWAYS

- Mark Brainard, President, Delaware Technical Community College (Del Tech)
- Cory Budischack, Chair, Energy Tech Department, Del Tech
- Matthew Burrows, Superintendent, Appoquinimink School District
- Robert Ford, Delaware Workforce Development Board
- Meg Gardner, Rehoboth Beach restaurant owner
- Joshua Grapski, Rehoboth Beach restaurant owner
- Paul Herdman, President and CEO, Rodel Foundation of Delaware
- Kim Joyce, former Assistant Vice President, Academic Affairs, Del Tech
- Jack Markell, Delaware Governor, 2009-2017
- Paul Morris, Assistant Vice President, Workforce Development, Del Tech
- Luke Rhine, Director, CTE/STEM Initiatives, Delaware Department of Education
- Gary Stockbridge, President, Delmarva Power
- Michelle Taylor, CEO, United Way of Delaware

## TENNESSEE PATHWAYS

### State-level

- Danielle Mezera, former Assistant Commissioner, Division of College, Career and Technical Education, Tennessee Department of Education
- Nick Hansen, former Program Director, Pathways Tennessee, Tennessee Department of Education
- Ellen Bohle, Program Manager, Pathways Tennessee
- Jay Bozman, Associate Director of Stewardship, Vanderbilt University Medical Center; former Program Manager, Pathways Tennessee

- Tristan Denley, Vice Chancellor for Academics, Tennessee Board of Regents
- Cassie Foote, Director of Policy and Research, Tennessee Business Roundtable
- Adriana Harrington, former Executive Director, Pathways Tennessee
- Victoria Harpool, Assistant Executive Director, Academic Affairs, Tennessee Higher Education Commission
- Heather Justice, Executive Director, Office of Career and Technical Education, Tennessee Department of Education
- Chelsea Parker, Executive Director for Work-Based Learning and the Tennessee Council for CTE, Tennessee Department of Education
- Anne Thompson, Director, Workforce Development, Tennessee Department of Economic and Community Development
- Ted Townsend, COO, Tennessee Department of Economic and Community Development
- Kyle Southern, Director of Policy and Research, SCORE
- Casey Wrenn, Assistant Commissioner, Division of College, Career and Technical Education
- Sterling van der Spuy, Director of Workforce Services, Tennessee Department of Labor

## Upper Cumberland
- Lillian Hartgrove, Vice President of Workforce Development and Education, Cookeville-Putnam County Chamber of Commerce
- Jerry Boyd, Superintendent, Putnam County Schools
- Adam Bernhardt, Director of Human Resources, ATC Automation
- Tom Brewer, Associate Vice President of Research and Economic Development, Tennessee Technological University
- Angela Bruce, Director of Human Resources, Tutco
- Stephen Crook, Vice President of Economic Development, Highlands Economic Partnership
- Sandra Crouch, former Director of Schools, White County Schools
- Becky Hull, Director, Cookeville Higher Education Campus
- Sally Pardue, Director, Tennessee Technological University STEM Center Southeast Tennessee
- Michael Torrence, Vice President of Academic Affairs, Volunteer State Community College
- Myra West, Director, TCAT-Livingston
- Deborah Whitaker, Supervisor of Instruction, Jackson County Schools
- Robert Young, Vice President, Custom Tool

## Southeast Tennessee
- James Barrott, Director, TCAT-Chattanooga
- Tony Cates, Human Relations Manager, Gestamp

- Sherry Crye, Director of Workforce Development, Cleveland-Bradley Chamber of Commerce
- Bill Seymour, President, Cleveland State Community College
- Annie White, Project Manager, Pathways

## GREAT LAKES COLLEGE AND CAREER PARTNERSHIP
### Northwest Suburbs of Chicago
- Kenya Ayers, Vice President and Board Chair, Northwest Educational Council for School Success
- John Breusch, Assistant Superintendent of Teaching and Learning, Barrington 220 School District
- Danielle Hauser, Director of Instructional Improvement, Township High School District 211
- Brian Knetl, Associate Provost, Harper College
- Andrea Messing-Mathie, Deputy Director, Education Systems Center, Northern Illinois University
- Alonzo Ramirez, Counselor, Palatine High School
- Fred Rasmussen, Director of Student Support Services
- Shayla Sanchez, Senior, Palatine High School
- Dan Weidner, Director of Academic Programs and Pathways, Township High School District 214

### Central Ohio
- Steve Dackin, Superintendent of School and Community Partnerships, Columbus State Community College
- Craig Heath, Director of Secondary Education, Dublin City Public Schools
- Sherry Minton, Director of Career Articulation, Columbus State Community College
- Marcy Raymond, Director College and Career Readiness, Educational Service Center of Central Ohio
- Todd Warner, Executive in Residence for Business and Community Partnerships, Columbus State Community College

### Madison, Wisconsin
- Cindy Green, Executive Director of Secondary Programs and Pathways, Madison Metropolitan School District
- Schauna Rasmussen, Dean Workforce and Economic Development, Madison College
- Pat Schramm, Chief Executive Officer, Workforce Development Board of South Central Wisconsin
- Jen Wegner, Director of Personalized Pathways and CTE, Madison Metropolitan School District
- Bridget Willey, Director for Allied Health Education and Career Pathways, University of Wisconsin Health

## Rockford, Illinois

- Kelly Cooper, Executive Director, Engineering Our Future, Rock Valley College
- Bridget French, Executive Director of College and Career Readiness, Rockford Public Schools
- Jon Furr, Executive Director, Education Systems Center, Northern Illinois University
- Anisha Grimmett, Executive Director, Alignment Rockford
- Reid Jutras, Director of Career and Technical Education, Rockford Public Schools
- Kari Neri, Executive Director of Curriculum, Rockford Public Schools

## AGRICULTURE CAREER PREP

### High Schools

- David East, Superintendent, Reef-Sunset Unified School District
- Juan Ruiz, Principal, Avenal High School
- Stephanie Bollweg, Ag Prep Coordinator, Avenal High School
- Erica Mendez, Counselor, Avenal High School
- Jennifer Vining, Teacher, Avenal High School
- Paul Lopez, Superintendent, Mendota Unified School District
- Jamie Anthony, Teacher, Mendota High School
- Claudia Robledo, Math Teacher, Mendota High School
- Lori Schultz, Principal, McFarland High School
- Matthew Navo, Superintendent, Sanger Unified School District
- Dan Chacon, Principal, Sanger High School
- Alisha Aguirre, Counselor, Sanger High School
- Mike Cantu, English Teacher, Sanger High School
- Matthew Canaday, Teacher, Sanger High School
- Jonathan Delano, Assistant Principal, Sanger High School
- Laura Henson, Teacher, Sanger High School
- Larry Paredes, Teacher, Sanger High School
- Daniel Polomo, Counselor, Sanger High School
- Ashley Wills, Teacher, Sanger High School
- Joey Campbell, Superintendent, Washington Unified School District
- Derek Cruz, Principal, Washington Union High School
- Steven Rizzo, Ag Prep Coordinator, Washington Union High School
- Kristen Barnes, CCPT Program Director, Wonderful College Prep Academy
- Saul Gonzalez, Executive Director, Wonderful College Prep Academy
- Jesse Gomez, Teacher, Wonderful College Prep Academy
- Doug Ihmels, Ag Pathway Coordinator, Wonderful College Prep Academy
- Angelica Rios, Ag Prep Coordinator, Wonderful College Prep Academy
- Shondra Walker, Principal, Wonderful College Prep Academy

## Postsecondary

- Sonya Christian, President, Bakersfield College
- Chris McCraw, Professor, Agribusiness and Mechanized Agriculture, Bakersfield College
- Sandra Caldwell, President, Reedley College
- Donna Berry, Vice President of Administrative Services, Reedley College
- David Clark, CTE Dean, Reedley College
- Mario Gonzales, Dean of Students, Reedley College
- Carole Goldsmith, President, West Hills College
- Clint Cowden, Dean, West Hills College
- Chris Cheney, Faculty, West Hills College
- Tim Ellsworth, Faculty, West Hills College
- Atif Elnaggar, Faculty, West Hills College

## The Wonderful Company

- Noemi Donoso, Senior Vice President, Wonderful Company, in charge of Wonderful Education
- Eric Barba, Director, Wonderful Education
- Rebecca Farley, Director, Wonderful Education
- Paige Gilkey, Wonderful Education
- Megan Mayzelle, Wonderful Education
- Emily Phelps, Wonderful Education
- John Lee, Wonderful Education
- Elysa Vargas, Director, Wonderful Education
- John Sprengs, Wonderful Education
- Kristen Barnes, CCPT Program Director, Wonderful College Prep Academy
- Saul Gonzalez, Executive Director, Wonderful College Prep Academy
- Jesse Gomez, Teacher, Wonderful College Prep Academy
- Doug Ihmels, Ag Pathway Coordinator, Wonderful College Prep Academy
- Angelica Rios, Ag Prep Coordinator, Wonderful College Prep Academy
- Shondra Walker, Principal, Wonderful College Prep Academy
- David Krause, President, Wonderful Citrus
- Andy Anzaldo, General Manager, Wonderful Farming International
- Robert Baker, Vice President of Farming, Wonderful Orchards
- Kristen Camarena, Crop Manager, Wonderful Orchards
- Sonya Carrillo, Financial Analyst, Wonderful Citrus
- Tomas Diaz, Field Scout, Wonderful Orchards
- Mike Dorion, Vice President, Wonderful Farming International
- Danny Garcia, Human Resources, Wonderful Citrus
- Joe Gonzales, Irrigation Senior Manager, Wonderful Orchards

- Brett Hampf, Crop Manager, Wonderful Orchards
- Vanessa Harikul, Director of Leadership and Organization, Wonderful Citrus
- Julie Kurchak, Senior Vice President of Human Resources, Wonderful Citrus
- Gladys Laurean, Director of Human Resources, POM Wonderful
- Jared Lorraine, Director of Continuous Improvement, Wonderful Citrus
- Gary Schengel, GIS Manager, Wonderful Orchards
- Matt Van Horn, Fleet Operator, Wonderful Orchards
- Arnold Viduya, Farm Accounting Manager, Wonderful Citrus

### Jobs for the Future
- Nancy Hoffman, Senior Advisor, JFF
- Elizabeth Santiago, JFF
- Julia Di Bonaventura, Program Manager, JFF

## MARLBOROUGH HIGH SCHOOL
- Karen Bento, Early College English Teacher, Marlborough STEM Early College High School
- Scott Brown, Science/Physics Teacher, Marlborough STEM Early College High School
- Kelley French, Former Director, PSW Youth Careers
- Stephanie Gill, Science/Biology Teacher, Marlborough STEM Early College High School
- Christina Hebert, Manager of Educational Partnerships, Quinsigamond Community College
- Elizabeth Kennedy DeHoratius, MAPP/STEM Counselor, Marlborough STEM Early College High School
- Heather Kohn, Math/Algebra Teacher, Marlborough STEM Early College High School
- Tess Le Duc, student, Marlborough STEM Early College High School
- Sharon Mattingly, Early College Business And Technology Teacher, Marlborough STEM Early College High School
- Aliyah Nisbett, student, Marlborough STEM Early College High School
- Laura Bilazarian Purutyan, Career Specialist, Marlborough STEM Early College High School
- Daniel Riley, Principal, Marlborough High School
- Miguel Lopez Rivera, student, Marlborough STEM Early College High School
- Kimberly Votruba-Matook, UMass Memorial–Marlborough Hospital

# NOTES

## CHAPTER 1

1. Ed Kee, *Delaware Agriculture* (Washington, DC: US Department of Agriculture, n.d.), https://www.nass.usda.gov/Statistics_by_State/Delaware/Publications/DE%20Ag%20Brochure_web.pdf.

2. Scott Goss, "DuPont to cut 1,700 jobs in Delaware," *The News Journal*, December 29, 2015, http://www.delawareonline.com/story/money/business/2015/12/29/dupont-cut-1700-jobs-delaware/78014766/.

3. George Sharpley, *Delaware 2024: Occupation & Industry Projections* (Dover: Delaware Department of Labor, Office of Occupational and Labor Market Information, 2016).

4. "Governor Markell announces initiative to expand Pathways to Prosperity program," *Delaware.gov*, August 11, 2016, http://news.delaware.gov/2016/08/11/governor-markell-announces-initiative-to-expand-pathways-to-prosperity-program/.

5. Enrollment in Delaware Pathways has continued to grow each year: from 13 percent of high school students (5,072) in 2016–2017, to 20 percent (8,328) in 2017–2018, to over 30 percent (over 12,000) in 2018–2019.

6. Nancy Hoffman and Robert B. Schwartz, *Gold Standard: The Swiss Vocational Education and Training System*, (Washington, DC: National Center on Education and the Economy, 2015).

7. In 2018, SPARC was restructured and moved to Delaware Tech.

8. In fiscal year 2019, Delaware Pathways benefited from a much more positive state funding environment and a $3 million investment from Bloomberg Philanthropies.

9. See a one-page snapshot of the 2017 outcomes report here: http://delawarepathways.org/wp-content/uploads/2017/10/DE-PATHWAYS-OUTCOMES-REPORT-V9-3.pdf

10. Grace Kena, William Hussar, Joel McFarland, Cristobal de Brey et al., *The Condition of Education 2016* (NCES 2016-144) (Washington, DC: US Department of Education Statistics, 2016); Joel McFarland, Bill Hussar, Cristobal de Brey, Tom Snyder et al., *The Condition of Education 2017* (NCES 2017-144) (Washington, DC: US Department of Education, 2017).

11. *State of Delaware College Success Report: Class of 2014* (Dover: Delaware Department of Education, 2016).

12. *State of Delaware College Success Report: Class of 2015* (Dover: Delaware Department of Education, 2017).

13. By Fall 2018, over 12,000 students were enrolled in Delaware Pathways.

## CHAPTER 2

The development of this chapter was supported by a generous gift to Harvard University from The James and Judith K. Dimon Foundation.

1. Caitlin Dempsey, "Fortune 1000 Companies List for 2016," Geo Lounge, September 9, 2016, https://www.geolounge.com/fortune-1000-companies-list-2016.

2. Jamie McGee, "Tennessee ranks No. 1 in foreign direct investment by jobs, *Tennessean*, August 11, 2016, http://www.tennessean.com/story/money/2016/08/11/tennessee-ranks-no-1-foreign-direct-investment-jobs/88579604/; Scott Harrison, "Tennessee is Top State in US for Advanced Industry Job Growth, Brookings Institution Report Finds," Tennessee Department of Economic and Community Development, August 5, 2016, http://www.tnecd.com/news/328/tennessee-is-top-state-in-us-for-advanced-industry-job-growth-brookings-institution-report-finds/.

3. "Tennessee Household Income," Department of Numbers, accessed November 28, 2017, http://www.deptofnumbers.com/income/tennessee/.

4. Arthur Laffer, Stephen Moore, and Jonathan Williams, *Rich States, Poor States* (Arlington, VA: American Legislative Exchange Council, 2017), https://www.alec.org/app/uploads/2017/04/2017-RSPS-INDEX-v5.pdf.

5. Robert Atkinson and J. John Wu, *The 2017 State New Economy Index* (Washington, DC: Information Technology and Innovation Foundation, 2017), 5.

6. Joni E. Finney et al., *Driven to Perform: Tennessee's Higher Education Policies and Outcomes—A Case Study* (Philadelphia: Institute for Research on Higher Education, Graduate School of Education, University of Pennsylvania, 2017).

7. Jason Gonzales, "Tennessee posts highest high school graduation rate on record for the state," *Tennessean*, September 14, 2017, http://www.tennessean.com/story/news/education/2017/09/14/tennessee-posts-highest-high-school-graduation-rate-record-state/663283001/.

8. Finney et al., *Driven to Perform*.

9. Ibid.

10. Ibid.

11. "Quick Facts: Tennessee," US Census Bureau, https://www.census.gov/quickfacts/TN.

12. Randy Boyd later became commissioner of TNECD and ran for governor in 2018. Boyd was defeated in the Republican primary but later in 2018 was appointed interim president of the University of Tennessee.

13. Oliver Schak, Ivan Metzger, Jared Bass, Clare McCann, and John English, "Developmental Education: Challenges and Strategies for Reform" (Washington, DC: US Department of Education, 2017), https://www2.ed.gov/about/offices/list/opepd/education-strategies.pdf.

14. *Drive to 55: Pathways to Postsecondary Report* (Nashville: Tennessee Department of Education, 2016), http://tn.gov/assets/entities/education/attachments/ccte_drive_to_55_report_state.pdf.

15. Emily House, "Dual Enrollment: Program Structure, Take Up, and Early Outcomes" (PowerPoint presentation, Tennessee Higher Education Commission/State Board of

Higher Education joint meeting, July 27, 2017), https://www.tn.gov/content/dam/tn /stateboardofeducation/documents/meetingfiles/July_2017_Dual_Enrollment.pdf.

16. Career Forward Task Force Report (Nashville: Tennessee Department of Education, 2016), 15, https://www.tn.gov/content/dam/tn/education/ccte/career_forward_task _force_report.pdf.

17. Ibid.

18. Tennessee Promise Annual Report 2017 (Nashville: Tennessee Higher Education Commission and Student Assistance Corporation), https://www.tn.gov/thec/research /redirect-research/tn-promise-annual-report.html.

## CHAPTER 3

The authors would like to acknowledge members of the GLCCPP coordinating team who provided early guidance on the focus and overall framing of the pathways stories in each of the GLCCPP communities: Amy Loyd and Leah Moschella of JFF, Julie Koenke of ConnectEd, and Jonathan Furr, Andrea Messing-Mathie, and Emily Rusca of the Education Systems Center at Northern Illinois University. Special thanks to Michael Deuser, formerly of Jobs for the Future and now chief of college and career success at the Chicago Public Schools, who provided an initial draft of the case background section and advised on the overall framing of the report.

1. The Joyce Foundation, "Investing in the Future of the Great Lakes Region: An Update," June 1, 2018, http://www.joycefdn.org/news/investing-in-the-future-of-the -great-lakes-region-an-update.

2. GLCCP, "Our Strategy," https://glccpp.com/our-strategy.

3. ConnectEd, JFF, EdSystems, *Quality Indicators for Pathways Design and Implementation* (Chicago: EdSystems, 2017).

4. Alignment Rockford, "Supporting Our Public Schools," https://alignmentrockford.com.

5. An interactive version of the 2018 Illinois Report Card is available at https://www .illinoisreportcard.com.

6. What Works Clearinghouse, *Dual Enrollment Programs* (WWC Intervention Report) (Washington, DC: Institute of Education Sciences, 2017), https://ies.ed.gov/ncee /wwc/Docs/InterventionReports/wwc_dual_enrollment_022817.pdf.

7. Northwest Educational Council for Student Success (NECCS): NECSS Mission (n.d.), http://www.necsspartnership.com/necss-partnership/about-necss/mission/.

8. Race to Equity, *Race to Equity: A Baseline Report on the State of Racial Disparities in Dane County* (Madison: The Wisconsin Council on Children and Families, 2016), 21.

9. Learn more about the Workforce Development Board of South Central Wisconsin's Youth Apprenticeship Program: http://wdbscw.org/youth-apprenticeship-program.

10. B. McCready and B. Vaade, *Personalized Pathways Year One Update* (Madison, WI: Research and Program Evaluation Office, Madison Metropolitan School District, 2018).

11. MMSD has adopted the Chicago Consortium's on-track model: attendance greater than 90%, no course failures, on pace for credits earned, and no out-of-school suspensions.

12. MMSD researchers did not report on the statistical significance of observed differences.

13. The Columbus Region, "Market Research," Columbus 2020, https://columbusregion.com/market-research.

14. R. Seils, J. Tafel, and D. Van Meter, *Navigating Central Ohio's College and Career Readiness System* (Columbus: Educational Service Center of Central Ohio, 2015).

15. The Central Ohio Compact, *The Central Ohio Compact, 2017: A regional strategy for college completion and career success* (Columbus: 2017), http://centralohiocompact.org/wp-content/uploads/2017-Compact-report.pdf.

16. Rockford Public Schools, "Profile of a Graduate," https://www3.rps205.com/academies/Pages/Profile-of-a-Graduate.aspx.

17. D. Thomas and J. S. Brown, "Why virtual worlds can matter," *International Journal of Learning and Media* 1, no. 1 (2009): 37–49.

## CHAPTER 4

This chapter was developed based on interviews, focus groups, site visits, and observations among Ag Prep education and industry partners over a four-year period, from May 2014 to December 2018. This includes dozens of site visits to schools, colleges, and industry sites in the San Joaquin Valley, and over 100 in-person or phone interviews with school teachers, counselors, vice principals, principals, and district superintendents; college faculty, advisers, deans, and presidents; Wonderful Education staff; Wonderful Company staff, managers, directors, vice presidents, and presidents; staff from JFF and other partners; and about 50 students (see appendix B for select interviewees). The interview materials were originally developed in collaboration with JFF and Wonderful Education to document the development of Ag Prep, resulting in several briefs available at https://www.wonderfuleducation.org/publications/. This chapter draws from these materials and from additional interviews conducted in the summer and fall of 2018. Information in this chapter is drawn from materials and content developed in collaboration with JFF. JFF has provided guidance and technical support to Wonderful Education in developing and implementing Ag Prep. For more information, see www.jff.org.

1. Fresno County Farm Bureau, *2017 Fresno County Annual Crop & Livestock Report* (Fresno, CA: County of Fresno, 2017), http://www.co.fresno.ca.us/Home/ShowDocument?id=30066; and Vegetable Research & Information Center, "San Joaquin Valley Agriculture" (Davis, CA: UC Cooperative Extension, UC Davis, n.d.), https://vric.ucdavis.edu/virtual_tour/sanjoq.htm.

2. The early college high school initiative began in 2002 and was led by Jobs for the Future (JFF), a national nonprofit based in Boston. See www.jff.org/earlycollege for more information.

3. National Radio Project, *How We Survive: Sprouting Up in Empty Breadbaskets*, season 12, episode 45 (November 11, 2009); Bureau of Labor Statistics, "Unemployment in the San Joaquin Valley by County: August 2015," https://www.bls.gov/regions/west/news-release/unemployment_sanjoaquinvalley.htm; and Public Policy Institute of California, "Maps of college enrollment rates in California's counties," based on data

from the California Department of Education and the California Postsecondary Education Commission (2018), http://www.ppic.org/data-set/maps-of-college-enrollment-rates-in-californias-counties/.

4. S. Burd-Sharps and K. Lewis, *Geographies of opportunity: Ranking well-being by congressional district* (Measure of America, Social Science Research Council, 2015), http://www.measureofamerica.org/congressional-districts-2015/.

5. T. Nodine, *College and Career Success in the Central Valley: How Wonderful Agriculture Career Prep (Ag Prep) is Changing the Educational Experience for Students* (Boston: JFF and The Wonderful Company, 2015), 4, https://www.wonderfuleducation.org/publications/.

6. Wonderful Company, "Social Responsibility: How We're Working to Make a Difference," http://www.wonderful.com/social-responsibility.html.

7. T. Nodine, *Partnering for Student Success: How Ag Prep Brings Together Schools, Colleges, and Industry* (Boston: JFF and The Wonderful Company, 2015). Much of the material in this section is drawn from this report. This report and other related briefs are available for download at https://www.wonderfuleducation.org/publications/.

8. C. Moore, A. Venezia, J. Lewis, and B. Lefkovitz, *Organizing for Success: California's Regional Education Partnerships* (EdInsights Center, 2015).Schwartz_BOOK.docx

9. R. Asera, R. Gabriner, and D. Hemphill, *What Makes Partnership Work?* (College Futures Foundation, 2017), https://collegefutures.org/publication/what-makes-a-partnership-work-2017/; D. W. Brinkerhoff and J. M. Brinkerhoff, "Public-Private partnerships: Perspectives on Purposes, Publicness, and Good Governance," *Public Administration and Development* 31 (2011): 2–14; and L. Mitchell and P. Karoff, "Accepting the Challenges of Partnership," *Stanford Social Innovation Review* (2015), https://ssir.org/supplement/the_power_of_philanthropic_partnerships.

10. N. Orfalea, "Where Two Rivers Meet, the Water Is Never Calm," *Stanford Social Innovation Review* (2015), https://ssir.org/articles/entry/where_two_rivers_meet_the_water_is_never_calm.

11. Nodine, *Partnering for Student Success.*

12. S. Colby, K. Smith, and J. Shelton, *Expanding the Supply of High-Quality Public Schools* (Bridgespan Group, 2005).

13. For more information about career academies, see the California Partnership Academy (CPA): https://www.cde.ca.gov/ci/gs/hs/cpaoverview.asp.

14. Source for wage data: Employment Development Department, California Labor Market Review, 2014.

15. An early college approach has been shown to increase college success among low-income youth, first-generation college students, English language learners, students of color, and other young people underrepresented in college. For more information, see M. Webb and C. Gerwin, *Early College Expansion* (Boston: JFF, 2014).

16. M. F. Rogers-Chapman and L. Darling-Hammond, *Preparing 21st Century Citizens: The Role of Work-Based Learning in Linked Learning* (Stanford Center for Opportunity Policy in Education, 2013); L. H. Lippman, R. Ryberg, R. Carney, and K. A. Moore,

*Key "Soft Skills" That Foster Youth Workforce Success: Workforce Connections: Toward a Consensus Across Fields* (Bethesda, MD: Child Trends, 2015); Center for Advanced Research and Technology (CART), *A Model for Success: CART's Linked Learning Program Increases College Enrollment* (2011); C. Cahill and S. Jackson, *Not as hard as you think: Engaging high school students in work-based learning* (Boston: JFF, 2015).

17. For more information, see T. Nodine, *Skills Mapping in the Central Valley: How Ag Prep is Linking Education to Careers* (Boston: JFF and The Wonderful Company, 2016).

18. C. Cahill, *Making Work-Based Learning Work* (Boston: JFF, 2016).

19. N. Hoffman, T. B. Wright, and M. Gatta, M., "Ethnographies of Work and Possible Futures: New Ways for Young People to Learn about Work and Choose a Meaningful First Career," in *Essays on Employer Engagement in Education*, A. Mann, P. Huddleston, and E. Kashefpakdel, eds. (Routledge, 2018).

20. For a sample work plan, see T. Nodine and J. di Bonaventura, *Ag Prep Internships: Work-Based Learning in the Central Valley* (Boston: JFF and the Wonderful Company, forthcoming).

21. California Department of Education, "2016-17 four-year adjusted cohort graduation rate (with county data)" (DataQuest, 2018), https://dq.cde.ca.gov/dataquest/dataquest.asp.

22. California Department of Education, "12th grade graduates completing all courses required for UC and/or CSU entrance (with county data), all students, State of California 2016-17," DataQuest, 2018, https://dq.cde.ca.gov/dataquest/dataquest.asp.

23. J. Fink, D. Jenkins, and T. Yanaguira, *What happens to students who take community college "dual enrollment" courses in high school?* (Community College Research Center, September 2017), https://ccrc.tc.columbia.edu/publications/what-happens-community-college-dual-enrollment-students.html.

24. Public Policy Institute of California (PPIC), "Maps of college enrollment rates in California's counties," based on data from the California Department of Education and the California Postsecondary Education Commission (2018), http://www.ppic.org/data-set/maps-of-college-enrollment-rates-in-californias-counties/.

25. California Department of Education, "2017-18 four-year adjusted cohort graduation rate," DataQuest, 2018.

26. Eighty-eight out of ninety students.

**CHAPTER 5**
This chapter was developed with funding from a Youth CareerConnect grant awarded by the US Department of Labor.

1. The source of this data is the Massachusetts Department of Elementary and Secondary Education Graduation Rate Report for 2007; Department of Elementary and Secondary Education, Graduates Attending Institutions of Higher Education Report, 2006–2007.

2. Source: the Massachusetts Department of Elementary and Secondary Education's District Analysis and Review Tools for English language learners.

3. In the 2014–2015 school year, the department stopped identifying students as "low-income" and created a new income metric called "economically disadvantaged." Therefore, the figures in the table before the 2014–2015 school year represent low-income status, and the figures after the 2014–2015 school year represent economically disadvantaged status.

4. Sample: Mentoring Assignment #2 Reflection: This mentoring experience was different from last in that you had much more time to spend with one (in some cases two) mentor(s) and to learn in more depth about a particular job sector/role. While the day is fresh in your mind, please write a reflection that addresses the following questions: (a) What did you learn about your mentor's school-to-career path? (b) What did you learn about your mentor's day-to-day responsibilities/activities? (c) Describe the industry problem that you and your group confronted, how you approached it, and how you ultimately solved it or came to some resolution, (d) What are your thoughts about the industry sector/career you had a chance to explore today? Is it something about which you remain curious?

5. In a March 2019 update, Principal Riley reports that the high school is being completely redesigned to incorporate work-based learning throughout all concentrations—STEM, Entrepreneurship, and Fine Arts—and to place all 9th and 10th graders in an all-Honors program.

# ACKNOWLEDGMENTS

First and foremost, our deep thanks to our case writers: Robert Rothman, Richard Kazis, Michael Grady, Thad Nodine, and Katie Bayerl. Except for Thad Nodine, who has been documenting the work of Wonderful Agriculture Career Prep (Ag Prep) for four years, the writers were new to their respective sites. All managed to convey the work on the ground in clear and compelling analytic narratives.

The editors selected the writers, all established journalists or researchers, for four of the five cases and worked closely with the fifth (Michael Grady) to help him adapt his case to fit the purposes of the book. Although all writers followed standard practice in checking all quotations and inviting site leaders to review their drafts for accuracy, in the last analysis these cases represent the observations and analyses of the writers themselves, not the funders, the site leaders, or the editors.

That said, the case writers have made it clear to us that, without significant help from two sets of people, they would not have been able to develop such robust portraits. In each site, key people paved the way for them, providing the necessary contextual background, opening doors to other informants, and reviewing drafts for factual accuracy. On behalf of our writers, We want to thank these folks for their enormously valuable assistance. They are:

- *Delaware Pathways.* Luke Rhine and Robert Ford
- *Tennessee Pathways.* Danielle Mezera, Annie White, and Lillian Hartgrove
- *GLCCPP.*
  - *Northwest Suburbs of Chicago*: Kenya Ayers and Brian Knetl
  - *Columbus*: Todd Warner

- *Madison*: Cindy Green
- *Rockford*: Kelly Cooper and Bridget French
- *Ag Prep*. Noemi Donoso, Eric Barba, Rebecca Farley, and Elysa Vargas
- *Marlborough High School*. Dan Riley

You can find their titles in appendix B, the list of all interviewees.

The second group of people who provided crucial support are the members of JFF's Pathways to Prosperity team that work with each of our sites. Over time, the team members assigned to each site shifted, but the key Pathways staff whose work should be acknowledged are:

- *Delaware Pathways*. Charlotte Cahill
- *Tennessee Pathways*. Tobie Baker Wright and Kyle Hartung
- *GLCCPP*. Kyle Hartung, Leah Moschella, Julia Di Bonaventura, Michael Deuser
- *Ag Prep*. Nancy Hoffman, Elizabeth Santiago, Daniel Trujillo
- *Marlborough High School*. Adelina Garcia, Anna O'Connor

Thanks also to our funders, without whose support this book would not have been possible. This case series was launched with a generous gift to Harvard University from the James and Judith K. Dimon Foundation. Its funding supported the development of the Delaware and Tennessee cases. The foundation's executive director, Abby Sigal, has been a close collaborator and supporter of the Pathways to Prosperity Network, especially in New York.

The Ag Prep and Marlborough studies have each been funded out of governmental grants. Ag Prep funding came from a grant from the California Career Pathway Trust to support the regional collaborative led by The Wonderful Company. The fiscal agent for the grant is West Hills College. Special thanks to Noemi Donoso, the leader of Wonderful Education, for negotiating support for this case. Funding for the Marlborough case came from a federal Youth CareerConnect grant to JFF. Neither the California

Department of Education nor the federal Department of Labor should be held responsible for the content of these cases.

The GLCCPP case is funded by the sponsor of the Great Lakes Partnership, The Joyce Foundation. It was Senior Program Officer Jason Quiara who commissioned this case and then graciously agreed to allow us to adapt it to fit the book, for which we owe him special thanks.

This book would not have seen the light of day if it were not for the continued advocacy of Doug Clayton, publisher of the Harvard Education Press. We can't imagine another press that would be easier and more supportive to work with, nor a publisher and editor who could be more collaborative than Doug and Editor-in-Chief Caroline Chauncy.

Another essential person in bringing this book to press is our excellent copyeditor from JFF, Sophie Besl. Under a tight deadline, Sophie worked nights and weekends to make this book as readable and typo-free as possible, so much thanks to her.

Finally, we need to thank the leaders of the two organizations who co-sponsor the Pathways Network. Maria Flynn, president and CEO of JFF, and Bridget Terry Long, dean of the Harvard Graduate School of Education, have been deeply supportive of the network and of the broader economic mobility agenda that drives it. It's a privilege to work in two such well-led and mission-driven organizations.

# ABOUT THE EDITORS
# AND CONTRIBUTORS

## ABOUT THE EDITORS

**Robert B. Schwartz** is Professor of Practice Emeritus and Senior Research Fellow at the Harvard Graduate School of Education, and Professor in Residence at JFF. Before joining the HGSE faculty in 1996, Schwartz served in a variety of roles in education, from high school teacher and principal to education adviser to the mayor of Boston and the governor of Massachusetts to founding president of Achieve, Inc. In 2011, he coauthored *Pathways to Prosperity: Meeting the Challenge of Preparing Young Americans for the 21st Century*, the report that led to the founding of the Pathways to Prosperity Network. In 2017, he coauthored with Nancy Hoffman *Learning for Careers, The Pathways to Prosperity Network* (Harvard Education Press).

**Amy Loyd** is vice president at JFF and leads the Pathways to Prosperity and college and career pathways work. In this role, she guides states and regions in developing and scaling effective policies, infrastructure, and practices to build sustainable systems of college and career pathways aligned with regional labor markets. Before joining JFF, Amy led a public-private partnership network of K–12 schools providing culturally responsive education and wraparound services to Alaska Native and American Indian students and their families.

## ABOUT THE CONTRIBUTORS

**Katie Bayerl** is an author, writing instructor, and editorial consultant. She has taught writing in public schools and a variety of community settings. A former member of the Early College High School team at JFF, Katie has served as editor of a teen-generated magazine, led the communications efforts of a Boston-based education nonprofit, and helped dozens of schools and nonprofits tell their stories. In 2017, she published her first young adult novel, *A Psalm for Lost Girls*.

**Michael Grady** is a Rhode Island–based education consultant whose work focuses on college and career readiness and transitions to adult success. In 2018, Grady retired from Brown University after serving nineteen years as deputy director of the Annenberg Institute and assistant professor of practice in education. Before his work at Brown, Michael was a senior research associate at the Annie E. Casey Foundation and director of research for the Prince George's County (Maryland) Public Schools.

**Kyle Hartung** is senior director of Pathways to Prosperity at JFF. He has twenty years of experience as a teacher, leader, consultant, and researcher in public K–12 and higher education settings, where he has worked to advance innovations in education. Before joining JFF, Kyle most recently worked as a researcher with Learning Innovations Laboratory at Harvard's Project Zero and as a consultant for Envision Learning Partners.

**Richard Kazis** is a senior consultant for MDRC and a nonresident senior fellow at the Brookings Institution Metropolitan Policy Program. He also serves as board chair for The Institute for College Access and Success. Before these roles, Richard spent many years as senior vice president of JFF, where he oversaw national and state policy work and also led JFF's program on community college student success.

**Thad Nodine** is a novelist and writer specializing in educational policy, practice, and research. For over twenty years, he has published stories of innovation in K–12 and postsecondary education—particularly efforts to help low-income students and those first in their family to attend college to achieve their educational goals. He is also a senior fellow at the Education Insights Center, where he blogs for the California State University Student Success Network and the California Education Policy Fellowship Program. His debut novel, *Touch and Go*, won the Dana Award for the Novel.

**Anna O'Connor** is a senior program manager on JFF's Pathways to Prosperity team. Before joining JFF in 2016, she worked at the Massachusetts Department of Elementary and Secondary Education, first in the Office of Planning and Research, then in the Office of College and Career Readiness, where she served as the early college coordinator.

**Robert Rothman** is a senior editor at the National Center on Education and the Economy and a consultant to several education organizations. A nationally known education writer, he is the author of four books and numerous articles on education policy.

# INDEX